Family Life Made Easy

A Fabulous Mum's Guide

Grace Saunders

arrow books

Published by Arrow Books in 2010

2 4 6 8 10 9 7 5 3 1

Originally published in Great Britain in 2009 by Century
with the title *The Fabulous Mum's Guide to a Fabulous Family Life*

Arrow Books
Random House, 20 Vauxhall Bridge Road,
London SW1V 2SA

www.rbooks.co.uk

Addresses for companies within The Random House Group Limited can be found at:
www.randomhouse.co.uk

The Random House Group Limited Reg. No. 954009

A CIP catalogue record for this book
is available from the British Library

ISBN 9780099519362

The Random House Group Limited supports The Forest Stewardship
Council (FSC), the leading international forest certification organisation. All our
titles that are printed on Greenpeace approved FSC certified paper carry the FSC logo.
Our paper procurement policy can be found at www.rbooks.co.uk/environment

Printed and bound in Great Britain by
CPI Bookmarque, Croydon CR0 4TD

To Isabella, Gabriel and Raphael – you are the
loves of my life.

Contents

How Did I Get Here?

Close your eyes and try to imagine where you were five or ten years ago . . . Were you getting hitched with flowers in your hair? Were you on a girlie holiday in Spain, smelling of suncream and dancing on the beach? Or were you on a last-minute city break with a secret lover?

Seven years ago, I was at a fashion launch with my fellow *Elle* girls, wearing the teeniest, skinniest jeans and the highest, pointiest stilettos and holding a half-empty long-stemmed champagne flute. Fast-forward to today and the scene is somewhat different. I'm sitting at my computer with my feet clad in an old pair of holey woollen socks, as they're too swollen to fit into even my most generous Ugg boots. As my unborn baby wiggles and squirms in my uterus I can also hear my two children as they fight over the last (shop-bought) flapjack downstairs. They've bickered all day and I have a pounding headache as a result. When the phone rings I can tell you with one hundred per cent clarity that it will be the head of the school's Parents' Association asking where my nominations are for class rep this year, because as usual I am the last member to hand them in. My mug of green tea has gone cold, but I can't face getting up to put the kettle on, as that'll involve making a third trip to the loo this hour. I might have made my name as the bestselling author of *The Fabulous Mum's Handbook*, but today I can tell you I feel anything but fabulous!

For almost all my fellow mums, unsurprisingly the transformation from twenty-something singleton to thirty-something (plus) mum rocked their world. One moment you're mulling over whether to have a glass of wine or a G&T for that 'all right then, just the one' after-work drink, the next you're agonising over childcare choices and which type of buggy you can afford if you give up those G&Ts for the next decade! In my original handbook my mission was to help new mums salvage an element of sanity and groove within their role, to help them gel their old world with the new and to fuse all these new identities and demands into one strong confident role model, whom we might call 'The Fabulous Mum'.

The outcome has been staggering. As I sat at my desk typing up my tips on fashion and interiors, chatted to fellow mums about their solutions for relationships and childcare, and spent months sourcing the cream of the crop in terms of experts to guide mums through each field, I couldn't have imagined in my wildest dreams the success the 'Fabulous Mum' concept would become. Reaching out and touching so many women as they embrace their new identities as mums has been humbling to say the very least.

A few years on, as my children grow from babies to toddlers and from toddlers to schoolchildren, my journey as a parent has begun to evolve and change once again. Around me the mothering lives of my friends, neighbours and colleagues have begun to shift too. As we 'grow up' with our children our concerns grow also. Not only do we want family-friendly interior solutions for our homes, but we also want to know how to cope with the hurdles of growing our family. Not only do we care about looking good and feeling confident in our clothes, but we also want to feel just as powerful about our choice of nurseries, schools and carers. Not only do we crave nourishment for our pregnant selves, but food has become a family concern for us all.

Friends and family started to ask me when I'd write a sequel to *The Fabulous Mum's Handbook*. Neighbours, mums at the school gate, readers via letters, emails and cards, all enquired as to when I would meet the demand for a new and evolved handbook that would help us with our ever-diverging and demanding role as mums. Questions were fired my way, such as 'How do I return to work after taking a break to raise my family?' or 'How do I travel long-haul with a brood of five?' Mums still wanted to know how to look good during pregnancy, but this time they wanted to know how to do it with a toddler in tow. They still asked me for endless tips on carving out time for themselves but equally desired solutions for staying afloat in this nightmarish era of competitive parenting. Add to this the daunting and ever-pressing issue of eco-friendly living: I've lost count of how many mums have begged me for tips on how to sustain a 'greener' family life without breaking the bank (and your goodwill!).

As I started to think about having a third child and all the ways my family life would evolve, once again, as a result of it, I felt a real impulse to try to answer some of these new questions and produce a handbook that would help those mums with the constant needs of a changing and expanding family. Just as I had done with the first handbook, I wanted to produce a guide that embraced all mums, whether they be in their twenties, thirties or forties, whether they be career or full-time mothers, single or married, fully staffed and living in the lap of luxury or, more likely, settling for a three-bedroom semi and a home full of clutter and chaos. No matter our circumstances, every mum has many a day when she's left wondering 'How the hell did I get here?' and even more so, 'How am I going to make it through another day?' I'm the first to admit that motherhood in all its growing glory can be overwhelming. How we do it all without simultaneously combusting before eight o'clock in the morning I don't know! But what I do know is that together we can work towards making motherhood viable and enjoyable, while still maintaining a sense of sanity and individuality throughout. So here we have it, *Family Life Made Easy*, the testament of endless conversations, late-night debates, phone calls, emails and texts with what must be hundreds of mums and experts from all walks of life. Expect lots of humour, tons of tips and an immense amount of common sense. Fabulous mums, let's enjoy the ride!

Go Forth and Multiply

When Is the Right Time?

Asking the question 'When is the right time to go forth and multiply?' seems the perfect place to start. Let me elaborate. At the precise moment of writing this chapter it's a Monday morning in spring. I sit at my computer, the top button of my jeans undone and my toes in a bowl of iced water. An extraordinary writer's fetish, you may well think. I wish I were that eccentric! In reality it's more an attempt to overcome the extreme nausea I feel as my eight-week-old 'baby' (or jelly bean as it's known in the Saunders house at present) grows an eyelid/hand/ankle. Not only is my tummy starting to swell but my cravings for strong cheddar cheese, home-made lasagne and Haribo cola-bottles are coming at such a rate I may have to abandon this chapter almost before I've begun in order to feed myself all three, preferably all at once.

Combine this scene with the fact that my three-year-old son, who had a playdate organised this morning at his 'girl-friend's' house, is in fact not knee-deep in craft activities with Aoife, but lolling on a makeshift sickbed beside my desk, as white as a sheet after vomiting all night. Throw into the mix the phone ringing, only to reveal the rather disgruntled voice of my five-year-old's school secretary informing me that I'd forgotten my daughter's packed lunch and her reading book bag at drop-off, so please could I return to the school immediately with both?

With all this family hullabaloo going on you may be wondering why on earth I am even considering adding chaos to chaos with a third child. My immaculately groomed, size-eight girlfriend Lotte (with a straight-out-of-the-pages-of-*Elle-Decoration* house) is totally satisfied with having one beautiful daughter. Five-year-old Ava organises her own clothes according to their 'colour pallet' (Ava's term, not mine) and insists her playmates take off their shoes before entering her bedroom and instead put on something from the selection of ballet slippers she has for guests (yes, there's even a black pair for the boys). Lotte and Ava go everywhere together: sushi lunches, Monsoon Girls to select a few diamante bracelets and hair clips, even matching blow-dries at Lotte's swish Mayfair salon. So you can imagine how Lotte rolled her eyes when I told her I was broody for my third child. 'But darling Grace,' she said, biting into a carrot stick, 'you're only just clinging on to your sanity as it is.' And as if to clarify her point my son charged into the kitchen wearing a Spiderman outfit and his sister's fairy bubblegum pink shoes, wielding a kitchen sieve as a weapon!

Still, my life was never meant to be a perfect scene from *Wallpaper* magazine. I like a little mayhem with my morning cup of tea. So the moment Lotte and Ava left to attend their mother and daughter yoga and meditation class (wearing matching Juicy Couture tracksuits, naturally!), I rallied together the children and my queasy mini-bump and headed two doors down to the ever-open front door of my neighbour, Amy. Unlike Lotte, Amy is a Mother Earth in every sense of the word. She had her first son Miles while studying for her degree at university and tells tales of writing her dissertation in student digs with her three-month-old attached to her breast as if it was as normal as getting wasted on cider at the Student Union. She gave birth to her second son some six years later and her third child, a daughter this time, arrived nine months ago on her kitchen floor in between helping Miles with his geography homework and cooking a Thai curry for supper!

Amy confesses to wanting 'a further one (or two) to complete her crazy family unit' and lets nothing more than her broody instincts determine when that 'perfect' time will be. Admittedly, Amy's garden full of excited rosy-cheeked children and the joyful shrieks of her baby daughter being entertained by her siblings makes my choice to expand my own brood feel even more right.

As some of you may well remember, I had my first two children very close together. (Not quite as close as my friend Jools, who popped two out in just over a year, but close enough to warrant a double buggy and only a few months between maternity jeans.) I can honestly say that getting pregnant with my son just over eight months after giving birth to my daughter wasn't something I'd anticipated. As I cherished my daughter's first seven months and my extended maternity leave, it never once crossed my mind that I'd be pregnant mere months later. I was still adjusting to my mammoth bust and the loss of my favourite slim clutch bag in exchange for a rather less dainty nappy bag. I would have told you to take a hike if you'd suggested embarking on morning sickness and life-altering exhaustion while still undertaking a three in the morning night feed and pureeing carrot and pear on a daily basis!

However, once I returned to work and weaned my daughter off the breast I had what can only be described as an enormous hormonal wrench. In short, every ounce of me seemed to cry out, '*I want another baby!*' Irrational I know, but I just felt an overwhelming desire to be pregnant all over again and to recapture all the intimacy that accompanies nurturing your newborn in the cocoon of your home. Looking back now, I'm sure the emotional and hormonal adjustment of giving up breastfeeding and returning to the world of work prompted this longing. But before I'd had time to rationalise my feelings, the thin blue line had appeared once again and the journey of becoming a mum for the second time had begun.

With my latest pregnancy the gap has been much longer. (My youngest will be four-and-a-half when his baby sibling arrives in December.) Not only will I be able to really enjoy quality time with the new baby while my older two are at school, but in many ways they will be little helpers too; my daughter has been practising her favourite nursery rhymes for weeks and my son asks repeatedly if he can hold the baby while he watches the Arsenal goals at the weekend! So you see I am starting to see the advantages (and disadvantages) of both age gaps.

From what I've discovered among fellow mums in my neighbourhood and through my Fab Mum network there are two major camps in the field of second-time-round conception. The first is that of women for whom conceiving is a hard slog of cycle-checking, ovulation kits, fertility testing and possibly even IVF. For these hopeful mums-to-be trying for the first and subsequent child/children is an emotional rollercoaster of disappointments and hormonal changes. I know several women who have taken two years (and sometimes many more) to get pregnant and that's not isolated to their first pregnancy either. The rule of thumb for these mums is not when they choose to conceive but when conception chooses them. It's about making it possible to have just one baby rather than ever truly having the luxury of preferring a one-year or even ten-year age gap between babies!

I've found the second camp of women tend to make one of the following three choices when deciding to have subsequent children: they either have them very close together (eighteen months or less between each child), leave the 'standard' two/three-year gap, or wait even longer, often for the first to be approaching school age or beyond.

Assuming you have a rough idea of your menstrual cycle and conception is possible, when do you think the right time will be for you?

Having them close

I admit the news that I was expecting my second child so soon after my first was received with mixed emotions. Was it fair to bring a new baby into my daughter's life before she could even walk? Was I a terrible mother expecting her to 'share' her mum so soon in life? And from a practical point of view, how easy would it be to breastfeed a newborn with a toddler reaching for the gas cooker ignition/glass vase full of flowers/dog poo in the park?

There is also an enormous amount to consider in terms

of your own physical and emotional identity. Having your babies close together barely gives you a second to enjoy squeezing back into your skinny jeans or venturing out for that rare blissful girls' lunch at your local gastro pub before your body is yet again preparing itself for motherhood. I know my neighbour Lara didn't even bother retrieving her sexy underwear or fitted frocks from the dusty refuse sack in the loft after she fell pregnant by accident when Jacob was just four months old. She merely resurrected her maternity jeans from the laundry bin and started the cycle all over again.

I vividly remember a super hot summer's day at the beginning of August, just days after my son was born. I was a bag of unpredictable emotions; elated after the birth, yet starting to feel the exhaustion of feeding round the clock combined with the appearance of my daughter's little head with the lark for cuddles each morning. While I sat inside feeding my newborn I watched my daughter, sister and mother splashing in the paddling pool outside. Gleeful and radiant, my daughter turned to find me and I saw her face fall when I wasn't there. For the next few hours I failed miserably to settle my son who seemed grumpy, hungry and full of wind all at the same time. It felt like an invisible line had been drawn and I was unable to reach my daughter. Suddenly my primary instinct was to feed my son, hold him as he cried, burped and gurgled in the haven of the cool indoors, yet it clashed with the unconditional attention I longed to shower on my daughter. Silly as it sounds, this scene still makes my heart lurch with sadness. I felt so tired and torn and I wondered how on earth I'd ever be everything to both my wonderful, beautiful yet inevitably needy children at the same time.

Many memories of being torn between children now feed into this one conundrum. How can I split myself in two? How can I possibly give enough time/energy/praise to each child in turn? How can I attempt to fulfil both their needs with one story/activity/song? And will I ever have any time left for myself? The answer is of course simple: you can't split yourself in two and it will be nigh on impossible to please both children all the time. You'll have to work twice as hard to give them both the attention they deserve and squeeze in that swim/yoga/glass of wine with a gal pal at the end of a long day impersonating Angelina Ballerina. However, you can only attempt to do your best and must praise yourself every step of the way for trying. The children *will* feel utterly loved, you *will* find small pockets of individual time with them both and you *will* (come hell or high water) squeeze in that swim *and* a glass of Merlot.

All this multi-tasking and these tearful memories must make having more than one child sound like some sort of horror show (and believe me, at times it feels like it!) but almost four years on from the birth of my second-born I can honestly say, hand on heart, that having my first two children close together was most definitely worth it! I am such a convert to the 'having them close together' ethos I could write a whole book on the benefits, but seeing as we Fab Mums have so much more to cover, I'll summarise them in five main points:

1. There is no memory of life as an only child. Leaving a gap of under two years often means the first child has little memory of life without a sibling. I know in the case of my two children this has meant a very limited amount of sibling

rivalry (or 'Please, Mum, can you send the baby back now?').
In short, all my daughter's memories include her younger
brother and she seemed to accept very quickly that he was
part of the family web. My great friend Katie is just eighteen
months younger than her brother, and her mother Elise (now
a grandmother herself) is adamant a small gap is the best
gap. Her theory that a child at the age of two starts to establish their own identity (with jealousy and attention-seeking
a large part of this 'phase') has a lot of grounding – why else
do we call it the 'terrible twos'? By already introducing a
sibling before your first-born hits two, the focus of the terrible
twos is not suffused by rage at the new arrival.

2. The children are best friends.   I know it sounds like
a cliché but my two kids are really and truly the best of
friends. As soon as the 'Oh my God, this is a nightmare
juggling act' phase had passed (give it a good six months),
the siblings are so close in age that they became the world's
best companions. Not a day goes by when they aren't building
a camp in the garden, wrecking either of their bedrooms,
ganging up to wreak havoc on the kitchen with under-fives'
world domination or sharing secret jokes under the duvet.
I regularly send them upstairs to play while I answer some
emails (or secretly indulge in the latest copy of *Grazia*, a cup
of Earl Grey and a slice of ginger cake) and on an exceptionally good day I won't be interrupted by either of them
for hours at a time. One of the sweetest memories I have
of late is my son creeping into his sister's bed of a weekend
night and her singing him to sleep! (I discovered them
entwined in each other's arms, and left them that way until
morning.)

There is less than two years between my brother and me and my mother says we were the same. Sharing a bed out of choice in the school holidays, composing funny rhymes to taunt our cousins and getting lost in our large country garden, only coming back to collect provisions at supper-time, are just a few of my precious memories. Our younger years were blessed with being the best of friends and even though we went through a few typical adolescent feuds, we're still as thick as thieves today. I agree with my own mother in that this early friendship and bond was made possible because we inevitably shared so much in terms of interests, hobbies and imaginary play. (It's always much easier to find fun and mischief as partners in crime!)

3. The baby phase is over and you can move on. It's true that by having your children close together you can get the breastfeeding/sterilising/nappies phase over and done with in one swift(ish) glut of winding, potty training and teething. For many women I know, the baby stage (and all the immense amount of baby-kit that goes with this) is one of the hardest parts of bringing up children. For them, the fact that you can do this once, with two children at the same time, never needing to return to this phase again, is a bonus. I don't know about you, but I certainly relished the fact I could pack away the changing mat, potty and double buggy, and wave goodbye to the under-twos' monkey music, tumble tots classes and gym babes sessions, safe in the knowledge we could now move on to a somewhat more mobile and unencumbered life! (I suppose I shouldn't be too smug: who'll be clapping along to 'If you're happy and you know it' this time next year . . . ?)

4. The fabulous mum emerges. A key plus point of having the children close together is purely a selfish one, I admit. You've burped, weaned and sleep-trained your two bundles of joy and now they're happily tucking into Sunday roasts and sleeping through the night (well, most nights). It doesn't take a genius to work out that after a tough few years of juggling two babies and a chaotic family life, you can finally start to think about you, the fabulous mum! A period of re-investing in yourself (your career, your wardrobe, your relationships, your nutrition and your home) is a brilliant incentive after what can feel like a good few years of trekking uphill with a double buggy and fending off mashed banana flung from an excited eighteen-month-old in a highchair!

5. Oh and one more thing . . . It goes without saying that if you're an older mum who has waited until her late thirties to start a family, having two close together is a good way of having more than one child while the risks are lower than waiting until your forties.

The two-year gap

Having outlined the advantages of a close age gap (but believe me there are disadvantages too: a toddler starting to wake up every three hours to accompany newborn night feeds, breastfeeding and spoon-feeding at the same time, a body that hasn't been out of maternity clothes for what feels like a lifetime . . . need I go on?) it seems only fair to discuss what seems to be the more common age gap between siblings. I have more friends than I can count who have waited the 'norm' of two years between their first and second child. They either aim to give birth to their second child around two years after their first, or plan to conceive around two years after giving birth to their first. My sister-in-law Sue is a classic example of this. She had her first child, Max, in her mid-thirties and always planned to have a second with enough time to ensure they would be good friends but leaving a big enough gap to really enjoy some quality time with Max before number two arrived. (Sounds sensible, eh?) Sure enough, Sue relished a wonderful first two years with Max. She put work on hold, threw herself into baby massage, baby aqua, Gymboree and the local playgroups. When Max was eighteen months old she settled him in to the local nursery two mornings a week, so she could enjoy a little time to get fit and get back into shape. She admits now that seeing Max settle so well into nursery and watching him grow as an individual outside their tight mother–son bond confirmed that as he approached his second birthday it would be a good time to try for number two.

Women who have taken a while to conceive their first may need to plan slightly longer to conceive again, but Sue, being one of those women who it appears only has to look at her husband in a certain way to get pregnant, suggested it and exactly six weeks later she was throwing up religiously every morning. Low and behold, nine months on, Yaeli, a sister for two-year-old Max (and Sue's teenage step-son Jack) arrived to complete what she vows is her 'finished' family unit!

Sue agrees with my numerous two-year-gap Fab Mum friends that these are the advantages of waiting until the two-year itch:

15

You have a good period in which to enjoy number one. As my friend Rosie puts it, 'Leaving a two-year gap means you can really enjoy the magic of being a new mum and totally indulge your first-born without compromising your emotions or being torn between siblings.' Her two-year-old Arthur is as bonny and loved as any child you'll ever meet, so with his second birthday fast approaching it seemed the perfect time to go through the trials (and in Rosie's case twenty-four-hour sickness) of early pregnancy once again. This is such a common voice in women who have opted to leave a similar age gap. In general they feel they've really relished their first-born, nurtured every roll/step/word and feel emotionally and physically ready to embark on motherhood all over again.

Equally, you can enjoy 'quality time' with the second baby. This point is simple: if you leave a two-year-plus gap between kids it's likely number one will be in nursery or pre-school for small chunks of every day, leaving you free to get to know your newborn (yes, without demands for the twenty-fifth reread of *Maisy* or cries of 'Juice *now*, Muuuu-uuuummmmmmy!' penetrating every magic gurgling moment!). You'll probably find it's good for the elder child too. They tend to enjoy the feeling that they have their own special space and friends by going to nursery.

They're close enough to be friends but not so close you feel like a breeding machine. A two-year-plus age gap works well if you're hoping for your first-born to be actively aware and involved in the arrival of a sibling. By the age of two or three they can start to recognise their role of 'older brother/sister' and help you to prepare for the new arrival. Although jealousy is inevitable in any configuration of siblings, you may well find that they can be good friends too (as well as arch enemies at times).

You can get your groove back before Take Two! Another added bonus is that a few years between pregnancies gives you room to breathe between them. In short, depending on your priorities, you can go back to your job and give your career a boost, work towards getting your figure and fitness back on track, or simply focus once more on your personal life. Pregnancy, childbirth and breastfeeding take their toll on your body, working life and relationships, and leaving a reasonable gap gives you time to reinvest in these and prioritise a little time for you.

Waiting for the first to start school

For some women the thought of rushing through babyhood and pregnancy is about as appealing as downing a pint of cod liver oil. I certainly felt that, after having my first two so close together, I'd put the brakes on my growing family until the two I had were both at school. In fact, I wish it had been such a rational decision; more realistically, I felt far too knackered for the first few years, and then euphoric at getting a semblance of my old life back for the latter two, to even consider breeding further!

My friend Clara waited five years between her first and second child. Her reason being? She absolutely couldn't understand, once her first child was happily skipping into nursery every day and she could get back to the job she loved, the man she adored and the Jimmy Choos she practically devours, why on earth she'd go and have another child straight away and be resigned to early nights and Birkenstocks once again.

However, once her first-born, Jasmine, began school, a wave of accomplishment at having brought up such a happy, gifted little girl was shortly followed by a wave of broodiness and longing to do it all over again. It took Clara a good year of 'practising' (and sadly one miscarriage), but Jasmine's seventh birthday was marked by her mum's labour pains and the arrival of her first (but not last) brother. To this day (even with an ex-husband in the dog house and over-time to do), Clara insists waiting five-plus years between births was the best thing for both mother and child's sanity. Not only did it give Clara a chance to enjoy each child and savour that baby phase one at a time, it also meant the elder siblings became the ultimate 'little helpers' when the newborn arrived. Now Jasmine is thirteen she's almost like a mini-mummy to her two little brothers. In fact I don't think I've seen Clara push the buggy or spoon-feed mashed up rusk to her youngest for months!

The bottom line is: choosing when to have your next child is almost as complicated as finding the 'perfect' time to have your first. There are so many emotional, financial and physical issues to take on board (not to mention for many women possible conception hurdles to overcome); it's a wonder the whole country isn't adhering to a one-child policy. Having said that, even with a stack of bills to pay, a five-year-old's lunch box still sitting by the front door (I know, I know, and the school secretary said *immediately*), a three-year-old who's now asleep wrapped in his duvet at my feet and a growling bean that's calling relentlessly for lasagne (despite the fact the fridge is bare and it's only eleven in the morning!), I wouldn't change things for the world. I suppose that's what we Fab Mums call 'the irrational yet overwhelming feeling of broodiness'!

When Three Becomes Four

I talked an awful lot in *The Fabulous Mum's Handbook* about the adjustments and challenges the new mum faces when

19

embracing motherhood for the first time. When I wrote the book, it seemed that almost all my girlfriends/neighbours/nursery mum pals had the same worries and questions about adjusting to a new life as a family of three. As the mums-to-be I knew approached parenthood for the first time, they constantly asked me for advice on what baby kit they should buy, what to wear through pregnancy, what to eat and what tips and tricks I could suggest for helping them to become new mums with their groove and sanity still intact. We're now all a few years on and the questions tend to be less about what brand of maternity jeans to wear and more about how to get your existing unit of three ready for the arrival of the tiny fourth member.

I'll talk at the end of this chapter about the importance of making time for yourself within this crazy, hazy time of family expansion, and woven into almost every chapter there will be tips and tricks on keeping your own identity as your family grows.

However, the key for many women to a successful transition from three to four is in the smooth adjustment of their first-born to their new role as eldest child. I know that for my good friend Jennie the imminent arrival of her second child has been far less about eating right (she learned the nutritional value of all the right foods the first time round) or sifting through the endless choice of baby paraphernalia (she'll just recycle any unisex clothes and equipment which have been safely stored in her mother-in-law's garage the past three years). No, this pregnancy has been about preparing her daughter Minnie for the role of big sister. Without investing time and effort in doing this right, you're bound to be so wrapped up with anxiety and guilt (not to mention a two-year-old who is utterly resentful at a baby who's stolen *her* mum) that you're likely to feel more big bad mamma than Fab Mum!

Here are some helpful pointers to assist you in preparing your first-born for the new arrival. Believe me, if you take the time to do just a few of these, the whole family will thank you for it.

Talk, talk, talk

Now I know I risk sounding a little 'Trisha' here, but talking about the arrival of your newborn will really help the older child get used to the idea of sharing her space within the family unit. Explaining the process of conception (which I did in its most simple form when my children were around three years old), pregnancy and birth will all help your child understand where the baby has come from and the motion of life evolving in the womb. (I'm even planning to take my two to the twenty-week-scan so they get an idea of who's in there!) A starting point for this explanation could well be a trip to the local bookshop to buy a good book on where babies come from and the arrival of a sibling. An old *Elle* colleague of mine, Abby Cocovini, has written a book for this very purpose, called *What's Inside Your Tummy, Mummy?* It's exceptionally helpful, giving kids a month-by-month guide to what to expect, and has certainly helped my two children with this learning curve.

Another nice idea (and one which I suggested to my friend Jennie when she found out she was pregnant with number two) is to involve your child in charting the progress of your growing bump. Getting your toddler or pre-school child to write the number of weeks/months in lipstick or face paint on your tummy and then asking them to Polaroid it for their very own scrapbook is a fun way of making them feel it's their own project too.

I know I'll be following Jennie's lead this time round with a whole array of banter which stresses the importance of being 'a helpful big brother and/or sister'. It's great to get them to think of all the ways they can help once the baby arrives, for example carrying the changing bag, pushing the buggy, helping to hold the baby's bottle or even turning the pages of a cloth book to entertain the baby while you're putting on a wash or dishing up the porridge. Children love to feel helpful and to gain praise, so this is an ideal time to utilise this!

Helping to prepare

Continuing with the helpful theme (you can see I'm going to run with this one), it's a good idea to involve your child with some of the fun parts of preparing for the new arrival. My friend Lyn, for example, has already got little Riley sorting through his favourite old Babygros for number two, whose arrival will be in time for Christmas. Likewise, my sister-in-law Sue swears that allowing Max to choose the mobile and 'special teddy' for Yaeli prevented any conflict about who the new gifts were intended for! (Bless Max, he even wrapped them up in Spiderman paper.)

I also love the idea of an exchange of presents between siblings after the birth of your second child. Although my daughter was only eighteen months when her brother arrived, I spent every waking hour in the days leading up to his birth erecting and painting a tiny wooden playhouse at the bottom of the garden for her as a gift from her new baby brother. I roped in my mum to transform an old Cath Kidston table-cloth into curtains, found a second-hand kids' table for seventy-five pence in a car boot sale, laying it with plastic cutlery and plates, and even put some potted plants outside. Bonkers, I know, (and lucky I didn't give birth as I perched on a ladder to paint the roof white), but believe me, when her brother arrived on a scorching hot July afternoon and I told her he'd wanted her to have a little 'extra surprise' she ran out into the garden with a teapot and an array of dolls and I didn't see her until September she was so enraptured with her surprise.

A garden playhouse may seem a tad extravagant (and maybe part of it was my guilt at having a second just a few months after her first birthday), but offering a special toy from the baby to the first-born and vice versa is a lovely way for your eldest to feel they are both showing and receiving love.

Avoid too much change at once

It's a good idea not to overload your child with too much change all at the same time. If you're planning to introduce your child to a new nursery, playgroup or school try (if you can) to do it a good few months before the birth, not on your due date! My gal pal Georgia made this mistake and when she tried to drop off Harry at pre-school a week after giving birth he screamed the place down with cries of, 'That nasty baby has stolen my mummy, I hate her!' The last thing you want is for your first-born to feel pushed out or replaced.

Similarly, if you're moving an elder child out of a cot to make way for the new arrival allow at least three months before the birth to do this. Establishing new habits and routines well ahead of such a life-changing event for your first-born is vital to ensure the arrival of their new sibling is not associated with the often unwanted changes. Avoiding resentment is key here!

If you're planning to take maternity leave from work, if at all possible take at least a few weeks before the birth so you can spend some extra time alone with your first-born. If you step straight from the boardroom to the labour room you'll not only be knackered yourself but you'll also have a child with a serious case of baby-envy!

Carve out time for your eldest

Now I know only too well that having a second child, no matter the age gap, is one huge juggling act as you attempt to keep breast pump, rusks, potties, *Spot* books and wet-wipes up in the air without dropping them all at once. To tell you it's important to carve out a little bit of one-on-one with your eldest probably sounds about as easy as jetting off for a girlie mini-break to the Algarve the week after giving birth, but, hand on heart, if you're organised it's not really that hard. Try to give your first-born just a few windows of 'special time' each week and they'll thank you for it in their own unique way. Even if all you can manage is to pass your newborn to your partner on a Sunday morning and make a smoothie together in the kitchen, or while your newborn is sleeping have a quiet story and cuddle with your toddler on the sofa (if you can stave off the urge to fall into a coma-like sleep!), you'll both reap the benefits and you may well prevent your eldest taking umbrage at the new baby who's wearing *her* old Babygro and suckling on *her* mummy's breast!

It's all very well advising you to spend extra time with your existing child during pregnancy and include them in the nesting process but in actual fact you and I both know that most of the time you feel like screaming, 'But I'm bloody knackered!!!!' There's no denying that being pregnant with your second (and subsequent) baby is even more exhausting than the first time around, simply because you have far less time to rest and relax. Nights are often still broken, the day is certain to start before it's light outside and instead of returning home from work or a day playing at the park and flopping, you've got to bathe, read to and put your toddler to bed. 'Heeeeeeeeeeeelp!' I hear you cry.

I certainly found that the first three months of pregnancy (when you deserve a medal for just getting dressed without throwing up/passing out) and the last few months (when all you want to do is eat chocolates and snooze in bed all day) are the hardest because of that life-shattering tiredness you only ever experience when pregnant. The best tricks I've learned to help ease this catatonic exhaustion are the following:

Rest when you can. If your existing child is at nursery or naps in the day take the opportunity to have a daytime rest too. Sure, you may be stuck in the office or have a hundred and one things to do around the house, but even a forty-minute stop-gap will serve you well in getting through the rest of the day. Likewise, take early nights and lie-ins whenever you can, even if you have to resort to bribing your partner with a roast lunch in order to get one!

Eat well. Obvious, I know, but by keeping your energy levels constant during the pregnancy you're sure to feel well fuelled throughout the day. Three balanced meals a day (and that means not grabbing a Big Mac at teatime because you've missed lunch and are close to fainting!) and nourishing snacks are crucial. Oatcakes with manuka honey, raw vegetables with hummus, banana and strawberry fruit salad with natural yogurt, and nuts and dried fruits are firm favourites of mine (did anyone say time for dried mango?). I find that a healthy yet filling snack at four in the afternoon keeps my energy levels from crashing during that all-important after-school rush and just about helps me make it through to the kids' bedtime in one piece.

Be productive while you can! At present I'm happily bobbing along in those middle three months of pregnancy I like to call the 'vitality trimester'. For most of us this is a time when we're over the extreme nausea of the initial twelve weeks yet not entering the phase of 'I'm so big I can't leave the house'. While I'm here and feeling energised I'm trying to do what I can to prepare for the months when I'll feel like a slug-cum-hippo. I'm doing as much work as possible to give myself a good few months 'off' at the end of the pregnancy, I'm 'nesting' (sorting through old baby clothes and making a mental list of what I'll need to buy) and I'm starting to plan wholesome meals that I can bulk cook and freeze in preparation for when I'll barely have the time and energy to reheat food, let alone prepare a family meal. My advice would be to get busy if you have the energy so you can make the most of resting-up towards the end of your pregnancy.

Take up offers of help.   Another thing I've been doing in the 'vitality trimester' is help my friend Jennie who is in what I call the 'beached-whale trimester' (i.e. the last few months). She's coming to the very end of her second pregnancy and it's now that she really needs playdates and trips to the park to entertain her daughter Minnie. Between her husband, mother, in-laws, neighbour and me, we've managed to keep Minnie well and truly entertained so Jennie can rest and preserve her energy for labour.

No one's saying the second/third/fourth . . . pregnancies won't be tiring (OK, life-shattering), but by easing up on yourself and taking short cuts here and there you should be able to claw back the occasional extra half an hour's rest. Let the house be slightly less pristine, the kids' supper be shop-bought for a change, a neighbour have your toddler over for some paddling pool action, and the boss roll his eyes as you slip home early on a Friday afternoon. With every new pregnancy you need to be even more resourceful in your search for zzzzzzzzzs!

Mother knows best

'When I fell pregnant three years after giving birth to my daughter it was a total shock. To be honest, my marriage was breaking down and the thought of being a single parent to not only one, but two kids scared me stupid. I decided after much deliberation to keep the baby and have absolutely no regrets as she's an adorable baby. However, from the start I was adamant I wanted my firstborn to feel totally involved. I devised a sticker chart that worked like an advent calendar throughout my pregnancy. Each week she ticked off the week and chose a sticker to mark it on the chart. At the end of every month we'd get a 'joint reward' of a treat (something like an ice-cream from the local Häagen-Dazs parlour or a new set of pens from Woolworths). My daughter felt so much a part of the whole nine months and really under-stood the cycle of new life. Well worth a try.'

Part-time working mum of two

Time for a People Carrier

I have a dream and it goes something like this: I am in my mid-forties (and haven't succumbed to Botox, yet). I'm sitting in my garden, the late Friday afternoon sun going down behind a weeping willow tree. I'm holding a (large) glass of rosé wine. I've laid the garden table for supper and the smell of roast chicken fills the air. Mulling around the house are my four children all in various stages of teenagehood. My daughter (who's just five now) will be close to twenty and probably in the midst of major boyfriend angst; my son will be tailing close behind and if his current boyish Brad Pitt-esque looks continue, will no doubt have teenage girls queuing up the garden path. The next two, well who knows; they are still fantasy at present.

What I'm sure of is that my children will be on their own journeys through life, possessing strong personalities and visions for their future. The other thing I'm sure of is that my house will always be filled with life. Laughter and tears, sibling world wars and teenage broken hearts, exams passed and failed, dreams dashed and accomplished; these are the things that make families feel wonderfully alive!

So there you have it. I didn't say a million-pound pad, I daren't suggest a garden with an outdoor pool and did I come close to suggesting a roast chicken cooked by my own in-house chef Gordon Ramsay? No, my dream is far more simple than that. It's to have four happy, robust, complicated and confident children and a husband who (still) loves us all to bits. For many women having 2.4 kids (let's say two for argument's sake) is more than enough. As such, most families can stretch to a holiday abroad now and then, give the children their own rooms and possibly maintain a family pooch. For a mum trying to be fabulous, surely four would be stretching the possibilities of fabulousness a bit? Time for yourself? A body you're happy with? A career? The odd grown-up night out on the town? With four kids? You must be joking, I hear you cry! Well, I'm sure I've told you I like a challenge and somehow, even if it seems like madness to you, I'm pretty damn sure that women who want a large family (and with it the obligatory people carrier) can make it work.

How better to illustrate this than with two wonderful role-model Fabulous Mums? The first, Celia, full-time mother of three daughters and a son; the second, Clara, working single mum to a daughter and two sons. Both these women have seemingly enviable lives. I don't mean they live in grand Georgian estates with staff in their own quarters and four cars parked on the gravel drive. No, what I mean is that they have wonderfully adjusted and happy children, and still maintain their own identity, passions and friendships. Sure, there are days when Clara pulls her hair out with the strain of juggling three children alone and holding down a successful, well-paid, full-time job, and others where Celia's attempt at a gym class is barred by a sick child off school with flu, but both confess that ninety per cent of the time they get the balance just about right.

So I thought it woulds be simple enough to discover the secret to why and how women have big families, and yet still manage to keep their groove intact. How difficult can it be to put a date in the diary for Celia, Clara and myself to brainstorm our experiences over a bottle of good wine (well, orange juice in my case)? Very, it turns out. It took three failed lunch dates, two cancelled evenings and probably at least twenty-five answerphone messages, texts and emails to realise that getting three women with nine children (nine-and-a-half if you count my mini-bump), two husbands, an on/off boyfriend and two careers is, well how do I put it? Nigh on impossible! However, in the end, over some long, late-night telephone chats and our brief and garbled conversations at the school gates, a page of A4 paper covered with ideas fused together to form the following pointers:

The Ten Commandments of The People Carrier Fabulous Mum

1. You don't have to be mega-rich to have a big family. However, you do have to have patience and a love of children (large and small) in abundance. If you have one or two children and your tolerance tank is running on empty, think about stopping now!

2. It must be a dual decision. There's absolutely no point breeding for Britain if your partner only wants one child. It will just end in tears (yours and his) and is likely to mean he'll spend less and less time at home and more time at work/football/down the pub or, I hate to say it, in the arms of another woman.

3. Sacrifices must be made (unless you're million-aires). Three-plus pairs of school shoes, a large car, bumper packs of bread/cornflakes/apple juice/fish fingers/Marmite and birthday parties three-plus times a year are just some of the extra ways in which your outgoings will increase. As we said before, you don't have to be mega-rich. However, you'll most likely have to cut back elsewhere to make ends meet.

4. Octopus mum. Having a big family means spreading your time and energy more thinly than you would with a smaller unit. Having said that, it's wonderful for children to learn how to share and cooperate early on. Make these skills key to your family ethos.

5. Round up the troops. Enlisting help from family, friends or the occasional paid helper is essential to meeting your own needs, those of your partner and those of your kids. If you work, you'll need a wonderful nanny (work out the sum of four times nursery fees and you'll see why!) or, if you're a full-time mum, you'd be wise to ensure you have a good support network of friends and neighbours to call on from time to time. After all, even stay-at-home mums need time off every now and then, even if it is to attend their eldest's nativity play.

6. Organisation is key. A rough routine to your week will help you so much in prioritising important tasks and dates. It will also help with having one-on-one time with each child and allowing a morsel of free time for you. Hurrah!

7. Don't be a control freak! Even though we all agree that organisation is key, expecting life to run like a military operation twenty-four-seven will leave you in a tizz when things don't go exactly to plan. Leave room for manoeuvre.

8. Don't give up on your career altogether. Clara is a prime example of the career mum with a big family. She works incredibly hard in the world of TV, yet has no partner to lean on when the going gets tough. Having said this, she swears doing the job she loves and maintaining her identity outside the realm of motherhood has benefited both her and the children, and seeing as her kids are so lovely that I'd happily have any one of the three move in tomorrow, I'd have to agree with her on that.

9. Be creative with space. You don't have to own a five-bedroom pad to have four children; however, you do have to be innovative with your space. Clara's boys share a room and have a wonderful boat/bunk/desk/den-type construction in their room. The eldest helped design and paint it one summer holiday before his brother arrived, which helped take the pain out of sharing.

10. Find great schools. Private or state, we'll all make different choices. However, what remains key no matter the type of school you choose is that you need to be content with your choice.

Celia, Clara and I all agreed this could easily become a list of one hundred commandments but I hope there are some points here that will inspire you.

Making Time for Each Child

I confess the past few parenting years have been far easier than the initial two. The reason being? Not only have we been rid of nappies and buggies to be replaced by pants and micro-scooters (hurrah!), I've managed at last to share myself pretty much equally between my two children. Up until this point I was working long and pretty stressful hours in the offices of a fashion magazine. My days 'off' were jam-packed with the weekly food shop, sorting out the household bills, trying to squeeze in a little leisure time and attempting (and failing more often than not) to have a little one-on-one with each child. Although my daughter attended a local nursery a few mornings a week, it was my babysitter who enjoyed the time alone with my son, while on the weekends both kids would tear their (and my) hair out for some individual attention.

So how have things changed? Well for a start I changed my job. I don't like to call it a stroke of luck because I worked bloody hard to make the dream of becoming an author and freelance journalist a reality. I realised very early on in my mothering life that if I didn't do a job I loved and that suited my family life better, I'd be miserable, my husband would be miserable and, lo and behold, so would my children. Working from home and having the support of great friends, neighbours and a super carer have meant I not only manage to get far more work done than I ever did chained to an office desk, but I also see an awful lot more of my kids.

Secondly, since my daughter started school and my son attends nursery in the afternoons, I've managed to devise a wonderful week-to-week rhythm that includes good chunks of time alone with both children. For instance, two days a week I write once the kids have gone to bed, allowing me to take my daughter to school in the mornings and then hang out with my son. I won't lie and say we while away the hours making model planes from matchsticks or that I teach him the history of the Royal Air Force, but we do have a lot of fun. Trips to the park to collect conkers, play-dates, making a mess of a brownie recipe, or simply sitting on the sofa with a cup of tea while he entertains me with a puppet show – whatever the chosen activity the important thing is we do it together.

Likewise, I delegate two afternoons a week to spend alone with my daughter. This is no mean feat, I'll have you know, when school hours and after-school activities fill up most of her day. However, we manage to go for hot chocolates (OK, admittedly with a double-chocolate-chip muffin thrown in for good measure) every Thursday, before I watch her spin and pirouette in her ballet class, and on Friday afternoons, when she gets a half-day at school and my son is at nursery until three-thirty, we simply hang out at home doing little more than playing with her dolls house or colouring in. (The former, I have to add, is only made possible by a rota of fellow mums picking up my son on a Thursday; thank you, Jennie, Rena and Vicky!)

All this will no doubt change once my son starts school in September and both children will be clawing for my un-divided attention from the moment I pick them up at the school gates. Having said that, this past year has taught me some important lessons that are here to stay. However manic you are, however much over-time you're doing and however many under-fives you have, it's still well worth trying to weave in a little focused time with each child. Even if it's just a brisk twenty-minute walk in the park in between the respective nursery/school (stopping at the swings for a whizz on the slide) or a fortnightly playdate for the rest of your brood so you can spend an hour with just one of them, it's a time neither of you will forget and that will benefit you both enormously.

My two are always so busy shouting for attention that with all the noise I can't always hear what they're really trying to express or they are too caught up in the moment to be themselves. In contrast, the moments of one-to-one give them space to pinpoint their thoughts with such ease and clarity it never fails to astound me. It was during a rainy morning of conker collecting that my son admitted he was scared of the dark (which finally explained the months of night wandering) and it was during one of our hot chocolate sessions that my daughter told me she knew where babies came from, in worryingly accurate detail for a five-year-old! Without these one-on-one sessions I'd probably still be turning out every light in the house each night and perpetuating the myth that a stork would be delivering our new baby!

My good friend Rena agrees that making time for each child is very important. Rena is a committed mum of two girls and a boy, and seems to spend her life encouraging her musical geniuses in every possible avenue in their lives. Sure, we still fit in the odd girlie lunch while the children are at school and she rarely misses her eight in the morning session at the local gym (while her husband feeds the children endless rounds of toast), but come school collection time she is there one hundred per cent for her three kids. Rena prides herself on taking every opportunity she gets to spend time alone with each child and making that time, in her words, 'unforgettable'!

It was half-term last week and I happily looked after her youngest daughter for a day while her son stayed at his friend's house. The occasion? To create an action-packed, super-fabulous day out for her ten-year-old Jemma. Jemma had just received an offer for a full music scholarship from almost every top private school in London; some achievement for a humble ten-year-old with brown saucer eyes and a talent for spotting glittery ballet pumps. Quite rightly, Rena felt her eldest daughter deserved one of their tri-annual mummy days. Armed with her favourite pair of red glitter ballet pumps and a huge smile, Jemma and her mother spent the day visiting the Tate Modern, picnicking in Green Park and taking a Rickshaw ride across central London. It may not be a regular weekly occurrence but when Rena makes the time the only way to sum it up really is 'unforgettable'.

Mother knows best

'I'm a working mum with two schoolchildren, so I find making time for each child increasingly difficult. Because my kids don't see much of me in the week all hell would break loose if I prioritised one over the other at the weekends. This is why my partner and I devised the 'golden ticket'. At the end of each month we fill a small sack with golden slips of paper; on each is written a

Making Time for You

Under-fives football, a meeting with your line manager after work, accompanying your six-year-old to ballet, writing up your latest feature proposal before the nine a.m. deadline tomorrow, trying to squeeze in a little messy play with your toddler *and* marinating lamb ready for supper with your in-laws at the weekend; with all this going on you probably feel that managing to wear shoes that match is nigh on impossible, let alone creating that all elusive 'you time'. It doesn't take a genius to work out that having one child makes finding time for yourself harder than it was as a singleton (with bags of time to spend drinking Pinot Grigio or pounding the treadmill in the gym), having two kids stretches your resources even more, and with three-plus kids, well now you really have to be inventive!

The crux of this issue remains the same: *Making time for*

you is the secret to being a happy, fabulous mum! Now, by this I don't mean giving up your job, employing a nanny to look after your children for the sole intent of lunching with the ladies or getting a manicure at your local salon (as if!). Nor am I suggesting prioritising time alone with your friends or partner after work above skidding in for the last ten minutes of the nativity play, or rushing home for bedtime stories. But what is important is that each week you try to place some 'me time' somewhere near the top of your to-do list as opposed to being an add-on in scribbled pencil right at the bottom.

It often feels virtually impossible to find a space for your own pursuits, especially when your week is one long wrench of feeling you have barely enough time for the children you have, let alone the Sainsbury's shop and the tax return waiting in your 'urgent' pile of paperwork. The thing is, without a weekly (or even fortnightly) bout of exercise, long bath, quiet chapter of the latest chick-lit book or late-night conversation with your best buddy in New Zealand, you start to resent all the utterly necessary weekly obligations (like helping with your eldest's maths homework, working that little bit of over-time or ordering your dad's sixtieth birthday cake). In short, life becomes one long chore instead of a choice.

My friend Paula is a high-flying career mother of three children (and in this mix is a set of twins). Her mornings are spent in a flurry of getting them ready for school and trying to select the perfect kitten heels. The moment she arrives at the office its non-stop 'fashion daaaaarling' until she whizzes out the door at half-five to be home for bath, bed and stories. By the time she's impersonated Horrid

Henry for her son, sung what feels like the thirty-fifth lullaby to her twin girls, listened to all their combined daily news and got them to sleep, she has just about enough time for a ready meal before falling asleep (often still in those kitten heels).

Not long ago she was hospitalised for a week after a severe bout of bronchitis developed into pneumonia. By Valentine's Day she felt so run-down and exhausted, something had to give. It was over one of our girlie lunches (which I should add here had been cancelled more times than I care to count) that we started to brainstorm ideas for her to carve some relaxed time into her week. Making time before work looked impossible, and lunches were out (bar our brief sandwich that day, she'd not taken a full non-work-related lunch break in almost three months). We both agreed that the evenings were also looking doubtful as a window for her own time (especially when her husband was knee-deep in editing a new TV show for the forseeable future). After much deliberation we concluded that the only option would be to bargain with her husband to have Saturday mornings 'off'; in return, she vowed to take all three children to the local park for Saturday afternoons.

To cut a long story short, once the husband was on board, and the kids firmly engaged in trashing their garden, Paula headed off to what has become her regular Saturday morning yoga group. She called me after the first session: 'You know what, Grace? As I lay there listening to my breathing I realised I couldn't remember the last time I'd actually been still, thinking about nothing.' Two hours a week doesn't sound like much, but to Paula it changes her mindset for the whole week. She tries her utmost to clear her mind for that short session and not worry about work deadlines, kids' phonics or mortgage payments.

I admit I have a similar tonic. (In fact, I have two.) As well as meeting my deadlines for this book, feeding my pregnancy craving for home-made lasagne, being class rep at both my kids' schools (I know, what was I thinking?) and listening to my daughter's theories on how babies are made, I still swear by my swimming sessions and a monthly night out with the girls to survive motherhood. My partner trades my Sunday morning swim with his Sunday evening football training and my monthly night out with the girls is easily granted as long as I rent him a Woody Allen movie and order some shredded chilli beef and steamed rice to arrive shortly after my departure. Well worth its weight in gold, I'm sure you'll agree?

I've heard a million different alternatives for a busy mum's formula to 'time out'. Clara, for example, swears by wine tasting; Celia, on the other hand, enjoys a local Bible group; and remember my pal 'Sexy Samantha' from *The Fabulous Mum's Handbook*? Well, I needn't say more about what she enjoys when she gets time to herself! The common thread is that as multi-tasking mums with growing families, we all agree the worst thing we can do is to neglect ourselves. The moment your life becomes one long stream of other people's demands (the boss, the partner, the mother-in-law, the headmistress and no doubt the kids) without a window for the old you, is the moment you know it's time to make a change. No one is likely to offer you a weekend at a health spa any time soon, so the only way to imprint a little fab mum time in the diary is to write it in red pen and make it happen!

Mother knows best

'After my husband left me I took a long hard look at my life. It dawned on me like a lead weight that I'd spent the past ten years prioritising my marriage and my children above all else. I utterly believe in being there one hundred per cent for your family but I realised I had done so at the expense of my own identity and self-esteem. It's taken a good eighteen months but I've managed to claw back some of the things I used to love. I do an art class one morning a week, some freelance proofreading while the kids are at school and a t'ai chi class at the weekend while the children do judo next door. My ex has returned like a sorrowful puppy, but the new me has bolted the door and changed the locks!'

Part-time working mum of three

Top ten growing family tips

1. Think carefully about when is the right time for you to have more children. Take into account your own needs and those of your partner and existing children.
2. Make the decision to grow your family based on your own family structure and ethos, not your close peers or demanding mother-in-law!
3. It's worth considering the pros and cons of differing age gaps between your children.
4. Designate time and energy into preparing your existing

child/children for a new sibling.

5. If at all possible structure your working life to help you to accommodate a growing family with changing needs.

6. Don't neglect your own health and well-being as your family grows (especially during a new pregnancy or those early newborn months when you're run ragged).

7. If you're going for a large family follow The Ten Commandments of the People Carrier Fabulous Mum!

8. Be persistent in trying to make tiny pockets of time for each child alone. You'll all reap the benefits of some sacred one-on-one time.

9. Aim to build a support structure around you that will help as your family unit grows (this could include parents, in-laws, siblings, neighbours, fellow mums or paid helpers).

10. Just because you have a growing brood of needy young-sters on your hands, that doesn't mean you shouldn't carve out occasional time for yourself. Remember you're worth it!

Grace's Guru: Rebecca Abrams

Rebecca Abrams is an award-winning journalist and writer. Her books include the bestselling guide to having a second child, *Three Shoes, One Sock and No Hairbrush* and the highly acclaimed *When Parents Die: learning to live with the loss of a parent*. Rebecca is well known for her articles on family life and until recently wrote a family advice column for the *Daily Telegraph*. She also writes fiction (her latest book is *Touching Distance*). Rebecca lives in Oxford with her husband and their two children.

What are your main tips for the following mums?

A mum who's trying to decide whether to have a second child The first step is to work out why the decision is giving you grief. Is having a second child a matter of 'when' or 'if'? Do you actually want a second child or would you be happy sticking at one? Are you keen to have a second child but anxious about the impact on your first-born/your finances/your professional life? Do you want a second child but your partner is reluctant? Is the memory of the first pregnancy or birth or a difficult postnatal time putting you off?

As well as the joy of a new child, any addition to the family, be it a second, third or fifth, will always bring new challenges. Being realistic about some of the likely practical consequences of a second child means you can, to a certain extent, prepare for them. Are you going to need to rearrange the house to make room for the second child? Will you need more or different childcare? Are you or your partner going to have to rethink your working hours and/or hobbies? Thinking through these issues in advance makes sense and will go a long way to alleviating stress further down the line.

Where the causes of uncertainty are more emotional or psychological, for example after a particularly difficult first labour or a period of postnatal depression, you should get support and advice from a professional via your GP, health visitor or local counselling service.

There are definitely a number of bad reasons for having a second child and it's wise to be honest with yourself about your motivations and hesitations. Having a second child to glue together a troubled marriage is rarely a great success.

Research has found that even in good relationships, marital satisfaction is at its lowest eight to twelve months after the birth of a second child, so if you're hoping a new baby will paper over cracks between you and your partner, think again. Because you want a child of a different sex from your first-born? Not a good reason. Because you feel you should? Not a good reason. Because your mother/mother-in-law/best friend thinks you should? Again, not a good reason.

Many people who would really be happy to settle for one child feel under pressure not to condemn their first-born to life as an only child, whereas in fact there are clear advantages to being an only child. Academically, only children do better and research has failed to turn up any proven emotional or psychological drawbacks. Any disadvantages to being an only child are more likely to be felt later in life when responsibility for ageing parents cannot be shared with a sibling. My advice to a mother who feels under pressure to have a second child when she's actually happy with one is to remain true to her own instinct. After all, there's no law saying 'thou shalt have more than one child' and what an only child might miss out on in terms of the hurly burly of larger family life they will certainly make up for in other ways.

A mum wanting to weigh up the pros and cons of leaving a small or large gap between her children
There is no such thing as a perfect gap. You need to take into account your own temperament, energy levels, lifestyle, and the needs and character of your first-born. For a year after my second child was born I barely left the house with the two of them because my first-born was a tearaway who

needed watching every second, which felt impossible with a small baby and pram.

A smaller gap makes for a more physically and emotionally demanding time for the mother but, on the other hand, the intensive early years of sleepless nights and nappy-changing will be out of the way sooner. There is a persuasive argument that having children very close together (less than two and a half years) is harder for the first-born, who does not yet have the emotional skills to understand and cope with the arrival of a younger sibling, nor the ability to manage the frustrations of no longer being the absolute centre of attention. On the upside, being closer in age makes it easier for siblings to be friends as they get older and also means they are at more similar stages developmentally – so you will have fewer of the conflicts of interest that come with a larger age gap.

The great advantage of a larger age gap is that the first-born is far more able to cope with the emotional transition of becoming a sibling. A child of four or older will already have routines, friends and interests, all of which will be less affected by the arrival of a new baby. You can involve an older child in caring for and playing with the baby, and you can explain and discuss with an older child his or her negative and positive feelings about the baby. In addition, an older child is more able to amuse herself while you're busy with the baby. A bigger gap also increases the likelihood that your older child will be settled in his sleep patterns, which means you're only going to be woken up by one child during the night, not two. I am worse than useless when sleep-deprived and neither of my children slept through the night reliably until they started school. When I look back now, I don't know how I survived those five years at all. If you're anything like me, the 'sleep factor' is an important consideration.

A mum who needs to prepare older siblings for a new arrival The key to preparing your older child is giving him or her plenty of information, especially about anything that might be causing anxiety. Explain what will happen when the baby is being born. For example, who will look after the older child, how long you are likely to be in hospital (if it's going to be a hospital birth), what the baby will and won't be able to do and not do when it first arrives. (Older children usually find it hilarious that the new baby won't be able to sit up or walk or feed himself.) Be positive. Don't anticipate problems with them at this stage that you may well not actually encounter. ('Mummy won't be getting any sleep after the baby's born so she's going to be very ratty for a while' probably isn't a helpful message at this stage!) Address any specific anxieties your child may have and in general stick to practical information and activities.

Books are always a good starting point for conversations and there are some really great picture books aimed at first children becoming siblings, so it's certainly worth going along to your local library or bookshop to check these out. However, do read them yourself first, as some will be aimed at specific problems that only much older children may experience after the baby is born. Pregnancy can also spark an intense interest in the whole question of reproduction. If so, make the most of the many excellent picture books for children on how babies are made. Before the baby is born you should get your first-born involved in the preparations; even a very young child can help with arranging the room, clothes and equipment for the new arrival. Indulge your first-born's curiosity about your changing shape – let her feel the 'bump' kick and let her talk and sing to it if she wants to. There is evidence that newborns respond more positively to voices they have heard during pregnancy.

A mum who wants to consider having a larger family (three-plus kids) If money, space, energy and time are already a strain then think very carefully about why you want to increase your family. If none of those are a problem, go for it. Many people assure me that the shift from two to three is a piece of cake compared to one to two. I am happy to take their word for it.

A mum who wants to defuse sibling rivalry The sibling relationship is a powerful and, at its best, precious bond. Growing up with brothers and sisters is how we learn to share, negotiate, accommodate, respect, support, love and be loved. Conflict is, however, a natural and unavoidable aspect of this learning process and as the parent you will inevitably find yourself in the middle of sibling rivalry sooner or later.

In my book *Three Shoes, One Sock and No Hairbrush* I distinguish between the different roles a parent can play when it comes to sibling rivalry and explain how some roles are more helpful than others. Sitting on the sidelines and letting the kids slug it out is just as destructive as positioning yourself between your children as the eternal referee. Instead, your aim is to be a kind of all-star coach, setting a few firm rules (e.g. no hitting, biting, scratching), seeing both children's perspectives, helping them to manage their frustration and anger, and teaching age-appropriate skills for resolving conflict without aggression. When my children were small I found it very comforting to learn that siblings under five average an argument four times an hour, or once every fifteen minutes. Suddenly it didn't feel like such a big deal. That said, you can certainly minimise sibling rivalry in a number of ways.

1. Make time for your first-born: five to ten uninterrupted wholly attentive minutes a day will make a big difference and help to reassure your first-born that they are still loved, wanted and important to you.

2. Involve your first-born in caring for the baby: let them help wash, dress, feed and change the baby.

3. Enlist your first-born's help in doing fun things with the baby: such as singing, reading and playing gentle games like 'peek-a-boo' and 'This little piggy'. (Obviously you need to watch out for any aggression coming through in these games and young children should never be left unsupervised.)

4. Sibling rivalry increases throughout the first year, peaking when the second child is around eight months old. A baby who is crawling and then toddling is a much greater threat to an older child. Make sure your first-born knows you understand this, and help them to put their favourite toys and games out of the baby's reach.

5. Much first-born resentment is seeded by the mother's protective bias towards the baby. Check that you aren't placing all blame for arguments on your first-born. Recognise how frustrating it is for your first-born to always be the one who has to make way for the younger sibling's needs and desires.

6. Make time to have fun with your first-born and to have fun with both children together. Laughter is a great sower of sibling harmony.

A mum who wants to make time for each child individually Undivided attention is one of the best investments a mother can make, not just when children are very young but throughout their childhood. Try and get into the habit of setting aside time for each of your children at some point in their day. If your younger child has a daytime nap, take the first ten minutes to play with your older child. If you're working during the day and time is short, enlist the help of a partner or grandparent to clear a bit of time in the evening – or at very least, at weekends. Even as little as fifteen minutes or half an hour a day will ensure each child feels seen and heard.

A mum looking to ease the guilt at sharing herself between children Guilt is what God invented to stop mothers forgetting they've got children and siblings are what God invented to stop children thinking they're God. When it comes to parenting, guilt is certainly a very common feeling but not a terribly helpful one. In the adjustment from one child to two, most of us will experience some difficulty at some point in shifting from having one child at the centre of your attention to having two.

The romantic model of an intense one-to-one bond is pervasive in our culture and very powerful. It colours our expectations of motherhood just as much as it does our expectations of adult relationships. Recognise and accept that you cannot mother two children as intensely as you did one, and that it's not even appropriate to try. If you find this rouses particularly strong and uncomfortable feelings for you, it is likely that you are confronting memories and feelings from your own childhood – perhaps of being displaced by a younger sibling, or of being emotionally exiled by your own mother. Facing down these ghosts from the past can clear the way to having more realistic expectations of yourself as a mother.

What are the crucial dos and don'ts for the mum having more than one child?

Do

- Have fun: make time to enjoy your children, individually and together. You will reap the rewards ten times over in the short and the long term.

- Keep your sense of humour: there's a lot of absurdity in family life and it's there to help you.

- Look after yourself: get enough sleep, eat regularly and healthily, make sure you get some proper exercise two or three times a week, and schedule in a bit of time out for yourself at least once a week.

- Remember that no phase – good or bad – lasts forever. Life with small children keeps changing and even the most trying times will seem short-lived when you look back. To help you through the worst patches, try keeping a gratitude diary – keep a small notebook beside the bed and list five things you're grateful for each night before you go to sleep – simple and amazingly effective.

Don't

- Don't label: Once there are two children it seems to be almost instinctive for parents to start labelling their children: he's the clever one, she's so musical, he's creative, she's selfish. It's as if we want to sort them into categories. Perhaps it's even pre-set in us as a kind of coping device. Labels from the child's point of view, however, are akin to emotional and psychological straitjackets. They are seldom helpful and they can cause lasting damage. I know people who have spent their entire adult lives trying to shake off the labels they were given in childhood by well-meaning parents. Don't do it! Describe behaviour you like in your child, by all means ('that was very kind of you', 'you did that beautifully', etc.) but leave the labels for the PE kits and the jam jars.

> **Rebecca's fabulous mum's family-life mantra:**
> 'We should think of our children as being like unmarked packets of seeds. It is not for us to decide what plant the seeds will become but simply to do everything we can to help the seeds grow into the plant that they are naturally meant to be.'

The Competitive Parenting Complex

And You Thought the First Year Was Tough?

I've been itching to knuckle down to this chapter since I first started planning this book. To be honest, it feels cathartic; a way to purge myself of all the ridiculous, surreal and unimaginable ways in which I've encountered (and admittedly at times, succumbed to) competitive parenting. But before I dive straight into accounts of unbelievable parenting one-upmanship, let me start at what for most of us is the beginning: the thin blue line.

In hindsight, I feel immensely lucky that when I read my first positive pregnancy test (some months into the pregnancy itself) I could actually count the number of my friends who already had kids on one hand. They consisted of my sister-in-law and three of my husband's old mates. My own core girlfriends were still busy enjoying their hedonistic twenties and climbing the career ladder. Similarly, my colleagues at *Elle* were largely footloose and fancy-free. Even though my editor at the time was on maternity leave, the fashion girls were largely occupied with guzzling champagne and getting front-row seats (and a free handbag) at the Chloe show, a far cry from pondering the merits of cloth nappies!

In some ways this meant my experience of motherhood was at times isolating (you need to be a very open-minded gal pal to want to hear about colic when you're on a boozy mini-break in Ibiza!), but in other ways it saved me from the vast and intimidating world of competitive parents. As my bump (and legs, arms, bottom, bust and chins) grew, there was no one to stand next to me with a minute bulge and wobble-free arms, quizzing me on how much weight had I put on in the first six months. As I made do with borrowing my sister-in-law's Moses basket and bunging a few white Babygros into the top drawer of my chest of drawers, fortunately there was no one to ask whether I'd seen the latest Chic Shack nursery brochure (where cots cost anything up to £899).

Although it sometimes felt like a maze of choices, I happily did what came naturally and followed my instincts throughout. I had my baby at the local NHS hospital, fought for a four-day working week and found a nanny share through a local advertisement. I breastfed for as long as felt right (seven months) and had my daughter snuggled safely in our bed for the same length of time. The fact that none of my friends, neighbours or colleagues had babies somehow made these instinctive decisions fall into place with real ease. There was no one telling me horror stories about NHS births (forcing me to feel I should beg, borrow and steal to fund a private birth), no one lobbying for me to give up work (or work the full five-day week), and no one to insist I shove my baby onto a bottle and into her own room before I felt either of us was ready. (The fact we had no spare room at the time would have made this extra tricky!)

As I enter my early thirties and my third pregnancy, things look very different. Take this as an example: It is my thirty-second birthday next week and to celebrate it I'm hosting a low-key supper at a local Italian restaurant for twelve of my closest girlfriends. Out of the twelve, seven will be anywhere between ten and thirty-six weeks pregnant. Bumptastic, I'm sure you'll agree! It doesn't take a genius to work out what the conversations will be like: birth plans, sibling rivalry, job options, childcare solutions, buggy choices, schools and maternity fashion are likely to top the agenda. (So much so, I must remember to sit the non-bumps together so they can broaden their conversation to summer holiday plans, Mulberry handbags, election choices and the latest gossip on Kate Moss!)

This illustrates perfectly how for many women having children is like going through the wedding phase at the same time as all your pals; in short, you become a cliché! Moving on from competing over Vera Wang-type frocks or honeymoon destinations you shift your attention to all things baby. Subconsciously you're checking out each other's bumps (the same way we eyed each other up as we tried to lose those extra few pounds to squeeze into our wedding dresses), taking note of how 'radiant' or 'knackered' each other looks and how much excess weight will have to be lost post-birth. As talk turns to baby accessories, it only takes one mum to confess to buying the latest designer buggy and another voice will own up to splashing out on a sheepskin papoose or French antique nursery furniture. Those mums who'll be buying their buggy from the local car boot sale or borrowing all their baby clothes from a friend suddenly feel incomplete and inferior in comparison.

Anyone who's had a child will know that sadly it doesn't end here. In fact, this is just the beginning of a long chain of competing, comparing, bragging and exaggerating. Take my 'holistic' yoga class that was a life-saver in my first and second pregnancies, until mums decided to return after labour to tell us their birth stories. Situated in a slightly shabby church hall in uber-trendy Notting Hill maybe I shouldn't have expected anything less, but somehow even in these serene bonding sessions mummy mania seeped in through the front door. Every week as yet another gorgeous boho mum came in and breastfed Jago/Indigo/Milo/Autumn, telling of thirty-two-minute labours and home water births (incense burning and Bach playing in the background), the urgency that we must all have such easy births grew.

Even though mine were natural labours there was no way I was going to come in with my colicky, irritable newborn (how come theirs were all sleepy and 'perfect'?) and tell of the searing pain, prehistoric roaring and endless four-letter swear words that constituted my 'real' birth. I would ask myself week in, week out, whether I was actually abnormal for expecting parts of the birthing process to be horrific, as opposed to altogether harmonious. Somehow, as women who feel the pain, scream for an epidural – 'Give me the God damn drugs nowwwwwwwwwwwwwwww'! – or, dare I say it, have to succumb to an emergency Caesarean, we feel we've failed.

So, we compete for the best bump, we compete for the best birth and then we compete for the best blow-the-budget buggy. Someone tell me it all ends there? Surely Germaine Greer, Sheila Kitzinger and Naomi Woolf taught us something about 'sisterhood' and 'bonding through gender'? Not enough, it seems. The first year of mother-hood itself is just as bound up with envy and insecurities. Like booby traps waiting for the new mum, everything from the breast-versus-bottle debate to which sleep guru you follow comes with baggage and guilt. When my friend Lyn struggled with breastfeeding (and spent the first three weeks in tears trying to establish it with her hungry first-born son), pressure from other mums and the media to breast-feed only compounded her anguish. 'Breast is best' was a happy motto she seemed to face at every turn. Yes, we all know that for many mothers and babies breast is best, but what if the mother is at her wits' end, close to cracking under the immense pressure of trying and failing to feed her newborn from her breast? How is a distressed mum and hungry, fraught baby ever 'best'?

Similarly, should you choose Ford, Leach or Ferber to guide you through those early months and sleepless nights? Each expert comes with a ready-made label and a backlash of preconceived attitudes. Surely you can't really be sleeping with your baby when she's almost celebrating her first birthday? Controlled crying – are you totally insane? Routine, ooh it's a rite of passage, didn't you know?

It's hard to find your way through that first year without the choices you make on everything from routine to child-care marking you out on the parenting mind map. Suddenly you're not just Clare, the office worker and mum of two; you're Clare, the follower of Gina with a Maclaran buggy and an 'unsuitable' choice of nursery. We pigeon-hole each other in our role as parents in order to try to make better sense of this huge life change, but the effect is far more confusing and misleading.

As if being told by fellow parents at the NCT group that their baby 'has been sleeping through the night since two weeks' (yeah right, without the use of Calpol?!) wasn't enough, you'll have fellow mums raising an eyebrow at everything from breastfeeding in public to going back to work a few months after the birth. All too often it can feel like every other mum implies that they do it better, have it more sussed, are far more 'in control' than you are. Unintentionally, we're pigeon-holed and we're made to feel inadequate. I summed up this rite of passage for all new mums perfectly when I was discussing it with my friend Katie: 'Just think of it as a baptism into the cult of competitive parenting.' Fabulous mums, it's only just begun . . .

Mother knows best

'I had no idea other mums could be so cruel. Even though there's a lot of camaraderie and sound advice out there, sadly there is a whole lot of smug competing too. I'll never forget not getting my son into the best local school and having to face all the other mums each day as I trekked to our alternative primary on the not-so-nice part of town. Of course I may have been slightly paranoid but I felt I was a real 'outsider'. Thank God we ended up making such good friends at the new school, and my gut feeling is they're all really down-to-earth and genuine. In away it's turned out to be a blessing.'

Full-time mum of one

Politics of Playdates

Before I elaborate on the modern madness of mums, let me wave a small white flag. I feel that if I go on illustrating the crazy methods we women learn to navigate our ways through motherhood I may put you off reading any further. Many of you will nod your head and feel a sense of relief that I'm acknowledging how ridiculous this competing has become. However, some of you will probably cry, 'Bloody hell, how depressing – can things really have got this bad?' The truth of the matter is, the moment you become a mum you feel a certain amount of pressure to 'keep up'. As fellow mums we often do what we swore we wouldn't, and that's rub salt in the wound. Instead of sticking two fingers up at this competitive streak, we can't help ourselves asking whether a child is walking yet, whether they can write their name or which school they're going to. The good news is there are many things we can do to be kinder to each other (and to ourselves), all of which I've outlined in the final sections of this chapter. My point here is that it's not all doom and gloom, competitive sniggers and what I like to call one-upmumship; however, I need to elaborate further on the extent of 'the competitive parenting complex' to really do this chapter justice.

With this note of hope and solidarity in place, I feel safe to move on from comparing bumps, Bugaboos and babies, to the next phase. You've managed to fend off advice about how to get your baby to sleep through the night and how to potty train your two-year-old in two days flat. And you'd be right to pat yourself on the back for getting your child to eat more than one type of vegetable and helping them 'grow out' of the biting phase. Surely you can expect to sit back now and let little Joe fend for himself through toddler-hood (establishing the odd boundary and providing the correct quantity of positive praise to leave him to carve out his own route to childhood)? If only motherhood was this easy! In my experience, the moment your child is walking and talking it's as if you get an invisible, obligatory licence to join the 'competitive parenting club' for real.

Suddenly, words of caution from another mum about letting your child eat chocolate cake at his first birthday party become positively ecstatic praise in comparison to the tirade of abuse you receive when your toddler pushes another child at a local playgroup. (Or in the case of my pal Carolina's toddler, shows his willy to the whole of his Monkey Music group!) The expectation of how your child should behave, what level they should be at with their speech/motor skills/manners/social interaction and how well they are doing in 'life' in general, is an invisible barometer present at most mummy gatherings. Never is this more apparent than at playdates.

Up until my daughter started nursery I'd been sheltered from the politics of playdates. In fact, I'd ambled along bliss-fully unaware of much of the politics of childrearing. I'd left my carer to establish local friendships with mums and nannies care of the local parish playgroup, while I wrote features on vintage chic for *Elle*. I'd hang out at weekends with my child-free girlfriends who doted on my daughter like the cute bundle of blonde hair and pink frocks that she was and when we saw friends who had children they were, by and large, much older than our own and our friends had gladly left behind the stage of asking about sleep routines or nursery applications. At this point the term 'playdate' was as alien a concept as 'grey hair'; it just didn't register in my life.

It was in this phase of blissful ignorance that my daughter began a local nursery three mornings a week and became obsessed with a little girl she called 'Beddy Sofarty'. Beddy Sofarty became a permanent fixture in my daughter's imaginary world. Beddy came with us to Tesco; she sat next to my daughter in the car; she even flew with us all the way to Ibiza for our August break and needed her own sunbed on the beach. By the end of the long summer holidays, I vowed to my three-year-old that Beddy would of course be invited to tea when nursery started up again in September. True to my word, on the first Monday back, I called the headmistress from my desk. No one knew who Beddy was and just as I was beginning to wonder if my daughter had made the whole friendship up (not as unusual as it sounds; so great was my imagination that I created three imaginary friends: 'Kambarugie', 'Margarine' and 'Saba', who went with me everywhere until I was eight years old), the headmistress called to say she had solved the mystery. My daughter's best friend was in fact a girl named Becky Steffani (I suppose they could sound familiar to a toddler!?) and she happily passed on the parents' details in order for me to invite the mysterious Beddy (or Becky as she must now be known) to tea. To cut a long story short, the very next Tuesday, Becky came for tea.

As far as I knew (in my limited experience of playdates) Becky would arrive, her mum would stay for a cup of tea, and the girls would play happily upstairs for an hour or so. I now realise there is a whole unwritten rule book on these sessions that I stupidly hadn't taken heed of. For a start, Becky turned up an hour late, by which point my daughter's face had moulded to the front room window as she watched for her friend's arrival. When Becky arrived with her dad and two sisters, I immediately felt ridiculous for expecting a fellow mum (this is the twenty-first century, you know). This was followed by anxiety at what the hell I would talk about with this dad in yellow cords for the ensuing two hours?

Mr S. proceeded to take off his coat and offer me a huge tin of delicious-looking home-made organic raspberry muffins. ('Oh, just something we made earlier!') This instantly made me realise I'd broken the first cardinal rule of play-dates (the first of many, I hasten to add): not baking anything myself. Needless to say, I quickly shoved my M&S choco-late biscuits back into the packet and hid them in the cupboard! To briefly sum up the next few hours would be impossible, but let me give you a few memorable snippets: My eighteen-month-old son pooed on Mr S.'s cashmere-mix coat and then proceeded to bite one of Becky's sisters on the bottom. While Mr S. was in the bathroom, I offered all the children fruit smoothies, little knowing Becky was 'fruit phobic'. (Can anyone tell me what this means?) For the half an hour that the girls played well (the rest of the time Becky was complaining that my daughter was 'rather too immature') I was stuck listening to Mr S. talk about the history of art and eighteenth-century astrology. When, to my relief, the clock finally read five o'clock, Mr S. put on his poo-stained coat and informed me he had some errands to run and would be back in an hour, and off he shot! Seeing as he'd already told me that his children *never* watched TV

(Why would they? They could all read by age two!), a very long final hour followed.

Not the best start to my journey of playdates, I'm sure you'll agree? (Needless to say my daughter carried on 'loving' Beddy for months to come, despite the fact that her father never reciprocated the invite. This may well have had something to do with the baby poo, or possibly the fact that Beddy moved on to another school in the area.) I confess that subsequent playdates have been marginally more successful, but nevertheless still full of their own specific minefields. There's been the time when my daughter locked herself in her room and wouldn't come out and share her toys with Milly (leaving me to play Barbies) and there's been four-year-old Sam who bucked, screamed and broke a picture frame when his mum came to collect him. But there have also been the regular playdates with my daughter's soulmate and best buddy Lily (who, unlike Beddy, reciprocates the love), which often end up with two gleeful fairy-clad, face-painted girls doing cartwheels in the garden!

For many mums I know, playdates are the ultimate in strategic planning. Just imagine: a mum who once headed up business meetings for city bigwigs now using her talents for tactically organising her daughter's social arrangements! For some this is a long-term project they are committed to. Inviting every child in the class to a playdate at some point during the term is essential for their child's popularity. It's also a great way for parents to check out the competition. (My friend Sophie's son was actually asked by a mum to write the alphabet at a recent playdate – some 'game', hey?) Many mums plan the playdate down to every minute detail, making sure the full mandatory two-hour session is packed with fun, education, nutrition and the key catchphrase, 'sharing'. My girlfriends and I realised that our kids had been offered sewing, baking, clay work, swimming (yes, at the 'in-house' pool!) and even t'ai chi at other friends' houses. It seems that if your child doesn't return from a playtea with a full tummy, a smiling face and a clay interpretation of Van Gogh's sunflowers then the hosting parent hasn't done their job properly!

Not only is carefully organised play a prerequisite, play-date etiquette is also key. If your child has good manners and remembers all her 'pleases' and 'thank yous', well then they can come again: God help the child who grunts his responses! Don't go forgetting the etiquette expected of us parents too! If you stay at the playdate you must be full of wit and charm. If you leave your child *they* must be full of wit and charm and don't you dare be late picking up (we have an hour's algebra to do before bedtime, don't you know?). Any invite *must* then be reciprocated (preferably that same day) and you must under no circumstances take longer than a month in which to do it! If you're hosting a play-date, you're not only expected to bake Nigella-style cupcakes (beforehand *and* during the date), you should also follow up the playdate with a call to the child's parent, saying how 'wonderfully' it all went and how 'adorable' their 'little angel' is. This always adds brownie points and will get your child invited over there, pronto!

Call me an old misery, but I do find all these unspoken rules mind-numbingly tedious and over-the-top! In my mind it's simple: your kid likes their kid, you see the parent/carer at the playgroup/nursery/school gates and you ask them over for tea. They say, 'Yes, is next Wednesday any good?', you check your relatively empty diary and, hey presto, it's a date! On said Wednesday, the child turns up, all offspring charge upstairs, wreaking havoc in the kids' bedrooms while you and the mum/dad/nanny talk light stuff like tantrums or TV. You make supper for all and lots of hurled fish fingers ensue. Both children then ask if they can 'please' leave the table (but only under duress). You offer chocolate buttons round, the children giggle some more and everyone goes home happy and with chocolate on their faces. Simple! Maybe we should all try this method at home; believe me, it is far easier than trying to create a perfect Martha Stewart-type scenario at the end of a long day!

But if even this 'go-with-the-flow' method leaves you bewildered then here are a few playdate tips to get you started:

Don't over-do the socialising. By the end of the school week my children are usually utterly exhausted, especially at the beginning of a new term, so packing their after-school free time with playdates just leads to meltdown all round. I find it's best to limit their playdates to one or two per week.

Keep some days sacred. Never mind the kids, I know as a busy mum I need a few days per week when we all just come home and flop. Maybe keep a couple of days as play-date days and assign to the others the odd after-school club or some much needed down-time at home. (In term time we make lazy days Monday and Friday in our house. Certainly by Friday the kids are ready for an early bath and a laze in their pyjamas in front of *The Wizard of Oz*.)

Double up. You may find if you have more than one child that letting both have a friend on the same day helps avoid potential conflict. If this isn't possible make sure you try your best to impose an 'all play together' rule at the start (and be prepared to mop up a few tears from the inevitably left-out sibling too).

Ask your child who they'd like to play with. My children tend to tell me straight out who they'd like to come for tea (and who they'd rather not). Don't force the issue; you can encourage friendships but you'll exhaust yourself by inviting the whole class over one by one. Children usually have a pretty set idea about who their close pals are, so follow their lead.

Remind your child of the forthcoming playdate. If it's a school day, I find encouraging the children to chat about how they'll go home together that day and what games they can play can aid a fun-filled, tantrum-free playdate.

Discuss the golden playdate word: 'sharing'. Some kids (especially younger ones) find sharing their toys with friends who come to play impossible. By calmly discussing and preparing for this before the playdate you can pre-empt some of the conflict. You could always suggest your child safely hide away any sacred toys (their favourite teddy or doll) which they feel unable to share, on the condition that they will share everything else with their guest of course.

Establish some ground rules. You know the kind of thing: no biting, no hitting, no bouncing on Mum and Dad's bed, no torturing siblings in pursuit of 'fun'.

Take a contact number.   Make sure you have a phone number for whoever is collecting the visiting child at the end of the playdate. It's always a good idea to agree a pick-up time too (or some busy mums may well not turn up until you're ready to hit the sack!).

Check on food fads and allergies.   My daughter's serious allergy to sesame means I always tell parents what she must avoid at meals (and leave her medical kit with them). Allergies aside, I find it's always worth checking what food guests like and whether they are vegetarian/allowed sweets, etc. – this can prevent all sorts of food tantrums.

Think of a few decoys in case the playdate goes belly-up.   Sometimes you may find the friend in question has a bit of a wobble mid-play or there's a friendship fall-out. Have something ready to distract them – some arts and crafts, a DVD, some music – and of course keep the cuddles on tap.

Let them be.   As I said earlier, playdates don't need to have a programme of stimulating, education-led activities. Generally, I try and leave my kids and their friends well alone. If I hear tears and tantrums from upstairs I know it's time for some mask-making or cookie-mixing, but I know that ninety per cent of the time they don't need me trying to entertain them with sensible activities. It's much better for them to interact without adult interruption. Their imaginations will run wild and usually the time flies by.

Mother knows best

'I'm on my third child, so I know only too well how playdates work. To be honest, by number three I was sick of trying to entertain my daughter and her friends with endless mask-making, beading and flapjack cooking. My main aim was for them to head off into the garden and let me get on with some ironing! My daughter and I have an unwritten rule that she invites the kids she really likes (what's the point of having a classmate she can't stand, just to make sure she gets to know every one of the thirty children?) and it's up to her to entertain them. She knows my rules: in her home she must be a good host and share well. These are good life rules, I think. My daughter has formed wonderful friends and they spend hours making dens outside, face-painting each other or playing dress-up. I don't need to get involved to create their fun; in fact she'd hate it if I did!'

Full-time mum of three

Party Pooper

I'd be a barefaced liar if I told you I didn't like a good party. Any friend or relative would be busy denouncing me to the local papers if I suggested otherwise. Holding or attending parties is something I love. Be it a three-year-old's tea party in a friend's garden, a baby shower at Claridges, a wedding in Norfolk or supper for eight at a neighbour's house, I'll be there with bells on. Things are no different when I throw my own parties. My wedding was an intimate boho country affair, but that didn't stop me dancing to Marvin Gaye (on the table tops!) in my diamanté-heeled Jimmy Choos, and at my rather chilled-out thirtieth birthday party I was dancing until dawn, barefoot in a floaty Matthew Williamson frock. Having children hasn't suppressed my party mood in the slightest. I may not stay up to see the sunrise quite as much as I used to but I still use any excuse to throw a celebration that will be enjoyed by all ages.

You may be wondering at this point why this sub-chapter is called 'Party Pooper'. Well, let me elaborate. Even though I like nothing more than a gaggle of four-year-olds racing around the garden, stomping glazed cupcakes into the flowerbeds or taking a party of six-year-olds to the woods for a 'pirates and fairies' birthday bash, I have a slight aversion to anything that doesn't bear the hallmarks of a home-made event – and by that I mean slightly improvised and chic in the 'shabby' sense.

Before you begin to pen me a hate letter about the pressure on mums to be the next Nigella at parties, hold it right there; I'm not implying you have to 'home-make' the whole party! What I mean is, don't buy into the popularised glitzy idea of how to hold the 'perfect' kids' parties. Hosting a mini-me celebration doesn't have to resemble the bar mitzvah of Philip Green's daughter (all private jets, chocolate fountains, A-list celebrities and Cristal champagne) to be fun. In short, you don't have to compete with other mums to have the biggest, best, most-talked-about children's party this side of the Oscars. The only thing that matters is that your child enjoys it and in my experience when it comes to holding a bash for your offspring less is definitely more.

Let me give you some examples of how many parents have lost the plot when it comes to planning their little one's birthday bash. Last year, for instance, I heard of a handful of local mums who were holding birthday parties for their kids in locations as diverse at the Science Museum and the Tate Modern, and as extreme as taking over the top floor of Hamleys toy shop. I was witness to jugglers at a party for a sweet little girl who had only just learned to walk and I kid you not when I say I attended a two-year-old's party which featured an original Venetian carousel and fire-eating stilt walkers (needless to say the birthday girl hid in fear for the duration of her party). Now when it comes to the obligatory party bags, I've seen three-year-olds leaving parties with bags that made a sham of the actual birthday gifts themselves. (I'm talking Power Rangers, Disney walkie-talkies and fairy fancy dress outfits all bagged up with cake, stickers and sweets to boot!) Admittedly, most of my fab mum friends are content with a church hall and Coco the clown. However, competing for the title of 'most amazing party giver' underlies many a child's birthday party.

I am by no means a party pooper; I just think that keeping up with the Joneses (or Greens) can get rather exhausting, not to mention time-consuming and expensive. If you have a large brood, hosting each of them a birthday bash that includes face-painting, fairies, balloon artists, home-made silver-iced cupcakes and thirty hyperactive kids plus their parents, would start to become a full-time job (and would cost a full year's salary!). For many mums, adding the role of 'party organiser extraordinaire' to their repertoire is just one thing too many when you consider the other one too many accolades they already have after their names (lawyer, wife, mother, sister, daughter, best friend, chef, cleaner, ironer, homework master, aerobic fanatic, sex kitten . . . need I go on?).

There's no reason busy mums can't throw a brilliant party for their children, but I urge you all not to get *too* competitive or obsessive about it. If the church hall is damp, then hey it's not the end of the world, if your home-made Victoria sponge fails to rise then nip to Sainsbury's and buy one (and dare I suggest even passing this one off as your own?) and if your entertainer fails to turn up there's always Uncle James and his magic tricks, isn't there? The crux of this is that you don't need to buy up Harrods and hire a fleet of circus entertainers to give your child a birthday to remember. Here are a few tips you could bear in mind to find the middle ground between party pooper and hostess with the mostess:

Think about what your child likes

Believe it or not I've been to several birthday parties which have been wonderful for the guests but an absolute nightmare for the birthday girl/boy. I'm lucky that my attention-seeking pair (where do they get that trait from, I wonder?) love a good party thrown just for them. However, if your child is super-shy and hates big crowds, inviting their entire class to their party is plain madness. My sister always felt just like this. A shy, gorgeous little girl with blonde ringlets and blue eyes to melt any heart, she was the type of child anyone would want to throw a celebration for. However, she had very different feelings on the subject. At her fourth birthday party she hid behind her hands and wept as we all sang her 'Happy Birthday'. Being centre of attention was her idea of hell. After that disaster, year in, year out, for Fleur's birthdays my mum would simply bake and decorate a pink cake and we'd have a small 'party' with just the immediate family: my mum, dad, brothers and me! So if you've got a child who hates big gatherings and being the focal point, then take this into account; this is a celebration for and about them after all. Think about having a family-only affair or a treat with a few close friends. (For example, if the child is older and still shy, a trip to the movies and a sleepover with a couple of best friends could be the perfect alternative to a big party.) And whatever you do, don't force the party-issue; the last thing you want is to traumatise the child on their big day!

Think carefully about the themes that interest your child. You may love the idea of all your daughter's friends coming dressed as fairies, but if she hates pink this is pointless. Similarly, if she is princess-obsessed, is this fair on the boys in her class? Maybe make it a superhero and princess party instead? Equally, it doesn't have to be all about Disney or gender stereotypes. My son couldn't care less about Power Rangers or Superman but is absolutely obsessed with puppets and drama. Instead of dressing him up like Spiderman or forcing him to sit through a magic show, I've asked his favourite drama teacher to help me put on a party involving acting and puppets, which I know he'll love from beginning to end.

Make it age-appropriate

Another mistake parents often make is planning a party that is too old for their child. Why bother with a Peter Pan entertainer when your three-year-old hasn't even seen the film or read the book? And is a disco really wise for a group of bum-shuffling one-year-olds? Think carefully about the stage your child's at and plan it appropriately. My friend Gayle, for example, was desperate to throw a small bash for her twin girls when they turned one. She knew forking out for a swish venue or a £250-per-hour entertainer would be wasted on them, so she did an intimate little gathering at home for all their one-year-old friends. (She only invited those who were close to one, which was a wise choice because it meant no older kids would get bored.) She took on the role of music maestro and her twin girls and their eight friends bashed away on instruments for twenty minutes. She then covered her living room with plastic sheets and had a finger food free-for-all. She admits it was pretty hard work for her, but perfect fun for her girls.

Set yourself a budget, and stick to it!

Everyone has different views on what's an acceptable budget for a child's party. The party spend can be regarded by some as an indication of how much the family earns; others may feel the need to over-spend to display their love for their child or to show off their generosity as a host; those more sensible will base it purely on what they feel is justified for a kid's birthday bash. My friend Jennie, for example, thought it silly to blow her monthly food budget on Minnie's second birthday. So she just invited friends over to the house, set out nibbles for all (pitta bread, hummus, raw vegetable sticks, berries, crisps and mini-quiches), got Minnie's godmother to take on the role of 'face-painter' and presented a wonderful pink castle cake courtesy of her mum. All in all, everyone had a great time without Jennie needing to blow her budget or spend hours preparing (and after all, a group of two-year-olds don't need much to keep them happy). At the other extreme, my pal Sophie had paying for the children's parties written into her divorce settlement, so she's more than happy to budget £500 per party! Admittedly, she doesn't go mad (no fire-eating midgets here) but you can always expect a first-class entertainer, a custom-made cake and helium balloons galore.

Whatever your budget, try to work out rough costs beforehand and stick to your calculations. It's easy to get sidetracked by multi-packs of tiaras or the idea of a talented out-of-work actress coming to braid hair, but with all these 'extras' costs can spiral. Children's parties are big business, so ask yourself before you start the planning phase what is really needed, and what you could do without. (My husband drew the line at my daughter's last party when I suggested offering wine to the grown-ups. He had a point – the party did start at ten in the morning!)

Share it out

Another way of easing the financial and time burdens of parties is to share them with other families. My two are constantly being invited to parties which are for a group or pair of friends. This helps cut the cost and organisation required immensely, and it's often really nice for the child to share (there's that favourite playdate word again) their birthday celebrations with a good pal.

Rally the troops

Getting a helping hand in preparations and on the big day is a tip worth bearing in mind. Asking your mother-in-law to bake a cake, your neighbour to help hand out the invites or a strong uncle to shift the chairs in and out of the church hall will all contribute to making this a team effort. At my son's last party I roped in both his godmothers for different jobs. (Clare was official balloon blower-upper and Jennie had the task of welcoming kids and storing the immense amount of gifts somewhere safe.) I managed to persuade my sister-in-law to make one of her famous cake creations (a fantastic pirate ship that would have cost me the earth if bought from a local bakery) and my old nanny, Helen, popped along and lent a hand clearing up.

Often you'll find that grandparents or friends without kids love to muck in (after all, it's not like they have to attend a kids' party every week, like we seem to). My mum would be devastated if her role as resident twice-yearly cocktail-sausage-bringer was made redundant and I think my sister secretly loves being honorary bubble-blower every year for my daughter (and with her princess looks all the five-year-olds swoon at her feet!).

Improvise and be inventive

Don't be scared to do something different. Anyone who's been to fifteen parties this year at indoor play centres and a further ten featuring 'Marvin the Magician' will thank you for daring to break the trend! I don't mean hiring the London Eye for a day or taking your son's class to EuroDisney, I just mean try being a little creative! Don't forget that often kids love a home party and this can be so much easier (and cheaper) if you don't mind the mess. One of my daughter's favourite parties was her fourth birthday when she had twelve girlies here for cupcakes and fairy fun. I hired one flower fairy entertainer, fed them all pink food (watermelon, fuchsia fairy cakes, strawberry jam sandwiches and raspberry smoothies) and let them trash my living room. In my mind it doesn't have to be OTT to be a success. You could always try a treasure hunt at a local park, hire a bouncy castle for the garden or take a group of older kids to the theatre.

Likewise, if you have the time, think about ways to make the invitation original (enough of the Bob the Builder '99p for ten' invites). You could just take a fun photo of your daughter dressed as Snow White and laser copy it or get your child to decorate invites with sequins and feathers. Similarly, on the day of the big event, I always try to mark my and the birthday girl/boy's stamp on the occasion. Interesting food (try star-shaped sandwiches or home-made veggie crisps), an innovative going-home pressie (for my son's this year we're choosing a Mini Treasure book by Red Fox for each child and wrapping them in a ribbon bow with an old-fashioned stick of rock) or just some snazzy table decorations are all simple ways you can make your party feel a little less conveyor belt and a little more original.

Give yourself time

Try to plan the party a month or so in advance. I know for some mums the thought of this much forward planning is unbearable but it will help you host a well-attended, fun and organised bash. One of my son's friend's was once invited to a party just three days in advance, by which point most of the pals invited had plans and the mums felt awful for the little boy whose birthday was going to be empty of children!

Equally, if you're going to book entertainment or a hall, you need to do this quite well in advance or you'll be left with the out-of-tune singer or the juggler with a broken arm!

Tips for the day

Don't let your child get over-tired. The worst thing about parties can be an over-tired, over-excited birthday boy/girl. Bear in mind what time of day they tend to be at their best before planning the times. If it's an afternoon party try to let them have a chilled morning (watching some TV, enjoying quiet play or even having a little snooze). Try to give them a good lunch too, or those party food e-numbers will send them crazy before the first guest has even arrived!

Have a vague structure. Try to work out a rough schedule for the day; it will help you keep calm and organised. There's nothing worse than turning up at a venue with ten minutes to set the whole thing up! By working out what time the kids arrive, when the entertainment starts, when they'll eat and go home, you can map out the party in your head.

Make it fun for all. Do remember that for kids under the age of five, parents often stay for the party. My friend Tanith always goes to town and offers parents champagne and mince pies (her daughter's birthday is in December), which is wonderful, but to be honest even a few olives and a Pringle would be enough for most! If you're choosing a venue make sure there are seats for grown-ups and somewhere for them to chat without getting in the way of the entertainment for the kids.

Enjoy it! Last but by no means least, try to enjoy it yourself! Take some time to chill on the day, ask a few parents you like to stay, share a drink or a laugh with you and remember to lap up your child's enjoyment!

Mother knows best

'I'm on my fourth child, so I really don't have the time, money or inclination to go all-out each time someone has a birthday. When my youngest daughter turned eight she had a slumber party which she's still talking about nine months on! She invited her five closest girlfriends; they stayed up watching old *Fame* movies, eating pizza and ice cream and braiding hair and then crashed out around one in the morning in a camp they'd made in the living room. Once they rose close to midday the next day they tucked into a picnic lunch in the garden and beaded necklaces for one another. Every girl went home with a huge smile and it cost me no more than the price of six Pizza Express Margaritas and three assorted tubs of Häagen-Dazs!'

Full-time working mum of four

Navigating Your Way through Education

Haven't we all wished at some point for a map to navigate our way through the education maze? In my view choosing the right carer, then nursery, then school for my children have been some of the most painstaking and important decisions of my parenting life. That's not to say I have always got it right and only time will tell if my two (soon to be three) children will turn out to be well-rounded, imaginative and confident learners or shoplifters with a drug habit! I'm sure that the magnitude of these choices and the importance that families place on getting them 'right' provides the perfect breeding ground for the biggest competitive parenting complex of all time: the epidemic of education, i.e. 'is my child at the best school?'

Private versus state

This is one of the main dilemmas for inner-city parents. The thing that keeps us awake at night, drives women to do insane and frankly ridiculous things (like organising C-sections on a specific day of the month to get a head start when applying to the best pre-preparatory in the area) and has families paying hundreds of thousands of pounds above the value of a three-bedroom semi near a good state secondary. I could write a whole chapter about the dilemma facing many parents up and down the country. For some, the choice of state education is as simple as waking up each morning; for others choosing private is what they have been born and bred to do. For others, like me, the lines are slightly more blurred, the decision-making rather fuzzier.

As a mum of two children (both at separate schools), one of four siblings (all of whom went to different schools) and a friend of a diverse cross-section of women (who were educated everywhere from leading independent boarding schools to the local Hackney comprehensive), I feel I can see the wealth of challenges that come with choosing between private and state schools. You may be wondering what my own education was like. Some of you may even be secretly hoping that I had the sort of privileged schooling that would allow you to say smugly, 'Well, what does she know?' I'm afraid mine was in fact slightly more 'mix 'n' match' than that.

I won't go into reeling off a lengthy CV, because that has little relevance here. What I will tell you is that after a relatively 'safe' state primary school education in Oxford my parents divorced and my new family unit relocated to South London. It was here that I joined a local middle-of-the-road inner-London comprehensive. In no time at all I learned that my Oxford accent would grant me the label 'snob' and that at all costs I must keep my Citroën-driving mother with a weakness for pearl earrings away from the school gates. In short, it was a school where the cockiest seemed to survive. I changed my accent just enough to stop being spat at by the boys, got my nose pierced and got legless on Thunderbird along the way, still managing to leave with grade As and a huge bank of 'life skills'.

From here I chose a rather 'different' path to university. My decision was to shun the sixth form at school (that was for wimps) and study my A-levels in the evening at a local sixth form college that offered classes at their 'night school'. I earned great cash and contacts in the day waitressing in the West End and still somehow managed to pull off top grades by attending college between seven and ten in the evening. A year in China and a First Class Honours degree at Manchester University followed – not so surprising for a nice middle-class lass; however, my route to the final destination wasn't the one taken by most ambitious girls I knew.

The point is, not a penny of family money was spent on my education (just the vast student loan that I was left to pay off with my measly first wage as *The Sunday Times'* fashion assistant) and I still ended up with the grades and a great social diversity of friends. It makes you wonder, doesn't it?

It came as a huge shock to me then, when after months of soul-searching and many a heated conversation with my local council, that I chose to send my children to private schools. On the one hand I asked myself was it really necessary or morally sound to fork out thousands of pounds each year for good schooling? Would my children grow up with warped views on race, creed and social identity? On the other, I wondered what would happen when the third local state primary turned us down for being six metres out of the 'catchment area' and we were left with the run-down, under-funded alternative that was in fact miles from our home. Combine this with concerns about how on earth my (then) shy first-born would survive and thrive in a class of thirty-six kids, many of whom were yet to learn English, and you can see how hard the decision-making was. Our conundrum was one faced by huge amounts of parents every year.

It goes without saying that for many of my mum friends going private just isn't an option. My friend Elaine paid way above the odds for a home near a 'good' state school; Lyn moved out of London so her children could get a great education for free (something that looked increasingly unlikely in her previous flat off London's Portobello Road) and for some mums reinventing their religious identity is a clever way of ensuring a place at the highly reputable Catholic school at the end of their road.

If you're lucky and can find a good school with wonderful teachers and a good mix of families (be it state or private) you should grab it with both hands. If it's a good state school, even if you wanted to move your child to a private school or top grammar school at eleven this should still be well within reach. If, on the other hand, you have the income to fund a private school of your choice and feel this is the route best for your child then feel blessed and ensure to choose it well. If you select a school with a good mix of children and a contemporary approach to learning then it's bound to be a lifelong investment. Just ensure that whatever decision you make, you keep your child well balanced with their feet firmly on the ground. Privilege taken for granted in a child can become a very nasty trait indeed.

As far as I can see, the decision is much simpler than it looks, and one that I learned from my own family's varied experience of education – my elder brother went to boarding school, my sister went to an inner-London all girls' independent day school, my youngest brother went to a mixed private school and my story you know. If you love your kids, give them as much warmth, energy, empathy and balance at home as you can, then they stand a good chance of doing well at almost any school you choose.

Pre-school: the first stepping stone

Selecting a good pre-school is a significant induction into how to choose the right primary school. Although some mums will choose to keep their toddler at home until they start at school aged four or five, most will opt to send their child to a nursery for a few hours each day to prepare them for some sort of formal out-of-home education.

I feel blessed to have discovered what I consider to be the cream of the crop in terms of pre-schools. Both my children attended different nurseries, both of which inspired absolute wonder in their quality of care and attention to detail. For me the main criterion was to find a stepping stone to a school that offered nurturing and learning through play. Encouraging my kids to love going each day was a top priority.

Although they both picked up their numbers and letters (and sometimes more), what they were encouraged to do above all was to enjoy play, share well, cooperate in a group and explore the world in ways I couldn't have offered them at home. (Having a doctor to come and talk to the class about the human body or have a Chinese parent take them to Chinatown and teach them to make egg fried rice are just two examples.)

The bottom line is to try to find somewhere local that emulates an extension of the care you offer at home. A head teacher who above all loves children and is knowledgeable about how children play and learn best, carers who actually 'care' (it's alarming how many nurseries have a high turnover of staff), a good selection of books and crafts, some outside space to play and a generally happy and fun-loving environment are all key for me. What I would avoid is a pre-school that is obvious about hot-housing their youngsters (anywhere that requests a list of intended schools before asking your child's name should be viewed with caution!) or anywhere that is mega-expensive and run more like a business than a nursery. Many of my pals have found that a tiny nursery with loving teachers set up in a church hall knocks spots off some of the chain nurseries where the kids often look bored and unhappy.

Assessments, exams, tutors and the rest . . .

You can't open a broadsheet newspaper this week without headlines about excess stress at British schools reaching peak levels. I don't know about you, but the thought of my children taking SATs at the age of seven, eleven and fourteen before even embarking on their GCSEs makes me want to move to Denmark where children don't even start formal school until the age of seven. Horror stories of eight-year-olds taking days off school for 'stress', eleven-year-olds suffering panic attacks about sitting exams, and self-harming reaching peak levels in youngsters really make me wonder if we're educating our children in the right way.

Don't get me started on the extra pressure facing children as young as two who are unbelievably facing 'assessments' for private nurseries and schools. I've heard whisperings among my North London mums about so-and-so tutoring her three-year-old for entry to a prestigious girls' school (where over three hundred girls are seen for twenty-four places) and hot-house nurseries demanding each pre-schooler writes their name beautifully and counts to fifty like a robot before facing selection at any number of independent schools.

I understand the need to 'select' the right children for their specific school. If it's a particularly academic environment which moves at a fast and furious pace, it would be wrong to subject all children to this way of learning. What

I object to is the vast number of parents who prep, tutor, coach and bribe their children into them. Surely any sane mum can see that bribing a child so young or tutoring a kid just out of nappies to sit nicely, hold his pen correctly and copy sequence patterns with beads is tottering on very rocky ground? Before even considering squeezing and squashing your little one into this 'perfect' mould, ask yourself if you really feel it's right for them. Sure, you'd love the prestige of them attending the country's best co-ed school, but at what cost? My feeling is, if it doesn't come naturally to a child, then don't force it. Remember, it's our job as mums to find a school to fit them, not to mould a child to fit the school.

Many modern parents may pay for a little maths tuition for their ten-year-old before they sit the local grammar school entrance exam (a few months, maximum) and I think this is pretty reasonable. What we must all resist are those hard-core pushy parents who will at all costs mould their offspring for entry to the best schools. It doesn't take a genius to work out that this robs kids of confidence, contributes to making them feel powerless and inferior (or in some cases too superior), and above all forces them out of the garden (and a good game of super warriors) and into a repetitive cycle of isolated coaching.

Each child is different

However much you want all your children to go to the same school, it may not always be possible. For some kids a fast-track, single-sex school suits them down to the ground, whereas for others this would be their idea of hell. My pal

Jodie was faced with a similar dilemma when her second child was drowning at her local primary school. Unlike her super-confident and ambitious first-born (just like her mum, then), her second had specific learning needs and was incredibly shy. After months battling to get her through the school gates, she opted for a small, local girls' school where classes of thirteen kids meant she'd get the special attention she needed.

I'm not suggesting driving around the county dropping all your children at different hotspots, I'm just recommending you consider each child as an individual case, and if necessary pursue an alternative option. As this section implies, each child is different and what suits one may not suit all.

So, what should we look for?

I confess, when addressing this question I looked further afield than my own experience and that of my fellow mums. It was in fact my own fabulous mum who held the most in-depth understanding of what to look for in a school. Not only had she sourced four totally different schools for my three siblings and me (taking into account our individual temperaments, gifts and challenges) but she's also a leading pioneer in the understanding of learning awareness and learning difference. (She works in-house for a leading independent school in South London.)

Booking lunch with one very busy lady (even if she is my own mother) is no mean feat, but with the offer of lunch in my garden, accompanied by school talk, I managed to coax her over to brainstorm the elusive question, 'What should parents look for when choosing a school?' With my children's 'useful' suggestions (while whizzing down the slide beside us) the following tips span three generations of advice:

Distance.   Ideally you should look for a school that is near enough to walk to or, failing that, incurs a journey manageable in day-to-day life. I've heard of parents who drive almost an hour each way shuttling their four-year-old to school, which seems madness. Obviously you may need to drive each day, but bear in mind distance before you look around (you could even do a trial school run). But it goes without saying that you want to avoid eating up all your and your child's free time sitting in a car listening to back-seat bickering about what CD to play next!

Facts and figures.   Always ask for a school prospectus if they have one or any leaflets/bumf on the place. Although it shouldn't be a deciding factor, looking at Ofsted reports and exam results (GCSE, AS and A2 grades and where students go on to when they leave) will also give you a good idea of how students perform. If enough students leave with good results you can feel more confident that your child will do the same. (Just to add a word of caution: don't let these be your only reference point. Ofsted reports can be misleading and exam results can be first class, but at what cost to pupils' well-being?)

Look around.   The atmosphere you encounter when visiting a school can often be a deciding factor. What you really want is a friendly, warm welcome the moment you step through the door. Look out for the rapport between students and teachers, a sense of pastoral care, how interesting the lessons seem, the behaviour of the children during lessons, how well girls and boys interact, whether there is praise for lateral thinkers (an ethos that cherishes the individual is key, I feel), the quality of the work on the walls and the teachers' approach to discipline (I'm always wary of too much discipline or a strict emphasis on results-only). If you're shown around by an existing pupil this is also a great way of deciphering what type of school it is and what sort of children they nurture.

Engage with the staff. I've found that by engaging with the staff and seeing how they respond to queries on everything from discipline to school lunches, you can get a real feeling of their warmth and tone. Rapport and a shared belief system with the staff are really important when choosing the right future school for your child. You could think about jotting down just a few questions beforehand to help you remember to address your key concerns on the day.

Bear in mind facilities and extra-curricular activities. If it's open space you want then an inner-city primary with no garden might not hit the spot, and if you really want your child to learn music but the school puts all its extra resources into drama, then you may want to broaden your search. Think about the extra activities and facilities you desire for your child and try to find a school that offers at least some of these things.

Talk to others. What other people say about a school can give you a good impression of its reputation. Obviously, everyone has their own distinct views on education and you should bear this in mind (there's no point in asking your neighbour who hates uniform and structure about the all boys', old-fashioned prep school down the road!), but asking parents, ex-pupils and teachers at your child's current nursery or school for their views may help you.

Remember your core family values. Always bear in mind your core family values. My husband and I place a premium on metropolitan, well-resourced day schools that nurture individuality and the creative spirit, so it would be pointless us looking around strict, single-sex boarding schools staffed by disciplinarians!

Make a list. You know how I love my lists; well, this is a great list-making opportunity! If you're torn between schools and can't decide then list the pros and cons and see if this helps.

Secondary schools. If it's the eleven-plus age you're thinking about, you may want to consider a few of the following points:

- Where are your child's friends going and why?
- Can your child get to school on their own, walking, cycling or using public transport? This will help promote independence and broaden their friendship networks.
- Is there much gossip about drugs and alcohol being associated with the school and/or pupils?

- What extra-curricular clubs are offered? Is there an additional charge? Are they held in the lunch hour or after school, and what are the implications of this?
- Is there a sixth form attached to the school? And if so, what A-levels are on offer?
- Is there a positive and effective approach to discipline?
- Does it cater for your child's particular gift and/or interests?
- Are there any weekend commitments?
- How does the option system work, for example, when choosing languages in Years 7, 8, 9 and for GCSEs? In comparison with other schools, does it seem that pupils have to make limiting choices (if they do art they can't do drama, if they do French they can't do Spanish, etc.)?
- What are the class sizes and do these change as the pupils progress up the school?
- Which sports are offered and how much choice is there? Are after-school clubs available and do they compete in leagues with other schools?
- Are there opportunities for getting involved in school plays and playing an instrument/singing, for example is there an orchestra, a drama club or school choir?
- Lastly, what does your child think?

The PTA

Whichever school you pick, being an involved mum benefits everyone. Now, there's a big difference between being 'involved' and being 'pushy'! What I mean by playing an active part in school life is giving as much time as is viable for you (and this varies greatly between mums) to understand how your child's school works and small ways you can be involved. Even if this just means helping on a theatre trip once a year when you can squeeze an afternoon off work, then great. You don't have to run the PTA to take an interest (although brilliant if you can!). My experience has been that, with both my kids, being involved has helped us all get to know the school better (and vice versa).

Try not to compare and compete

How many of us have taken a sneaky look into another child's reading bag just to check what level they're on? Come on, admit it; the desire to compare and compete can just become too much. Anyone who has ever helped their kid draw the most fantastic mask for Hallowe'en or embroider the most exquisite costume for the Christmas panto can come clean now! While we can be honest and share a laugh about this now, try, try, try to make your competitive streak end at the peeking in the book bag. Too much fierce competition will drive you to an early grave and turn your kids off school for good!

Prepare your child

Whether you choose the church primary school at the end of your road or a private girls' school in the next town, attempting to boost your child's confidence before they start school is a great tip to bear in mind. I made an effort to do the following and it helped my kids settle with ease.

Help them make friends. Getting a class list from the school and organising a few playdates and teas with local families will help both you and your child feel more familiar with the new names and faces.

Do some play activities to help early school skills. Things like hand–eye control, simple counting exercises, pre-reading skills and recognition of letters and words, sharing, concentration or even some teacher–pupil role-play will help.

Teach your child to play in one spot for ten to fifteen minutes. If you can give them a game or activity, instruct them how to undertake it and encourage them to complete it over a ten to fifteen-minute period, it should help them to understand what may be expected of them come September.

Practise routine self-reliance skills. Things like getting dressed, putting on their own shoes, using a knife and fork, and going to the toilet (as well as washing their hands after-wards!) will be expected within school from day one.

Prepare them for separation. Talk things over and explain clearly the procedure for dropping off, saying goodbye and returning at the end of the day.

Be true to yourself

One last note on education, and one which I have to remind myself of often (especially when I was asked at the nursery gates for the tenth time the other day, 'Where will your new baby be going to school?'): Stay true to yourself. Before you ring that tutor, bribe that headmistress, put your house on the market with the intention of moving to the nearby 'hot' primary school, remember what really and truly matters to you and your family. For me it's not the bowler hat uniform, the bragging about exam results, what the other mums think of me, or even whether my child is on Reading Scheme Four or Forty, it's that they are happy and confident kids. This is being true to me and to them (and working on phonics with a three-year-old for all the wrong reasons is not!).

Mother knows best

'There was no way we could afford to send our children to private schools, but what we could do was ensure we lived somewhere with good access to state schools that offered diversity and warmth. When we moved to Oxford we made this a top priority and although we had to compromise on a slightly smaller house, we now live within walking distance from both primary and secondary schools, where our children are very happy, secure and have very high learning confidence.'

Full-time mum of two

School Gate Mafia

I must confess, when my son started at his pre-school last year, I was terrified. You may be wondering if this terror was that he'd cry when I left him, that I'd forget his gym kit or a fear of my own wrench (that my youngest was off in the world). It was in fact none of these. My terror was at the thought of the other mums! It now seems ridiculous because the mums in his class are by far some of the nicest, warmest and most down-to-earth women I've ever met, but prior to meeting them I was a nervous wreck! What should I wear? I needed to strike a balance between coming across as not too glam, not too mumsy, and seeing as half of them had Dr before their names, I worried they would all think I was a bit of a media-mummy. And what the hell do you talk about as you meet and smile nervously for the first time? Heeeeeeeeeelp!

Anyone who's encountered these first-day-at-school nerves (yours, not the child's) will empathise with that only too familiar feeling of being the 'new girl'. You wave your child off and look around to see twenty-odd other tear-stained faces, all of whom will be your fellow 'mummy mafia' for the years to come. I won't imply that you'll get on with everyone (like any workplace, classroom, even family unit, there will be people you just don't 'click' with) and I'd even go as far as to say you may well find some of the fellow school-gate mums impossible.

Take my friend Sophie. She's a working, single mum, so in her mind that gives her two black marks against her name immediately. (She reckons the school gate mafia value only full-time working mums who are a size ten, happily married and bake muffins every Tuesday.) After her second child got a music scholarship to a brilliant independent school she was thrilled. However, Sophie quickly discovered the toughest part about moving him from the relaxed state school up the road to the 'posh' (her words, not mine) alternative was meeting a whole new set of parents. As the new girl in town, all eyes were on her and she says to this day she never feels well groomed, well spoken or even well baked enough to totally fit in. One mum in particular constantly berates her (between forced smiles) for missing the school panto or getting the childminder to make the Hallowe'en costumes, and don't get Sophie started about the way she calls her house 'quaint' when she picks her daughter up from playdates. It drives her to despair!

If your fellow school gate mafia aren't competing about handbags or house sizes (and to be honest, I don't think mine would know the difference between a Chanel padded chain-clutch bag and a Topshop maxi-bag!) then they may well fall into the competitive parent category. By this I mean they bypass the usual chit-chat on car types ('Which four-by-four do you have?') or holiday destinations (thank goodness, when you're off to Center Parcs again and *not* the Maldives Four Seasons!), and move straight onto what languages their child is learning and how many schools they'll be sitting for at eleven-plus. Oh, God help us!

We all know one or two competitive super mums who'll use the school gate as leverage for one-upmumship. Whichever school it is, it's impossible to be blessed with thirty mums who are all as relaxed about grades and ambition as you'd like them to be. However hard you try to avoid them, they pop up and gleefully inform you that their little one is already fluent in Japanese (at the age of four), can read *Harry Potter* (at the age of five) and swim one thousand metres (at the age of six). Not only this; they have immaculate manners, beautiful nit-free hair and can tie their double-jointed toes into a bow! Now, I have nothing against gifted children; I only mind parents who want to tell you every detail of their child's gift as if it were a medal worn with pride.

Maybe it's because many mums leave or downscale their working lives to have a family, making their child's achievements replace their own? Maybe the bragging is a sign of misguided pride or maybe they are just super-competitive? Who knows? The only thing I do know is it's very off-putting for other mums!

What I've found useful is an ethos of unity with fellow mums. Just by my nature I'm inclined to cut through the small talk and competitive edge as quickly as possible and move onto developing genuine warmth and familiarity with the women I'm going to see rather a lot of over the coming years. Sourcing familiar ground (not about our child's skills in long division, but possibly about our careers or interests), inviting them round for tea or sharing a jokey email all help you feel united rather than like a gaggle of competitive bees swarming the entrance of the school. Getting onto a real friendship level with a handful of these mums should really help you fit into a school and share common ground with someone. I've honestly made some really wonderful girl-friends via my children, many of whom I never would have met had it not been via the school gates. Making that extra effort to be friendly, relaxed and not super-competitive is a great way to break down those initial nerves. Organising a mum's night once you've got to know each other over the first term is also a great way to build on those friendships while letting your hair down. (Although getting drunk and confiding all your deepest, darkest secrets at this gathering might be slightly over-familiar, for now anyway!)

Down-time

Let me give you a window into my perfect Saturday (although minus one husband as he has to work most Saturdays). While I hear other mums in my street piling their kids into the car for swimming lessons/violin tutoring/drama groups or play-dates we tend to do the following:

- Get up and eat breakfast in our pyjamas.
- While the kids play (puppets, dolls house, 'baddies', 'alien war zone'), I'll read a novel/have a long bath/cook up something yummy for later in the day.
- If we're feeling brave we'll saunter up to the Broadway to buy a newspaper and some lunch from the local deli.
- Head home for an afternoon of further kids' play and Mum reading up on the Culture section/catching up on emails/making a cake to be devoured while still hot or

if it's nice we all venture into the garden, me catching up on the weeding while the children 'help'.

Really not too complicated, is it? I can honestly say that most Saturdays this would be our normal agenda. Pencil in a visit from my sister Fleur, possibly a movie in the afternoon and maybe a little reading practice for the kids, but honestly not a lot more. What I can't understand is what the rest of the nation are doing zooming around shopping centres just for the fun of it or, worse still, signing their kids up for an endless array of out-of-school activities to fill their time.

I suppose my favouring of 'down-time' comes from an innate belief that as parents we have a tendency to over-stretch our children. I risk sounding like a real old bag here, but when I was growing up we mucked about on bikes, made camps in the garden, ate Nutella on toast in front of *Fame* and generally had a lot of childish fun. It's a total myth that you need to stimulate your children *all* the time. Not only is it expensive to fork out for kung fu, ballet, French and vocal training at the weekends and after school, it also fills up the family timetable, leaving little or no time for free play. How do you think children learn to share, create, imagine and, I hate to say it, overcome boredom, if their senses are being stimulated in adult-formed group activities every moment of every day? You see my point?

We've all fallen victim to the extra-curricular trap at some time. Only last year my daughter was attending ballet, drama and swimming sessions after school every week. It was in the car as we waited in the one-hundredth traffic jam en route to her ballet class that she asked, 'Do you think we could just go to the park next week?' I looked out the window at the afternoon sun and wondered why the hell I felt I had to drag her from one group to the next, just in case we captured the inner Darcey Bussell/Kate Winslet/Sharron Davies in her?

Children today work so hard at school that surely they deserve some really extended playtime once they leave at half past three? As mums too, we deserve some time just 'hanging' with our kids without rushing to and from art classes or yoga for under-fives. My son likes nothing more at the moment than coming home from nursery, getting back into his pyjamas and putting on a show for me with his endless collection of puppets. Not only are his stories wonderfully vivid (something I doubt he'd get to explore in a more structured drama class), but he has me all to himself, with my positive attention totally on him and this is something that would be impossible if I was screeching at him to get his music practice done before dashing out for football training.

Somehow we seem to feel if we're doing 'nothing' at home with our children then we're wasting precious time. It's almost like a race to create the most gifted, cultured, talented and multi-skilled primary-schooler, and in order to have a shot at winning we fill their time with every imaginable activity. I've heard of mums who think nothing of piano for two-year-olds or a double-whammy of sport-and-arts after a long week at school. *I'd* be exhausted with some kids' schedules, never mind how it must feel for a small child who's at school five days a week! It's always been my philosophy that too much over-stimulation does more harm than good. I'm amazed on a daily basis by the games and plays that my kids make up during down-time at home. The paintings they do, the little worlds they create in their bedrooms, the taunts they devise to get me off the computer, are all brilliant for developing their own personalities. Even if they get bored, being resourceful and 'finding' fun is an important life skill.

My rule for the new school year is 'two clubs each kid, *maximum*'. Their schools offer a range of diverse activities during the school day, so I feel two extra activities are ample. Luckily, because they're so close in age and share many of the same interests, they've agreed they'd both like to do drama and swimming. I'll make sure they can go to a class at the same time which leaves three nights and the whole weekend for homework and down-time in equal measure. It also means I have time to spend with them (which doesn't involve sitting in a car en route to karate or sitting in a cold corridor waiting for a ballet class to finish). Ideal for all, don't you agree?

Mother knows best

'My kids go to a school which has very few activities beyond the National Curriculum. I vowed I'd make up for this lack of choice with out-of-school clubs, which we've managed well. Having said that, I do make weekends sacred and try to leave these for fun. In my book, the week is for work and extra-curricular activities and the weekend is about playtime. It seems to work OK and means I can actually have some 'me time' at the weekend too.'

Full-time mum of three

Top ten tips to *avoid* the competitive parenting complex!

1. Becoming a parent seems to give you an obligatory licence to enter the competitive parenting race. Focus on your own instincts as opposed to the overwhelming advice of others.

2. Try to avoid the pressure to become a 'perfect parent' with 'perfect children'. We are all human and ultimately muddle along the best we can (making huge mistakes, as well as great achievements along the way) and this *is* OK.

3. Don't make your kids' playdates into a strategic operation. Play-Doh and My Little Ponies should be a priority, not long division and spelling tests!

4. Kids' parties should be age-appropriate and above all fun (not an opportunity to hire the Barbican, show off your canapé repertoire and network!).

5. Education is a minefield and therefore the perfect breeding ground for anxiety and competition. Try not to use your child as a pawn in this contest.

6. Choosing the right school takes a lot of thought and energy so combine my tips with your own family's ethos and stick to your guns!

7. Avoid the desire to coach your child; remember their academic school life is about *them* not *you*!

8. Strike a good balance between being involved with school life and fellow parents and letting your child carve out their own identity within the school.

9. Don't over-stimulate your child with endless after-school activities. (Violin lessons, Kumon maths, ballet, meditation and horse riding each and every week for your four-year-old are the guilty sins of pushy, or preoccupied, parents!)

10. Make down-time a priority for the whole family. Kids need large chunks of time to enjoy and explore free play at home.

Grace's Guru: Lucy Cavendish

Lucy Cavendish is a writer, journalist and mother of four children: Raymond (eleven), Leonard (four), Jeremiah (three) and baby Ottoline. She lives with her husband Michael, a graphic artist, in a cottage in the Chiltern Hills. When she is not cooking, washing up, doing the laundry, shopping and helping with homework, she interviews celebrities for the *London Evening Standard*. She also writes for the *Guardian*, *Sunday Telegraph*, *Observer*, *Tatler*, *Harpers Bazaar*, *Woman and Home*, *Marie Claire* and many other publications on a range of subjects. She has also written two novels, *Samantha Smythe's Modern Family Journal* and *Samantha Smythe's Incredible Expanding Family*, which are both published by Penguin. She is currently writing her third novel as well as becoming a talking head about children's issues on television. She has been on *LK Today* and *BBC Breakfast* talking about competitive parenting syndrome as well as being on the BBC2 series *The Madness of Modern Parenting*.

What are your main parenting tips for the following mums?

A new mum wanting to navigate her way through the advice-overload of the first year My top tip here comes in two words: Penelope Leach. In my experience she is the only baby guru worth reading. Everyone else throws so much conflicting information at you that it is impossible to know whether a baby should sleep in your bed or in a cot, should be pushed to feed every three hours or have food on demand. The problem with all this advice is that every mother and every baby and every relationship between mother and baby is different. We all bring many things into motherhood; our own expectations, our experience of how we were mothered ourselves. Maybe we have friends and/or family and we have seen at close hand how other people parent and we will have picked up our own dos and don'ts from that.

For example, I always have my babies in bed with me for the first six months. I don't really know why I do, but every bone in my body tells me to keep them close to me. I cannot imagine carrying a child for 40 weeks safe and snug and warm in my belly and then pushing them out into this bright, cold alien world and putting them in a cot in a separate room. I also demand feed – I cannot bear hearing a newborn mewl for food and not be allowed to feed.

My best advice is to listen to what your nature is telling you about your baby and you. Every baby is different so you must treat every baby as an individual. Mothers know their babies. If they are under the weather, the mother knows. Do not let anyone tell you that you are wrong about this. Also, use your health visitor. They are knowledgeable people who are there for you. If it is your first baby and you feel you are struggling then ask for help – it may well turn out to be a life-line.

Above all, just remember this: all babies are unpredictable. You may find yourself thinking you have the key to your baby – sleeping through at six weeks, going three to four hours between feeds – then all of a sudden, a few weeks later, the baby is screaming all day and night and you think, 'What on earth has gone wrong?' Well, nothing has gone wrong. Your baby has just changed the shape of the lock, that's all. You must learn to find a new key. Remember that if you trust your baby, your baby will learn to trust you. I talk to baby Ottoline all the time and I know that she understands what I am saying. If she is frightened by something, her instinct is to look for me. In return I talk to her soothingly and hold her close and then she is reassured. It's all about getting to know one another.

Also remember that good parenting is down to confidence. Keep telling yourself that you are a good mother and don't give yourself such a hard time.

A busy mum who wants to throw an enjoyable but inexpensive kids party Ah, the children's birthday party, what a nightmare. I have spent a fortune on them. I have hired clowns (mostly dreadful) and booked discos. I have leafed through the *Yellow Pages* and consulted the Internet. I have asked friends and family and yet still it has taken many years to hone the art of the perfect party.

It seems to me that with pre-school children you can get away with just about anything. My third son Jeremiah has a late-July birthday which is bad in terms of him being young for his age within the school year but great in terms of party opportunities. This year he turned three and we arranged a picnic tea by the river for him. My husband hired a little phut-phut boat (fifteen pounds for the afternoon) and then he brought him and his brothers slowly and gently down the river. Meanwhile, I set up a picnic – nothing major, just a picnic blanket, cucumber sandwiches and a birthday cake – on the towpath and, when my husband arrived, we all had tea. We invited a couple of other families with small children and they brought bats and balls and we all had a lovely afternoon for not much expense.

However, when children get older, especially in that first year they start primary school where everyone in the entire world is having parties, you have to be a bit more experimental. But it is possible to take the summer picnic idea and transpose it. For Leonard's fourth birthday party in March, we had lunch in the woods and then played hide and seek; the adults were the monsters and the children hid and then, after we pretended not to see them, they stalked us back to our 'lair' and they were very pleased with themselves. For Raymond's tenth birthday in October, we all went and built a camp with long branches and peat from the woodland floor and then we made a fire and toasted marshmallows and cooked sausages. That was a really exciting thing to do but it does take a lot of organisation.

Local halls are worth checking out too; there are church halls dotted the length and breadth of this country and they are very cheap to hire for an afternoon. Then you could organise your own party games and maybe get a face-painting kit and ask a talented friend to make the children up. One year, I made a treasure map and a guess-the-weight cake and did a mini-fête in our local village hall, which went down very well. I also draw the line at party bags. They can end up costing a fortune so I usually just dole out bits of cake and maybe a fancy pencil and a rubber. One year I bought some juggling balls to hand out and everyone loved them. Do not get competitive about party bags. No one wants their child to go home with ridiculously expensive toys and/or lots of sweets.

Once the children get older, the pressure eases off a bit. I find now that a trip to the cinema with a friend works for my eldest son or a game of bowls or a day in London. This year I am taking him to the National Portrait Gallery and that's free!

A mum looking for a good school for her children
This, surely, must be the most confusing, loaded thing a parent can do and in many ways what I am going to say will not be popular because, when it comes to primary education, it is probably best just to send your child to your local school unless there are very good reasons not to. There are many reasons to send your children to the local school, the main one being that they will meet local friends and all children need friends who are easily accessible. They will also feel part of their local community and that is very important.

Whether you choose private or state, make sure you look at Ofsted reports. You will probably have an idea of which schools you are interested in so it is worth looking up what the school inspectors have said about them. Then you will need to make a shortlist and go and visit the school. Before you go, decide on what factors are important to you. Do you want your child to go to a faith-led school? Is sport important? What about school meals? What is their attitude to bullying and what do they do about it? Are you interested in the head teacher's role and success in defining the school's ethos? A good head teacher can turn around a formerly failing school so don't just write a school off before you have visited it. But, if you really like a head teacher, ask them how long they are intending to stay in the job.

The other thing to do is to go and stand at the school gates when the children are coming out from school. How do you feel about being there? Do you feel you fit in? Do you like the look of at least some of the other parents? Maybe talk to some of them. Explain that you are looking at the school for your child and ask them what they do and don't like about the school. Then watch the children as they come out. Do they seem happy? Do they come out chatty and lively or down and depressed? Essentially, can you see you and your child fitting in at the school or not?

Do remember that what suits one child may not suit the others. My eldest son went to the local school but ended up in a fee-paying independent school in our local town owing to the fact that there were some question marks over his learning ability. My second son, however, is not following his brother to the school in the town but going to the local village school as, at the moment, he doesn't seem to have any special educational needs. You need to find the right school for each child.

A mum who wants to avoid being an OTT competitive parent I think the key to being a good parent is just to let yourself relax into it. That sounds terribly easy but, in many ways, it's very hard. Without realising it many parents start imprinting themselves onto their children. So many times I have said to my eldest son, Raymond, 'I never did that when I was your age!' or 'I always handed my homework in on time, why can't you?' Sentences like this usually leave Raymond quite rightly growling at me, for Raymond isn't me. I am me and he is him and, yes, I was a terribly studious child but why do I expect Raymond to be the same as I was? I think Raymond is just no more or less than a typical boy.

And yet, for years I have been endeavouring to shape him. I have enrolled him for virtually every single course going. From the age of three he did Tumble Tots and swimming and football and since then we have gone through chess club, French club, Mindlab, sailing, tennis, cricket, more football, rugby, kayaking, water-skiing, judo and karate, piano lessons, the guitar and guess what? He's given up all of them. I have spent a fortune on him and yet he has done one course of each and then refused to re-enlist. When I have pointed out to him just how much money I have spent on him, he looks pained and then says, 'But I never asked to do any of this. I'd rather you'd spent the money on buying me a Playstation.' At least he is honest! But yet again he has a point. It's not Raymond who wants to be an Olympic swimmer, it's just me who wants him to be. No one gets to the top of their game without being pushed along by a parent, but of course, this is the problem. In this day and age, we are all so busy helping our pre-school and school-age children find their true potential that we've forgotten to back off and let them find it for themselves.

So, after years of pushing and tugging Raymond off to tennis and the like I have sort of walked away from my other children. I have learned that you really can take a horse to water but you can't make it drink, and so Lennie and Jerry and the baby, obviously, spend their lives just being rather than doing. I often feel guilty about this. I watch other parents enrolling their small children into baby music programmes and gym classes, but I have decided that not only are they a waste of time and money but also they are not that good for my children's mentality. I like to see my children explore the house/the garden/their relationship with each other. And yet, I still feel that somehow I am letting them down. This is the rub, of course; the more you decide not to play the competitive parent game, the stronger and more resolute you have to be.

When you are surrounded by children who, aged about six, seem to be accomplished in just about everything while yours are doing nothing more than playing hide and seek in the garden and maybe doing a basic jigsaw puzzle, it is hard to follow your own course of action. What can you boast about? And it's not just the boasting. It's the real fear that somehow you are short-changing your child. But ask yourself this: are these other children really that accomplished? Are you sure? Maybe their parents are over-egging the pudding in order to feel better about the fact that they have bought into it all and are slightly threatened by the fact that you haven't. It's a complicated web, parenting.

I think my best bit of advice is for mothers to try and avoid guilt. We are all trying to do the best for our children but that doesn't necessarily mean filling their days and weeks up to the brim with goal-orientated after-school activities or stunning achievements within the classroom. Parents feel a great need for their children to be high-achievers but that is not something that should be of any concern until the child is of secondary school level. In fact, if I am wearing my other hat of celebrity interviewer, I can say with some assurance that what marks a large percentage of these people out is their lack of ability to perform as a child.

A mum looking for the balance between nurturing her children and enhancing their potential Any child that is loved and cared for will, in the end, be able to enhance their own potential. The worst thing any parent can do to a child is to constantly put their child down. If you ruin your child's self-confidence, then however much you push them and encourage them, they will not be able to move forwards in their life or have the ability to try new things and pursue their own goals in later life. All children need a tremendous amount of nurturing, especially when they are under seven years old. They need constant love and attention and reassurance. They will look to their parents for approval all the time and that approval must be given. Be unrelentingly positive. Small children don't need to know that the world is a tough and hard place. They need to know that they are loved and fed and cared for. Their world needs to feel safe and warm and ultimately fantastic.

If you have laid this warm and loving foundation down for your child then helping them find their potential is not very difficult. Children tend to find out what they like to do and, once they have found that out, then your job is to encourage them and reassure them. I find that it helps to make suggestions to them about what they might like to do. I took Leonard to Stagecoach because I truly felt he would enjoy it. He wasn't sure about going but once he went, he loved it. I am not expecting him to be a child actor, it is just that at the age of four, nearly five, I felt it was time he ventured out a bit more into the world of extra-curricular activities.

But there comes a time when the nurturing changes a bit as children start to stand on their own two feet. I find that with Raymond, I still have to support him massively but now he has his own independence. He makes decisions about what he does and doesn't want to do and I listen to his reasons and we take it from there. If I want him to learn the piano because I think he has a musical ear but he just doesn't want to, there is no point in me pushing him into it. He needs to come to that realisation by himself and I have to trust him to do that. Raymond actually tries many things even if they scare him. When I see him looking insecure, I don't make a fuss. I just touch his arm or give him a wink. I do something to let him know that I am here with him and everything will be fine, then I see him visibly relax into undertaking a challenge he feels insecure about.

A mum looking for innovative ways to enjoy down-time with her kids The main thing to do here is think about what your children like to do. My baby likes to have a milky feed and then gaze at me while curling my hair in her little fist. This is her down-time. Jeremiah likes to help me cook dinner, Leonard likes to paint and Raymond likes to read a book or veg out in front of the television. There are so many ways of enjoying down-time with kids but the most important thing to do is to focus on it. What children really hate is a mother who says, 'Ooh look, let's enjoy some time together,' and then wanders off to answer the telephone or check emails. If you are going to spend quality time with your children then you had better make sure you can actually do that or else you may well find your telephone calls interrupted by loud wails and the plug being pulled out of the computer. So, when you are spending time with your children, don't answer the telephone or go and look at your computer because the message you are then giving them is that they are less important to you than whoever is on the telephone. If you absolutely have to talk to someone on the telephone, let your children know how long you will be – five minutes maximum – and then they will know when you are coming back to them and most children can deal with that.

Also, think long and hard about what you are going to do with them and then throw yourself into it whole-heartedly. Then again, you mustn't be prescriptive about what you want the children to do. For example, I once spent an hour cutting out potatoes for us to make potato-print pictures with. I did stars and Christmas trees and it took an age because I am not remotely talented when it comes to anything artistic. Once I'd finished, though, the children did a print each and then they all announced they wanted to walk the dog instead. I could have cried. I wanted to say to them, 'I've just spent ages doing this!' but I had to accept that although I wanted them to make pictures, they wanted to do something else and we had a lovely time in the woods with the dog anyway.

But some structure to down-time is a good idea. I have an arts and crafts cupboard full of paper, paint, glue and glitter. I also have a dressing-up box and a corner with a tape player and cassettes in, so that there are many activities we can all do in the house. I also bought a small pretend-kitchen for the smaller two boys to play in. They love it. They make me tea and cakes virtually every day and they put on their pinnies and they are very proud of themselves. All small children love imaginative play. You don't even need anything for that. You can be an ogre/fairy/giant/princess and they can fight you/rescue you/paint you green, etc . . . It's great fun. You also have to be prepared for them to make a mess. Paint and felt and Play-Doh and train tracks and princess castles made from papier mâché are all messy so just let them get on with it and don't have a go at them. You can all make a game of clearing up later.

Teaching the children how to cook is also lots of fun. My little ones even grow vegetables in their own vegetable patch and it's amazing to see children make a connection between what grows and the food on their plate. If you don't have a garden then why not get your children to come to the supermarket with you and choose the food they want to cook. Have a look at a kids' cookbook and ask the children to choose what they want to cook from it. Then you can all go and buy the ingredients and they can make (or try to make!) dinner for you. My children love doing that and even if it is a disaster I still smile my way through undercooked spaghetti covered in a too-salty sauce because I love the fact that they tried.

Other things I find good to do include puzzles, junior sudoku and lots of reading and then talking in an imaginative way about the book. If the weather is good we are outside a lot building camps and pretending to have campfires. We often 'pack' and 'go on holiday' in the garden. Really, children are so imaginative all you need to have is a bit of commitment and energy and the days roll past full of fun and enjoyment.

What are the key dos and don'ts for the mum seeking balance with her children?

Do

- Remember that they are your children. You chose to have them and, therefore, you want them and wanting them means loving them in the way they need to be loved.

- Have fun with them! I see so many miserable people with their children but children are, by their very nature, fun! So remember that and laugh with them, a lot.

- Praise them, praise them, praise them. Children really just want to please so let them know when you are pleased.

- Have consensus with your partner on how you bring your children up. You must show a united front even if, in private, you don't agree.

- Have boundaries – it's up to you where you draw that line in the sand but that line must be drawn or else your children will not learn what is acceptable and unacceptable behaviour.

- Recognise when to give up. There is little point in trying to have a rational conversation with an overtired/hungry child. Pick your moments carefully.

- Feed them! I don't know what is happening these days but many of my children's friends don't have three sit-down meals a day. Some of them snack all day, others barely eat or they come to our house and say, 'I don't eat dinner, I just have crisps.' It's unbelievable! Children cannot survive like this. Try at least to have one meal a day as a family. I think it really helps glue a family together.

- Change your life. I am sorry, and this is not going to be

popular, but you need to be with your children. You can work all your life but who is going to remember that in the long term? Take some time out to be with them properly rather than having your mobile constantly ringing with work calls. They need to feel that they are worthwhile in your eyes.

- Let them be naughty once in a while. Naughty can be good. No one ever likes a goody-goody.
- Give them time. Stop and listen to them. Turn off the computer and don't answer the telephone so that they know you think they are worth listening to.

Don't

- Don't sweat the small stuff. I see so many parents telling their children off over the smallest of things. Get off their backs sometimes.
- Don't continually disagree with your partner in front of your children over the way you bring them up. Children are astute and conniving little people. If they feel their parents are divided on issues they will start exploiting that.
- Don't confuse them. You must have consistency. If it's not OK to eat cake before supper one day then it's not OK the next. If your boundaries change all the time then they will become confused and angry.
- Don't match anger with anger. If your child, of what-ever age, is having a tantrum then walk away.
- Don't ignore them, talk down to them or belittle them. It's crucifying seeing people do this to their children. It's quite a middle-class thing, that subtle chilling put-down. Just don't stamp on their dreams.

- Don't tell them how to be. Our children never really turn out how we imagine them to. I want my children to be musical but they are not, at the moment, interested in playing an instrument. I have to accept that. They are not mini-mes; they are their own people.

> Lucy's fabulous mum's parenting mantra:
> 'You are a good mother. You are a good mother. You are a good mother!'

Mother Earth

Changing Times

Once upon a time the words 'mother' and 'earth' or 'green' and 'living' said together evoked an image of hippy types with long underarm hair and raffia sandals. A picture would emerge in one's mind of a long-haired mother still breast-feeding her three kids (Moon, Indigo and Tulip) way past their third birthdays, smelling of patchouli oil and insisting everyone around her eat only organic, home-grown seeds and nuts for tea. Fast-forward to today and green living conjures up a totally different stereotype. Now I picture a Boden-clad mummy of three, her uber-trendy, eco-friendly maxi-bag slung over her shoulder (because, let's face it, she queued for three hours in the rain to buy it *and* it's made by a top-name designer). She walks the school run and after drop-off whizzes to her local organic fruit and vegetable market to buy sweet potatoes and goat's cheese for supper. On Tuesday she attends a yoga group (and no doubt brushes shoulders with the likes of Sheherazade Goldsmith and Laura Bailey while in the cobra position) and on Wednesday she gives talks to local mums on the power of recycling. There's no denying it, in today's world, the green mum is the truly fabulous one!

Putting chic to one side for a moment (I confess I'm not one of the thousands who queued for the ultimate in eco maxi-bags, being far too busy finishing an article for *Junior* and picking the kids up from school), there can't be many of you reading this who haven't felt yourself becoming more 'green aware' since embarking on motherhood. I certainly didn't give the idea of leading a more natural, environmentally friendly life much thought as I wafted from one fashion launch to another, hailing cabs twenty times a day and buying my lunches at M&S (chucking the excessive plastic and cardboard packaging in the nearest Soho bin). The closest I got to 'being green' was buying cocoa butter from a duty-free Body Shop before departing for four days in LA.

But the moment I realised I was pregnant my priorities changed. I suppose slowing down and thinking more about my body, what I was putting into it and the tiny seedling of new life within promoted a rather more healthy and natural approach to life. Instead of browsing in Topshop on my lunch breaks, I found myself in the local organic supermarket, cautiously sniffing organic body oils and filling my basket with multi-vitamins and chunky organic veg soups. In the same way your instinct and common sense tell you not to consume vast amounts of booze, sugar, caffeine and colouring and additive loaded drinks and foods, it can push you to explore a more natural diet and healthier lifestyle as well. I'm not saying that once we're pregnant we all become teetotal and drink only wheatgrass with added omega-3 oils, but often we'll up our intake of fresh goodies (making many of them organic) and smother our bumps with natural, organic almond oil instead of chemical-laden, perfumed designer body creams.

I remember being most struck by this environmentally aware streak just three days after giving birth to my daughter. I'd eaten as much organic, local produce as possible throughout my pregnancy (bar the daily tub of Ben and Jerry's ice cream), undertaken weekly yoga classes, rubbed my stretching skin with natural oils, mentally committed myself to breastfeeding and read up about organic baby foods. I'd managed to give birth naturally and had kitted my beautiful daughter out in natural, white cotton Babygros for the first three days of her life. As she snuggled into my husband's chest, secured safely in her papoose, we ventured out for the first time.

Half a mile up the high street and nearing our local branch of Blockbuster, I was struck for the first time by just how polluted, dirty and smoky the streets were. Up until that moment I'd been far too busy chatting on my mobile or running for the number 19 bus to notice before. Cars lined up at red lights pouring exhaust fumes into the air, discarded crisp bags blew in the wind and cigarette smoke whacked you in the face as you passed yet another twenty-a-day Benson & Hedges smoker waiting at the crossroads. I felt an overwhelming urge to get my daughter out of there. Only three days ago she'd been protected in the womb by the most natural fluid on earth and now her tiny lungs and perfect skin were exposed to all the fumes, germs and grime of the busy, noisy street. I was horrified!

Of course, part of this is a new mum's protective instincts kicking in ('Oh my beautiful, pure baby, let's just stay in this double bed bubble forever') but part of this is a sign of how once we start a family mums become more aware of the planet, the environment and how we live, breathe and eat. I certainly began to view the world into which I was bringing my kids in a different way. Questions like: 'What kind of planet will it be when they're parents?'; 'Will there even be parts of the planet still in existence (not to mention dolphins, polar bears and marine life)?'; 'What will the cancer statistics be like in twenty years?'; and 'How much more will we know about how our diet and environment affect all these factors?' sprung to the forefront of my mind. Suddenly you find yourself seeing the world in a much broader sense. It's not just about 'you' any more, but the future of the next generation.

Now, I won't pretend that this has led me to dress exclusively in homespun cotton, kit out all my kids in cloth nappies (boycotting Pampers by organising weekly rallies while I was at it) or even enforce a one hundred per cent organic, veggie kitchen at home. I'm the first to admit that I still chuck the occasional trashy magazine in the dustbin (and not the green recycle bin outside the front door), eat M&S fruit daily (despite the fact much of it isn't sourced locally or organic), and occasionally spend a bomb on a designer bag without questioning how or where it was made. However, I have changed my lifestyle for the greener (and better) in ways that I wouldn't have thought possible pre-kids.

For many of you, going entirely green just isn't an option. You may be feeding a family of six on a tight budget, in which case eating exclusively organic food will mean you'll have to sell the house and move to a caravan just to fund it. You may live twenty miles from your child's school, in which case walking the journey would entail getting up almost before you've gone to bed. Alternatively, you may be changing the nappies of twins (what feels like a million times a day) and the thought of washing cloth nappies on top of everything else is likely to tip you over the edge of sanity. I'm not about to tell you that any of these choices are 'wrong'; we can't all live the life of an eco-farmer with bags of cash to spend on frocks made of Cornish hand-spun, organic cashmere. Having said that, I will urge you to think about some of the small ways you can achieve a greener, more natural life. I promise with a little bit of recycling here and there, the odd purchase from a cool and inexpensive natural clothing company and the occasional input of organic meat into your diet, you'll start to feel you're making a difference. As minuscule as it may be, in the large scale of the earth's problems, it will affect the well-being of your immediate family and planet at large every single day. In the end don't we all want to set a good example to our children about caring for ourselves and our environment?

Mother knows best

'I've always been vegetarian and have been aware of the earth's crisis points since joining Greenpeace at university. When I had my daughter in my late twenties, I became even more anxious to do my bit for the planet. Although cloth nappies and organic purees were time-consuming and more expensive, I felt I wanted to start her life as I hoped she'd go on. Of course I can't stop her living on junk food and buying all her clothes in Primark when she gets older, but by showing by example how I feel you should treat yourself and the world around you, I hope she'll follow suit.'

Part-time working mum of one

Where to Start?

Making an effort to help the planet is all well and good in principle but where does a busy mum of three start?

Cloth nappies

Well, if you're my friend Jennie, the place to start (even if it's for the first time with number two) is reusable cloth nappies. I hold my hands up in shame here and confess that the thought of all that palaver with my number three is stretching my planet-friendly attitude somewhat. (I'll be hard-pressed to buy regular Pampers with a two-school-drop and 3,000 words to write on a daily basis!) But if it's good enough for my own mum and one of my closest girlfriends, then surely it's worth a try? I won't bore you with endless facts and figures, but just bearing this in mind might make you consider it as an option: apparently, eight million disposable nappies are thrown away every day in the UK, and by the time your child is potty trained around five thousand of these nappies will have come from your home. That's a hell of a lot of waste now, isn't it?

If you're worried about the extra laundering, then don't. There are many nappy services that will collect, wash and deliver clean nappies for around a tenner per week (which is about the same as you'd pay for disposable nappies). If you can't face going completely natural why not try the favourite brand in our house, Moltex? These are eco-friendly disposable nappies that you can buy from many an online eco store, local pharmacy or green baby shop.

Carry it all

If your children are well and truly out of nappies then there are still lots of little things that can be done day-to-day that will make a huge difference in the long run. For a start, re-using your plastic bags will save on hundreds of wasted plastic bags each year. (Multiply this by every mum you know and we're really starting to make a difference.) Even better, always carry a reusable fold-up cotton shopping bag with you and use that instead of grabbing a new plastic bag every time you pop to the shops.

My friend Celia even shops with a wheeled shopping trolley. She jokes that it's her 'old lady shopper' but as she glides around the Broadway, one hand free (instead of bowed down with three Sainsbury's plastic bags on each wrist) wheeling her funky striped contraption, she looks far from old-ladyish!

Washing and drying

Another small task that will save on water and fuel is the washing and drying. Now, you don't have to tell me twice to wash the family's clothes less. I'm sure you can identify with me here: there are days I feel I've had my head stuck in the washing machine drum more than in front of my computer! If you can try to reduce your washing by making more of one load, then great. Alternatively, use a cool wash; it's a total myth that clothes need to be constantly cleaned on a hot cycle. (I try to wash everything at thirty or forty degrees.) I also try to avoid washing small loads just for the sake of it. If, for example, my daughter's ballet kit needs cleaning for the next day, but not much else, I'll do it quickly by hand rather than putting the washing machine on. If you can dry clothes outside on warm days or on radiators or a clothes rack in an airing cupboard or spare room, then this will save an immense amount of tumble-drying (a method of drying that uses up alarming amounts of energy). These small changes also add up to be big savings to your pocket too! Another tip is to avoid clothes with a 'dry-clean only' label. Not only is it a pain to organise and very costly, dry cleaning is also incredibly toxic for the environment.

Recycle, recycle, recycle

It goes without saying that recycling as much waste as you can is an easy part of saving the planet without giving it too much thought. Many councils now impose fines for households found not to recycle their rubbish, so even if it feels like an extra hassle, it could save you a hefty fine. To start with simply make a daily ritual of sorting through your paper, glass and plastic rubbish, distributing them into separate recycle bins (most of you will have these supplied by the council anyway). I find the kids love to help with this and from a very early age started to be aware of how and why we recycle. (My son was even given a toy recycle truck for his birthday one year.) Each day it's one of the children's jobs to collect paper and place it in the recycle bin and I can tell you they prefer it to tidying up their toys any day. You could also keep any interesting boxes, tubes and containers for craft activities, or offer them to the school for their art lessons.

As well as the obvious recycling of rubbish, there is the

extended reuse of everyday bits and bobs. It depends how far you want to take the idea, but greener than green pals of mine swear by reusing envelopes (especially padded ones where you can just replace the address label), reusing bath and washing up water for their household plants, sharing and hiring DVDs and books instead of buying them new each time, and passing on kids' toys between them instead of buying new plastic toys once their kids are bored of or have grown out of the ones they've got.

Compost

My pal Jennie is a pioneer of garden composts. She has a garden the size of a postage stamp (if I won the lottery, one of the first things I'd do would be to set her up with a huge garden), but she utilises the space she has brilliantly. Her compost is retained in a green waste bin and then reused in her flourishing garden. If you're interested in learning more about composting then borrow a Monty Don book from the library. As Jennie says, 'He is the master of composting'!

A green home

Simple things like keeping some houseplants to purify and revitalise the air (peace lilies or bamboo plants) instead of plugging in an air freshener, and turning off lights, the TV standby and mobile phone chargers whenever possible, all help to save on household energy. It's worth looking into how you insulate your home too; keeping heat in is a priority for reducing energy output. Even though I'm not a fan of double glazing, I am looking into having my beautiful, original single-pane bay windows insulated with a heat-saving lining, which could well bring my heating bill down and save on precious energy reserves.

Think about packaging and waste

I know it sounds obvious, but by watching how much you buy and trying not to over-buy food/clothes/gifts, you'll help save on waste and excess packaging without lifting a finger. My friend Elaine, for example, is very mindful of buying food which has been excessively packaged. She always buys loose fruit and vegetables wherever possible. Jennie is Mrs Listmaker: writing precise shopping lists means she can avoid over-buying at the shops. She once told me that one-third of all food grown for human consumption in the UK is thrown away, so it's worth making these minor adjustments to help reduce your household wastage.

Another handy tip is to mend clothes before chucking them out and regularly requesting that shops don't give you a massive carrier for a small pair of briefs! I know it can be hard when a Whistles pink cardboard bag looks so glam, but if it's a self purchase, why not compromise by getting it wrapped in pretty pink tissue paper to place inside your own bag instead. This in itself will save on large quantities of packaging every time.

Novel gift ideas

I don't think any mum needs much persuasion to cut down on toy consumption! When buying for your child, or as a gift for someone else's, why not opt for wind-up toys, building material, arts and crafts, wooden treasures or books as opposed to battery-operated items or those brand toys which are excessively packaged as a sales tool? From an aesthetic point of view, I know I much prefer my daughter to receive a Russian doll to add to her collection rather than yet another plastic-engulfed, over-packaged Barbie doll. When it comes to my son, a wooden train or fancy dress costume are always first choice over a chunky, bleeping, battery-fuelled remote-control car.

You could also try something my friend Katie opts for, which is giving 'experience' birthday and Christmas presents (a holistic massage or a trip to the theatre for adults; a movie ticket or voucher for a 'treat day out' for kids). Or how about a gift that supports a worthy cause, such as sponsoring an endangered animal or planting a tree in an area affected by drought? My elder brother went down this route last year for all his Christmas gifts and it made a refreshing change from receiving some bath salts or a GAP T-shirt!

And if you want to go the whole hog . . .

Some of my dedicated eco-mummy pals share useful tips at our weekly coffee mornings and, listening to them, it's a wonder that they find time to go to work! Jennie, for example, insists we all make a 'no junk mail please' sign for our doors (to save the onslaught of home-delivery pizza leaflets that must surely cut down a rainforest per year to produce). Elaine, on the other hand, is devoted to buying bamboo products after discovering that it is the most eco-friendly of all the materials on offer (bamboo plant pots, bamboo flooring, bamboo cutlery:

you name it, she's bambooed it!). My neighbour, Susie, has gone as far as making her bathroom a 'bath-free zone', so disgusted was she at the amount of water used every day for her evening soak (her bath would take an average of 150 litres, as opposed to her five-minute shower taking 40 litres). What's more, she'll even tell you off for flushing the toilet, unless you've done a number two!

I know it would be unrealistic to expect you (or me) to do all of the above in our mission to lead a greener life. Having said that, even if you manage a little recycling here, the odd save-on-a-plastic-bag there and watch how you wash and dry clothes on a day-to-day basis, you'll be making a fantastic start.

Mother knows best

'I can't afford to feed the family purely organically and we don't have a garden, so grow your own vegetables and compost production is out. What I can do easily, however, is change our laundry habits. I wash at lower temperatures since finding out that eighty-five per cent of energy used by washing machines is devoted to heating the water and I only clean a full load. If clothes are really dirty I give them a good soak first and never, ever tumble dry. The other thing I do less of is ironing. I leave out the sheets and smalls and this serves a double purpose; it saves on the planet's energy as well as my own!'

Full-time working mum of two

Organic and Local Produce

It wouldn't be possible to discuss leading a greener life without touching on switching to organic and locally sourced produce. A decade ago we all began to rave about eating organic greens and meat, and organic supermarkets like Fresh & Wild were the height of shopping fashion ('Oh, was that Jamie Oliver I just spotted fondling the mushroom selection?'). Some years on and now a mother of two and counting, I do try to buy organic food whenever possible. The reason why? Broadly speaking from what I've read and researched, it seems that organic food is better for the whole family. It is certified by the UK Soil Association, it doesn't contain genetically modified ingredients, there's recent research which points to organic food containing more natural vitamins and minerals, and it goes without saying that it undeniably tastes better. The obvious fact that it's farmed with TLC and lacks the input of pesticides and hormones must surely mean an organic chicken and vegetable stir-fry beats battery-farmed chicken nuggets and deep-fried chips any day. (The fact that over 430 chemical sprays are used on non-organic crops compared to four on organic gets you thinking, doesn't it?)

Although I try to buy as much fresh organic food as possible, I confess that a part of my larder is still non-organic. When you're whizzing around Tesco on a Monday night, it's impossible to buy *all* your produce organically and even if you could, a packet of HobNobs and some Cheerios are still essential weekly must-haves in most homes. Saying that, I do try my best to buy the following products with an organically certified label. (For two reasons: the first simply because they taste better; the second because produce grown non-organically or sourced from non-organically reared animals comes with a double whammy of being pumped with things such as growth hormones and pesticides as well as incurring terrible battery conditions for the animals as they're reared.)

- *Meat* (especially chicken and beef)
- *Salmon*
- *Some fruit and vegetables* (especially things like apples and strawberries that not only contain huge amounts of pesticides if bought non-organically, but also make up a day-to-day part of the kids' diets)
- *Milk*
- *Cheese*
- *Eggs* (they should at the very least be free range)
- *Yogurt*
- *Bread*
- *Chocolate* (apart from the obligatory box of non-organic Celebrations for the weekend!)

Having told you the positive part, I must add that there are hitches with the organic regime, as well as pluses. There are three main problems with organic food: The first is cost – organic food is far pricier than non-organic. (Just check out the difference in price between a battery-farmed chicken and an organic bird.) The second is access – many mums don't have the time or means to nip to an organic butchers/market on a weekly basis. (Organic fish is tough to find at your local Iceland.) The third is appearance. (Admit it, don't the non-organic plump, ripe strawberries look more enticing?) With all these obstacles you can see how eating one hundred per cent organic is tricky for the modern, multi-tasking mum.

Faced with these dilemmas, I follow a similar line to my food guru, Jane Clarke. She advises mums to buy organic where practically possible but also to place importance on locally grown produce. You'll often find that if you buy fruit, for example, that is grown locally (Wales or a neighbouring county, not Cuba or New Zealand!), even if it's not been given an organic stamp it won't have been flown thousands of miles in tons of packaging. Not only this, buying goods from local farmers supports small farms and businesses and encourages a less mass-produced way of life.

As well as local produce being on my food hit list, I also try to make sure much of the produce we eat is in season. This often goes hand-in-hand with buying local produce. If it's summer, British strawberries are in abundance, so make the most of this and eat up! (You could make it a fun trip out and go *en famille* to pick your own at a local picking farm.) Likewise, in winter go for parsnips and root vegetables that are in abundance at that time of year. Not only will this ensure that the produce is fresh and largely sourced locally, it will also teach your kids about the foods and seasons. Sure, I'll still buy bananas in December (even if they come from South Africa – sorry, but we hardly have the climate to source them locally!) and I won't stop my daughter grabbing green grapes that come from Southern France, but whenever possible I will take note of how far the food I'm buying has come to reach the shelves in N10.

My good friend Katie has even gone as far as starting a vegetable patch at her home in Gloucestershire, where her little Archie can sow his own beans and watch them grow.

He's not yet two, so who knows how much soil will end up in his mouth and how much will end up under the beans, but never mind! The idea is to encourage a family ethos of growing your own vegetables, even if the total number of beans doesn't reach ten (for this year at least!).

Not only is food an issue when thinking about organic and natural produce, you should also factor cosmetics and health-care into this too. There's little point breaking the bank buying organic Essex farmed meat and insisting you and the kids eat only organic broccoli if you then clean the kitchen with chemical-packed cleaning products and soak in a potent bubble bath before bed. Many of us (myself included) tend to start off motherhood with a very natural, holistic approach to pregnancy (yes, it's that reference to no booze and almond stretch mark oil again!), move onto wiping our babies' bottoms with tap water and cotton wool and by the end of year one have resorted to Pampers wipes, Heinz jarred baby food and a long Radox bath before we hit the sack!

I like to advise everything in moderation; therefore I'm definitely not suggesting you chuck all your toiletries and cleaning products in the wastebin and reach for the nettle fragrance and natural lemon oven cleaner instead! 'No way,' I hear you say! However, I would suggest casting a fresh eye over your bathroom/kitchen/medicine cupboard and just thinking about what could be replaced by a more natural alternative next time you run out of something.

Perhaps you could try out an eco-friendly organic washing detergent, just for a week at least. How about swapping that Clarins body soap with an organic lavender one by Duchy Collection and comparing it for fragrance? Or simply change your known brand toothpaste for a month for one by Green People? You could even start substituting a plaster with arnica cream the next time your little one falls or making a hot lemon and ginger tea (using fresh lemon, ginger and manuka honey) when you get a cold, instead of reaching for the painkillers and max strength Lemsip. I'm not saying the natural alternative is viable or desirable every time, but on the other hand you may be very surprised by the results. For a start, you're bound to feel better about the amount of pesticides and chemicals you're *not* putting into your body (and those of your nearest and dearest). Not only this, you may well feel the physical difference too. Many children (my daughter, especially) are far less sensitive to natural products and remedies and I find her skin is a million times clearer when I use small amounts of natural products, as opposed to mass-produced chemical ones. (My friend Elaine swears baby wipes were the root of her child's endless nappy rash.)

Let's not all stampede the local organic supermarket at once . . .

Mother knows best

'Organic was an alien word in our house until last year. As a full-time working mum of three, just getting around Sainsbury's in one piece was a miracle, let alone selecting pricey organic goods while I was at it. This all changed when my youngest was diagnosed with food allergies and eczema. She was a very sickly baby and as a toddler reacted badly to almost everything. Conventional soap gave her itchy skin, milk gave her hives, wheat gave her stomach cramps and even my washing powder had her up all night sneezing. I was at my wits' end, tired of applying steroid creams and administering Piriton and inhalers to such a small child.

In the end, I was forced to look at the natural approach and I'm so glad I did. My daughter now eats largely organic wholefoods and we use only natural remedies and products on her skin. I won't lie and say the whole family is totally green, but we certainly all watch what and how we eat much more carefully. The main thing is my daughter is a different child, with unhampered breathing, clear skin and eyes and for this it's been worth the extra few quid on groceries and hours researching natural cleaning products on the Net.'

Full-time working mum of three

Health and Vitality

I confess that before I fell pregnant with my first child, my answer to any cold and flu symptoms was found on the shelves of Boots. A sniffle and I'd get some Tunes, a headache and a box of Nurofen would be in order, an impending flu bug and I'd be straight to the front of the queue armed with Lemsip Max and some Night Nurse. Eliminating the symptoms was of top priority (usually so I could continue to meet the deadlines of the January issue of *Elle* without needing to take a day off work). I'd push to the back of my mind any thoughts of long-term prevention or why I was developing my third cold that winter but still hadn't given up booze, had an early night or bought a hat and scarf to keep warm!

The idea of 'natural healthcare' was about as alien to me as the concept 'a winter without flu'. Back then it wasn't a possibility that registered in my conscience.

Oh how life changes! Even for the most conventional of women, pregnancy, childbirth and childrearing often brings out a desire for a more alternative approach to health and well-being. We must all know a few mums who have surprised us with this change of heart. You know, the friend who lived off caffeine and cigarettes and suddenly, six weeks into pregnancy, is tee total and sipping nettle tea? Or the one who took recreational drugs obsessively in her twenties only to harp on about her 'natural, drug-free' twenty-six-hour labour? Or how about the run-of-the-mill mum who took organic multi-vitamins and herbs hand in hand with conventional medicine pre-kids but suddenly wants to explore homeopathy, aromatherapy and Indian head massage now she's a mum?

As I've mentioned before, becoming a mum rocks your world and forces a shift of priorities. Almost all the mums I know start to embrace a more eco-aware way of living (even if this is just the odd bit of recycling and the switch from non-organic to organic meat) and together with this comes an awareness of alternative, natural healthcare too. Initially this may take the form of an increased awareness of natural pain relief in labour, herbal massage oils to prevent stretch marks in pregnancy, osteopathy to ease that terrible sciatica pain, homeopathy to help with your newborn's colic or meditation to help with that insomnia caused by the broken nights.

As your family grows you may well find this leads to an interest in all kinds of alternative therapies to treat everything from childhood eczema, bumps and grazes to teenage exam stress. In short, exploring natural ways to keep you and your family in tip-top physical and emotional health becomes a priority.

After dipping my toe into the alternative healthcare pond during pregnancy (where I embraced yoga, massage, alternative forms of pain relief and good old raspberry leaf tea!), I began to turn in this direction once again when confronted with the health issues of my newborn daughter. Unlike her brother (who has the skin type and disposition of his robust, happy-go-lucky father), my little girl was sensitive and reactive to almost everything. Particular washing powders made her itch, she had raging colic and at eight weeks old developed terrible eczema that became infected and made her look like she had some ghastly medieval disease.

Whenever I visited my GP with these symptoms I'd walk away with a pile of prescriptions for lotions and oral medicines that seemed utterly excessive for a baby not yet into her third month (especially when most of these tubes carried 'steroid' in huge letters). After carrying this little babe in my womb for nine months it felt absurd to cover her in all this toxicity, even if it would help her symptoms in the short term. Where was talk of long-term prevention or recommendation of natural remedies without resorting to steroids? Where was a discussion of my diet (and therefore hers via breast-milk) and the environment she existed within?

My solution was to make it my mission to seek out a more natural, holistic approach to her ailments. In short I embraced homeopathy, osteopathy (which uses very gentle manual techniques on the body to help the immune system work more effectively) and nutrition to try and get to the root of her problems. I admit that in the fast six years we've had to resort to antihistamine for her food allergies, the odd cycle of antibiotics for her infected eczema and the occasional dose of steroids for seasonal hay fever that's hindered her breathing (I know, poor kid!) but more often than not the complementary medicine route has worked wonders. This summer, for example, we put all inhalers, medicines and nasal sprays to the back of the cupboard and treated my daughter's eczema, hay fever and seasonal asthma with homeopathy and 'lifestyle changes' which involved removing her bedroom carpet and being strict about the quantity of soft toys and soft furnishings she has in her bedroom in order to reduce the dust. We also keep a pet-free home and reduced the amount of dairy in her diet (though she still gets her recommended daily amount). It's now almost November and (touch wood) we've avoided all conventional drugs for one full pollen cycle, hurrah!

You may not have a child prone to any of the above but you may still find a place for natural healthcare in your family life. Maybe it's just some arnica in your medicine box to aid with the inevitable bruises incurred by your tree-climbing energetic son. Possibly it's some natural massage oil to ease the stresses and strains of everyday family life. Or it could just be some traditional Chinese medicines to help with your PMS migraines. Trust me when I say it's worth a try.

If you're not sure where to start in this new-age world of alternative healthcare, check out my brief summary of therapies and remedies for older children and adults below and maybe it will inspire you to get started.

- Propolis-enriched honey dabbed on cold sores can help to reduce inflammation.
- Arnica cream can help to reduce bruising.
- Witch hazel ointment or tea tree oil – use as an antiseptic.
- Lemon and ginger tea – perfect for a sore throat. (To make, just place a few thumbnail slices of ginger, a large dollop of honey and a generous squeeze of a lemon into a mug of freshly boiled water.)
- Rescue Remedy – great for shock or stress.
- Lavender, eucalyptus and tea tree oils – use together as a steam inhalation to ease sinusitis and catarrh.
- Finely chopped onion mixed with a couple of table-spoons of runny honey and leave for an hour to make a soothing cough syrup – take one teaspoon to treat a non-severe tickly cough.
- Chamomile tea – helps tummy aches.
- A foot massage – provides relief for headaches.
- Sleep-inducing foods (like pasta, dates, bananas and hot milk) – good for battling insomnia.
- Peppermint oil on a handkerchief – for travel sickness.
- A daily intake of Vitamin C and natural yogurt – helps build your immune system so you're less vulnerable to common colds.
- Floradix – it's a great multi-vitamin supplement made with herbs and natural produce that is packed with iron so it's great for iron-deficiency (a great boost just after giving birth too).
- Cotton clothes and lavender oil in your bath water – helps reduce irritation caused by eczema.

- Manuka honey – eat as a part of your regular diet to aid digestive problems or apply to scars and burns to help speed up the wound healing.
- Omega 3 capsules – take daily to boost brain power, improve your skin and boost the immune system.

Please note, these remedies are not suitable for babies under the age of 18 months and professional advice should always be sought when treating any child or when symptoms are not relieved within a few days.

Homeopathy

I'm a big fan of homeopathy and greatly value the basic premise of this philosophy of treating ailments. Before you're given treatment by your homeopath, they will spend a lot of time talking with you and trying to get to the root of your problem. (It can almost feel like therapy at times!) They will then offer you a specific remedy (usually tiny pills or liquid drops) to suit your exact needs. The assumption is that when you take the remedy over a controlled period of time it will help the body to cure itself, leaving your own immune system intact. You may have to let a symptom get worse before it gets better but homeopathy will work at the root of the problem, not just at disguising the immediate symptoms.

Acupuncture

My friend Sophie swears by acupuncture for everything from her own insomnia to her child's seasonal tonsillitis. She also describes a general sense of well-being after a treatment session. Acupuncture uses superfine needles at specific points on the body to encourage the natural healing process. Like homeopathy, it's a method that doesn't mask symptoms but aims to stimulate the body's own immune system in order to fight them. (The fact that acupuncture is now available on the NHS means it's certainly worth a try, don't you think?)

Osteopathy

I've found cranial-osteopathy and osteopathy have helped with everything from my pelvis pain which started when I was six months pregnant to my daughter's colic at six weeks old. Any osteopath will tell you that their work is based on the principle that all ailments are a caused by an imbalance in the body. A soft and subtle hands-on approach is used to correct this imbalance and get the body working in better harmony with all its connected parts.

Massage

Oh, yes please! Massage is great for everything from bonding with your newborn, re-connecting with your partner or simply treating backache, stress or headaches. The added bonus is that you can get it for free at home (if you're partner is nimble with his hands!); otherwise, ask at your local doctor's surgery if they know of any good massage therapists or baby massage instructors.

Traditional Chinese medicine

I taught at a village school in Southern China in my late teens so based on my experiences there I have a great deal of time for the Chinese holistic system of medicine. It's worth looking into this ethos of diet, massage and herbs when considering alternative approaches to healthcare.

Hypnotherapy

I'm rather suspicious of this, but my pal Elaine gave up smoking three years ago after a session of hypnotherapy and can wax lyrical about it at any given opportunity! I've also heard of it being beneficial for older children who still bed-wet or have irrational fears (my neighbour found it worked well at curing her eight-year-old's fear of flying).

There are plenty of other alternative routes you could try (herbalism, natural healing, reflexology, Alexander technique, etc.) but the ones I've mentioned here have received the most acclaim from mums I know. If you fancy giving it a go, turn to my 'Useful Addresses' section and you'll find websites that will help you source a reputable practitioner near you. So, next time you have a soaring headache and reach for the paracetamol or your child gets prescribed with the tenth inhaler of the year, why not explore a more natural approach to your family's health?

Mother knows best

'The Buteyko method of breathing was a life-saver for us. My son had terrible asthma and my husband was a chronically bad sleeper and thanks to a few lessons on breathing correctly à la Buteyko they're having far less trouble with both. I've always been open to new ideas

Clothes with Conscience

If it's hard to find an opportunity to buy yourself a five-pack of knickers then it's even harder to shop with an environmental conscience. Having said that, the recent craze for the eco-friendly, reusable 'I'm not a plastic bag' shopper designed by Anya Hindmarch indicates that people want to feel they're doing their bit for the planet while still looking and feeling stylish. My close mum friends and I have certainly become much more alert to items made in sweatshop conditions or items that cost a fortune and come with a guilty environmental conscience.

I know for most women, owning a one hundred per cent environmentally friendly wardrobe of clothing essentials doesn't seem like a viable, or possibly even very enticing option. Finding that perfect smock top in the high-street scrum is hard enough without having to make sure it's made of organic cotton. I'm not suggesting we all retire to natural-soled sandals or hand-woven-in-Devon hemp dresses, I'm just raising the issue of ethically and ecologically friendly dressing and shopping and discussing whether it's possible as a busy mum to make this achievable in some small way with our shopping needs. As mothers we owe it to our planet and our children's futures to have style with conscience.

When picking clothes for you and the children you could always try to balance your high-street purchases with those from exclusively eco-friendly labels (American Apparel, People Tree, Friendly Cottons, Viridis Luxe, Aravore Babies and Organics for Kids to name but a few). Even if you get your stylish coat from Marc Jacobs and your shoes from Office, you could make your denim selection from Sharkah Chakra, your knitwear from Lutz & Patmos and undies from GreenKnickers (all of which make ethical, ecologically friendly, yet uber-stylish garments). Good old Jennie makes a few investment purchases from Viridis Luxe each year and I've never seen someone get so many comments about garments. She mixes them well with jeans and great accessories and when fellow mums find out her key item not only looks great but is also environmentally sound, and uses eco-friendly cashmere and hemp, they're racing to jot down the details of the label!

Recycling clothes, bags and shoes is also a great way of helping the planet and easing the strain on your wallet. I don't mean unstitching that denim mini to make a pair of dungarees for your toddler (although I bet Jennie has tried this); no, I mean handing down clothes between siblings and friends. Obviously, it's not fair for the youngest child to be constantly kitted out in her elder brother's sports kit, but there are always good unisex pieces that last well and can be passed on (and by this I mean no holes, pasta bolognese stains or broken zips!). Alternatively, you can pass things on to friends and extended family. My son has a whole selection of designer jeans courtesy of his elder cousin Sam; likewise Jennie's daughter Minnie looks great in an array of my daughter's old dresses and patterned tights. If your school doesn't hold second-hand uniform sales then maybe think about starting one or suggesting it at the next PTA meeting.

If you don't fancy giving or receiving second-hand clothes from your nearest and dearest, then how about selling your hardly used items on eBay, at a local car boot sale or, as Jennie would rave about, a local NCT sale? My friend Esme makes a small fortune selling her little girl's old GAP clothes at their local Sunday boot fair, and both mum and daughter have a ball while they're at it. If you've been fortunate enough to kit your child out in Rachel Riley velvet smock coats or Clements Ribeiro designer cashmere then you could always place them on eBay and see what bids you get. If making cash isn't a priority then donating old clothes to charity shops or collections for the Third World are ideal ways of giving something back.

The same ethos applies to your old clothes. We all confess to owning heaps of items that are too big/small or have just become too out of touch with our present lifestyle (it's those three-inch snakeskin stilettos again!). You could easily pass them on to friends, donate them to charity, sell them for a small fee on eBay or at boot sales, or do what my friends and I do and hold a 'swap-shop'. In short, this is when I get together with some close pals at one of our houses, the kids safely tucked up in bed, and we mums swap clothes. Everyone brings a bottle of plonk or some nibbles and piles up their wares. (I advise limiting it to ten garments each or it becomes more jumble sale than intimate shopping experience!) You then work out what you fancy swapping and more often than not everyone goes home with fewer unwanted clothes and a few 'new' items for their wardrobe.

The crux to all of this is to try to be aware of how (and

how much!) you shop, how you look after and how you recycle clothes. There's nothing worse for the environment (and let's face it, the wallet) than the all-consuming yummy mummy who trawls the designer boutiques for endless new styles, wears them once and then goes back for more. By planning your wardrobe well, shopping with awareness about where garments are made and thinking about how much you'll use them, how much you'll need to clean them and what you'll do with them once you've finished, you'll find you can shop with a far clearer conscience.

Mother knows best

'Until I had kids I never monitored how many clothes I bought or how often I washed them. Then suddenly I seemed to be buying one new Babygro after another and the washer/dryer was in constant use. I think being a mum started to make me view the world in a more humble way and I felt in all honesty pretty disgusted at how much I bought and spent. I now ensure that my daughter has only three or four outfits at a time (and for nursery she wears a uniform of sorts in that I dress her in one of two tracksuits) and I try to ensure that these are bought from one of three organic environmental clothing companies. This way I don't buy items unnecessarily and I know that each garment is made with minimum harm to the planet.'

Full-time working mum of one

Fancy Footwork

All this recycling, clothes-mending and water-saving can be an exhausting business. No sooner have you returned from the farmers' market laden with fresh, organic peppers and a loaf of wholemeal, seeded bread, you're expected to water the garden with the morning's bath water and peel the stamps off the day's post in order to reuse the envelopes for your party invites. What on earth am I going to ask of you fabulous mums now? To give away that prized Prada bag and don a recycled wicker basket instead? To write to your local MP, requesting a compost bin asap (not a bad idea, actually!). Or to rid yourself of all your No7 mascara and go au naturel instead? Ha ha!

I promise, my aim is not to make this eco-life too much of a sacrifice for the average modern mum; after all, we all like a little Clarins body oil, some non-organic Pinot Grigio and a beautifully, yet extravagantly boxed, Tesco Finest chocolate cheesecake every now and then! I merely hope to offer insight and solutions that could be easily achieved. Now, please bear all this in mind as I continue . . . OK, I admit that while cloth nappies aren't for all of us, the idea of saving on fuel and petrol when hitting the roads may be a more viable option when trying to 'do our bit'. Just think about it for a second. How many times have you 'just nipped' to the local corner shop for the Sunday papers but opted for the car, instead of a cold walk in your pyjamas? How often do you drive the kids to school on a hot summer's day, the air con on full blast, when, if you're honest, you could have walked the route in less time or even taken the bus for a change? And really and truly have you ever jumped on a flight for that romantic mini-break minus the kids, when you could just as easily have gone to a lovely country hotel in the UK?

You see my point? We're all guilty of it. The kids are ratty, you've been up half the night with a newborn and it's drizzling outside. So what if the school's only a mile down the road? 'Everyone in the car, noooooow!' Or how about this familiar scenario: you're off to a friend's house for supper but instead of walking the mile to their house, you'd rather wear your new stiletto boots and get a cab (or even better, persuade the other half to drive). Cars and 'lazy travel' (as I like to call it) are so much a part of our daily lives that we've forgotten what it would be like to get around by using any other means.

Take my area of North London as an example. Being a proud resident comes with the added bonus of hosting a whole load of private prep schools in some of the double-fronted Victorian residences. Every morning without fail the clock strikes eight o'clock and the mummy mafia descends in their four-by-fours, clogging up the road and all the parking spaces. I have nothing against these mums per se, but seeing as I know many of these mums live but a stone's throw away, surely some of them could a) walk to school or b) (God forbid) catch a bus or c) trade their cross-country tanks for a smaller more fuel-efficient model. (Please stop me if I'm wrong, but not many of these mums can be off to work on a remote farm after drop-off.) I admit I'm guilty of using a car for the school run, but I have the reasonable excuse that our new chosen schools are a good five miles from home and before the kids started there we religiously walked to their old school (all two and a half miles each way) at least three times a week.

Even now the schools are unreachable by foot or public transport, I still vow to share the journey with fellow mums or carers whenever possible. Almost every night this week, for example, my daughter has brought a friend home or has been dropped back by a fellow mum. Of course, we'd all prefer the door-to-door comfort of travelling everywhere in our plush cars (snacks, drinks and CDs obligatory) but this is causing the planet no end of trouble (not to mention traffic congestion, endangering the safety of our children around school entrances and parent road rage!).

If school runs, commutes to work or just trips to the local shops to buy milk and stamps seem impossible by foot, how about buying a bike, getting the kids to scooter or checking out public transport routes? Even if you're just making the pilgrimage to Grandma's once a week via the local buses, or choosing to walk to work once a week, it makes a difference. Not only this, you may well find you have time to think, chat and see the world in a way that was impossible in the car, where the children would tear chunks out of each other's hair in the back seat. I certainly found that by walking to school with the children we chatted and bonded far more than if they'd been blankly staring out of the car window watching the world whizz by. Combine this with the fact that when you walk you're also getting a good morning work-out thrown in and you can start to see how appealing it may be!

Mother knows best

'I felt terrible about the fact we owned two cars in our family and worried about all the unnecessary pollution this was causing. Last summer we decided to do something about it. We sold our four-by-four and clapped-out vintage Mini and bought the hybrid electric Toyota Prius instead. My husband is committed to cycling to work and if he needs the car for business trips then I'll either walk the kids to school or we'll catch a train. It takes rather more forward planning but I feel so much better about our carbon output now.'

Part-time working mum of two

Every Little Helps

I was interviewing one of my gurus at a rather chic coffee shop in central London yesterday. While we tucked into double espressos (her) and rather delicious pink-iced cupcakes (me), I realised at the table next to us was the archetypal 'yummy mummy'. I'm not one for eavesdropping (much!) but she was talking to her perfectly coiffed friend (whose baby slept soundly in the latest designer buggy) so loudly that I couldn't help overhearing most of their conversation. In short, the proclaimed a catalogue of 'divine summer jaunts' (which included three weeks in Barbados and ten days in Capri), her must-have fashion buys for autumn (a Burberry trench, Mulberry bag in black croc and a pair of wedged Manolo Blahniks) and her mission to get two new cars before the end of the month (not forgetting the latest Mini Cooper for her eldest child).

While finding this woman rather excessive and larger than life in the extreme, I also found it somewhat depressing. It seemed she represented so much about consumerism that I'd naively thought we'd begun to shy away from. It occurred to me how easy it is for every single one of us to 'do our bit', and made me even more certain that we should. It's no hardship to advertise to our friends the beautiful cut of a coat bought from an eco-friendly fashion label, the pluses of staying at a country house hotel in the UK (instead of a similar place hundreds of air-miles away in Italy), or some of the wonderful organic smellies we've stumbled upon at our local pharmacy. No matter how chichi or wealthy, budget income or cost-cutting we are, no one should be exempt from trying to do more for the environment.

You may not be even remotely yummy (thank goodness!) but you may still have a million and one reasons why making family life greener seems like a distant reality. I certainly know many mums who can't afford to budget for a fully organic food shop each and every week and others who only just about manage to find the time and money to kit their kids out in Hennes, let alone trawl the Internet for cheap, stylish, environmentally friendly alternatives. I certainly have to remind myself exactly why and for whom I'm doing all this as I lug another pile of washing down to the washing line to dry or insist the kids walk to a friend's house, even though it's raining.

I'd be lying if I said I was as green as my guru for this chapter and eco role model, Tamsin Blanchard (I shouldn't think I'd even make it onto her green radar), and my nose would grow even longer if I said I didn't cheat and take short cuts almost every day. I'm sure like most of you I'm guilty of giving in to that easy, over-packaged ready meal because I've had a long day. I'm also partial to that non-organic bottle of plonk and bar of Galaxy to polish it all off. Yes, I do team my eco-jeans with a GAP roll-neck and co-ordinate my ridiculously expensive Miu Miu bag with some mass-produced Converse trainers. I also leave lights on by accident, give in to my daughter's request for a Little Mermaid made in Taiwan, just to achieve a peaceful life, and book a week in the sun flying return with easyJet because I'm on my knees with exhaustion and the thought of some sun anytime in the next six months will prevent me from reaching for the Prozac!

But before you go on to accuse me of being a hypocrite ('do as I say and not as I do' and all that), give me some credit for my honesty! I would be a rather cunning writer if I told it to you as I'd like it to be and not as it really is. Having said that, I do my absolute best every day to live the greenest life I possibly can (within reason and means) and my occasional easyJet slip-ups or confessions as a white-wine junky merely make me try harder at the parts I can commit to with ease. As I mentioned before, the recycling and water preservation, the washing and drying techniques and the shopping seasonally might not rid the planet of all its sins, but make me feel I am doing my small bit for mankind. They also remind me of the examples I'd like to set for my children about caring for themselves and the planet in which they live. Seeing me tuck into a chocolate HobNob or hail a cab once in a while isn't going to undo this in an instant.

The trick is to remember that every little counts. Even if by necessity you drive everywhere (because let's face it, some people do live in splendid isolation, twenty miles from their closest neighbour) but use your extra garden space to grow your own vegetables, then that really counts and most importantly you're doing what you can. Similarly, if you cannot face substituting your cosmetics with a new organic brand (after all, you've been faithful to L'Oreal for fifteen years!) then don't beat yourself up about it, just pride yourself on recycling just about everything (including the little boxes your cosmetic products come in) *and* cooking a fully organic roast every Sunday.

As a busy mum, the key is just to try your best. Making a concerted effort to be aware of the planet and how we treat it, what chemicals and pesticides we expose ourselves and our environment to, and how we live in harmony with all of this is a brilliant start. Just by reading this chapter you've made a step to becoming more aware of the little things we can do to help. Even if you do just one of the tips on my hit list (or maybe you'll try a few more), it's a great beginning to leading a greener life and must surely be a step in the right direction.

Mother knows best

'I'm far too much of a consumer and fashion fox to turn totally green overnight. However, that doesn't mean I'm not aware of my vices. To counteract my fetish for designer goodies and deli food, I vow (and usually keep) to holidaying in the UK once a year, taking the train to our destination and recycling just about everything from newspapers to discarded kids' clothes. I'm hardly a Green Goddess but I do my bit and that's what counts.'

Full-time working mum of one

Top ten green-living tips

1. Prioritising leading a greener life is essential in today's changing world.
2. Pregnancy is often a good place to start (the term 'earth mother' didn't come from nowhere).
3. Set an example to your kids and make environmental concerns part of every day life (you can even get them to help with things like recycling from very early on).
4. Even if cloth nappies aren't your thing, you could instead consider recycling more, washing on low temperatures and reducing how much packaging you buy.
5. Think about how and what you feed your family and how this impacts on the environment. Buying more locally grown and sold produce is a good start.
6. Even if yours isn't a totally organic kitchen, try and buy organic meat and fresh, local produce as much as you can.
7. Embracing alternative healthcare (finding one of the diverse forms to suit you and your families needs) is a great way of leading a more 'natural' life.
8. Don't ignore fashion and style. Dressing with an environmental conscience is so easy these days (even high-street retailers like GAP and M&S offer organic and recycled ranges these days).
9. Walk, walk, walk (or failing that run a car that has a good fuel efficiency rating, uses LPG or is a hybrid).
10. Remember the motto, 'Every little helps'.

Grace's Guru: Tamsin Blanchard

Tamsin Blanchard is a journalist and author specialising in fashion and design. After training at the internationally acclaimed London fashion and art college, Central Saint Martins, she went on to the dizzying heights of becoming the fashion editor of the *Independent* newspaper. No sooner had she got used to free Jimmy Choo shoes and endless designer launches at one publication, she was then snapped up as style editor of the *Observer*. After six years reporting on every up-and-coming trend imaginable (and making fast and furious notes in the front row of the international fashion shows each season) she moved on to the *Daily Telegraph Magazine* to take on the role of style director.

Tamsin still finds time to be the fashion correspondent for the *V&A Magazine*, a contributing editor to *10 Magazine* (one of the UK's most forward-thinking, innovative fashion publications) and to teach fashion students at the University of Westminster and MA students at her old stomping ground, Central Saint Martins.

In the past few years Tamsin has written a host of acclaimed books, including *The Shoe: Best Foot Forward*, *Love Your Home* and her recent, highly successful and cutting edge eco-fashion book, *Green is the New Black*.

She lives in East London with her partner Mark and their five-year-old daughter. Juggling a full and happy family life with work is a constant preoccupation for her. Somehow she manages.

A mum who wants to know why it's important to consider the environment when raising her family
Any mum (or dad) will quickly become very aware of the importance of the environment. As soon as you hold that innocent, pure little bundle, the idea of exposing it to any kind of nasty chemical or pesticide becomes abhorrent. You want to keep them as pure as the day they are born. You also begin to realise how important it is that we look after the planet, if not for our own generation but for the future generations – your own baby's and even your future grand-children's! What's the point of creating future generations if we continue to pollute and destroy the air they will breathe?

A mum who's looking for easy but worthwhile ways to make a difference
1. Start with nappies. Eight million disposable nappies are thrown away every day and make up fifty per cent of all the rubbish in a one-child household. It may take anything from two to five hundred years to decompose a single nappy. If you don't have time to wash your own, there are companies who will take them away and wash them for you. You can also invest in reusable nappies that come with disposable liners. They seem expensive but will be cheaper in the long run than buying disposables. There are also disposable nappies (and who blames any mother for wanting the easy convenience of a disposable nappy?) that are much more biodegradeable than some brands. Look out

for nappies made from bamboo and for Moltex Öko disposables and Tushies.

2. Treat your baby and children to organic cotton undergarments. Non-organic pesticides used in the production of cotton poison cotton farmers and their families across the world, so buying organic cotton basics whenever possible helps and you will want the garments that go closest to your baby's skin to be as pure as can be. Check out www.greenbaby.co.uk.

A mum who wants to lead a green and natural pregnancy Eat organically, use organic lotions and potions for a bit of pampering so that you feel looked after and relaxed, swim, exercise (gently) and join an antenatal yoga class, a good way of meeting like-minded mums.

A mum who wants to feed her family as organically and ethically as possible

1. When weaning it really is easy to make your own organic carrot, sweet potato, apple and pear purees. Simply boil or steam the fruit and veg, whizz them up with a hand-held blender, and freeze in ice-cube trays to defrost and use as and when you need. Much better, healthier and less wasteful than buying processed versions from the supermarket.

2. Take the baby/toddler for a walk to your local farmers' market instead of the supermarket. You'll get some fresh air, your baby/toddler will love the hubbub, and you will be able to buy locally produced fruit and veg that you can take home and make into lovely nourishing soups – great for the whole family.

3. Avoid sweets from the start. What they don't know, they won't want and you can put off pester power at your local corner shop for as long as possible. Their teeth will thank you for it.
4. Vary their diets so that if there is something they don't like one mealtime, they will hopefully have something they do like the next one. That's the theory anyway!
5. Keep a stash of healthy snacks that you can give as treats – fruit, berries, raisins, cheese fingers, breadsticks, rice cakes, sunflower seeds, etc.

A mum who wants to dress herself and her family with environmentally friendly style Green Baby (www.greenbaby.co.uk) is a great place to start dressing environmentally soundly from the first weeks. Babies are better catered for in this arena than older children and grown-ups, so make the most of it. Tatty Bumpkin (www.tattybumpkin.com) has some fun clothes in bamboo for toddlers and older children too. For party clothes, Equa (www.equaclothing.com) is good for both children and mums. Howies (www.howies.co.uk) is great for casual stuff for Mum and Dad. People Tree (www.peopletree.co.uk) is the place for basics and for accessories and also for a small selection of really great designer pieces. You can also find some good organic cotton ranges on the high street – everywhere from H&M to Oasis. Also, don't forget to look at car boot sales and charity shops, particularly for children's clothes. Babies grow out of clothes so quickly that their clothes are often only worn a couple of times, if at all. And it's always satisfying to hand cast-offs and maternity clothes on to friends who are having babies.

A mum who wants to involve her kids in going green Children who go to nursery and school are pretty well versed in all things green and environmental. They learn about recycling and about not polluting the planet. But it is really key to involve them at home too. Get them to join in recycling. (There is a really useful star chart on CBeebies, www.bbc.co.uk/cbeebies/ecobeebies that you can print out and give stickers as rewards for recycling, turning taps off, etc.) Get your children cycling (it's good exercise too) and try to use other methods of transport apart from the car from time to time. Walk to school. Involve your children in buying your weekly shop – look out for the Fairtrade logo and talk to them about organic food. Plant seeds with them – cress seeds are great for even the most impatient child, and then they can make organic egg and cress sandwiches with their crop too. Children learn by example so it should become second nature to them.

What are the key dos and don'ts for the mum wanting to lead a green life?

Do
- Buy organic wherever possible.
- Make organic living part of the fun of teaching your children about the world they live in.
- Make it fun.

Don't
- Don't preach; it's boring.

- Don't buy things that are processed or over-packaged.
- Don't be wasteful.
- Don't buy things you don't need – that goes for toys and children's clothes too.

> **Tamsin's fabulous mum's green mantra:**
> **'Green is the new black!'**

Have Kids, Will Travel

Will We Ever Leave Home Again?

Once upon a time, in the days before going on holiday entailed packing enough nappies and snacks to fill Wembley Stadium, travelling took one of two moulds. The first was almost like preparing for an impromptu Friday night out; it entailed little more than booking a last-minute flight and a cheeky cheap beach hotel, requesting an extended Bank Holiday weekend from the boss and nipping to Topshop for a selection of itsy bitsy string bikinis. You know the type of break? The one where you get that essential pre-flight bikini wax before the crack-of-dawn flight the next morning and buy SPF and the latest 'three-for-two' chick-lit novels at the airport. You return a week later with various bikini strap marks and a few extra pounds in weight after far too many sweet cocktails, all with dodgy names like 'Sex Bomb' or 'Summer Goddess'.

The second type of break, and one I was rather more partial to, was the well-planned far-flung, once-yearly holiday. The process of picking a destination would occur sometime around Christmas when the weather was getting us down and we were recovering from yet another Christmas party hangover. My live-in lover (now husband) and I would snuggle under the duvet on a Sunday morning with a heap of Lonely Planet guides and plan our summer adventure. Would it be a road trip through Morocco? Or an exploration of the deserts of Rajasthan? How about island-hopping off the shores of Greece? Or living it up with a week of partying and shopping in New York or LA? Oh, those were the days!

Whether your pre-children holidays were more Mykanos than Maldives, or more budget back-packing through Thailand than five-star safari in Kenya, the likelihood is you'll have scrimped and saved all year to make it happen. You'll have savoured every moment of either a) lying on your lounger doing little more than flicking through *Grazia* and *Bridget Jones's Diary*, or b) climbing Kilimanjaro with a bandana around your head. The simple fact is that pretty much all travel choices were within reach. Let's face it, without a teething one-year-old and almost-walking toddler, the world was our oyster.

So where does this leave us busy mums now? Back-packing with the baby in a front-papoose? Lying on a lounger at a Club 18–30 resort, blushing as your toddler has his third tantrum and knocks your pina colada into the pool? Or staying at home where your children have all their toys and friends, can eat their favourite fish fingers and ketchup combo, and where you can grab the occasional half hour to read a chapter of your novel in peace without worrying about jet lag or your pre-schooler drowning in the villa pool? You certainly can't be blamed for feeling that life would be far easier if you didn't actually leave your neighbourhood for the next sixteen years!

Take some of my first holidays with my newborn as an

example of 'how travel would never be the same again': our first break-with-baby was a week's holiday in Ibiza. As a couple we'd been going to the northern part of Ibiza for years (my father has a traditional farmhouse out there). We'd do little more than enjoy the hidden beaches, low-key restaurants and lounge bars, all the time turning a golden brown, me in my boho vintage sundresses. Surely now we had a five-month-old our holiday haven wouldn't be that different? However much I clucked at the cute little sunhats I was now allowed to buy and fantasised about my husband and me drinking cocktails in cool beach bars, while my daughter slept soundly in her buggy, I had a niggling feeling it might be slightly different this year.

True to form, having a babe in tow changed the holiday dramatically. My adorable daughter didn't fancy sleeping soundly while we lounged on Moroccan scatter cushions eating seafood; in fact she wanted to be wide awake half the night and delighted in throwing her rattles at fellow diners (who were less than amused when a saliva-covered teething ring landed in their paella). Not only this but the heat made her crotchety, the sea salt made her eczema itch and after eating a handful of sand and a garden lizard (don't ask me how!) she got the shits. Hardly boho holiday heaven, eh?

Pretty soon afterwards (and with a six-month baby-bump and almost-walking toddler in tow), we decided to venture long haul, to the Caribbean island of Anguilla to be precise. My good friend and fellow travel editor at *Elle*, Sue, had just done a feature on the hotel we'd booked, so not only guaranteed its child-friendliness (she'd taken her own one-year-old when she'd reviewed it), but also managed to cut us an amazing deal with the tour operator. Glossy brochures in hand, a heap of oversized pregnancy bikinis in my luggage and enough board books to last the nine-hour flight, we headed to our luxury paradise island.

Now, I'm sure the flight would have been bearable had it not been six hours delayed. My daughter also decided that it was the perfect opportunity to take her first steps, resulting in my husband and me spending much of the nine-hour flight walking up and down the aisle behind her, hopelessly trying to catch her as she fell against the legs of our fellow passengers. On arrival at the main airport in Antigua some fifteen hours later (and with an interconnecting flight and boat trip still to go), none of us had slept a wink (do remember here that I was six months pregnant, too!). A good five hours on from this we all arrived 'in paradise'. However, we were sadly far too strung out and jaded to really appreciate the iced tea cocktail waiting on a tray, held by a gorgeous-looking waiter. All we could think of was sleep. Granted, the hotel was breathtaking and the beautifully isolated island second to none. Having said that, marble stairs might look great as they swoop down to the pool, but can be a nightmare when a toddler is trying out her first steps. In the same vein, white sandy beaches are perfect for couples, but not ideal with a one-year-old who still has a weird fetish for eating sand. To top it all off, while the time difference incurred by retreating as far as the Caribbean can seem nothing when you can sleep it off on a sunbed, it plays havoc with a child who's only just about got to grips with her UK routine (and whose parents were finally enjoying the occasional full night's sleep).

Admittedly, I have rather overplayed the drama, and don't want to take away the many great memories I have of our first holidays as new parents, but I must admit they were definitely hard work! Sure, witnessing my daughter's smile as she first saw the ocean is a priceless memory, watching the waiters in Ibiza dance with her to jazz at midnight was certainly pretty special and letting her take some of her first steps in between palm trees and exotic flowers are all amazing memories to have. Counter to this though are the other memories of pacing the flight for the eighth hour behind a strung-out toddler, ordering the tenth meal of the day in the hope that my daughter will try something other than banana and sweet potato and having our luggage 'mislaid' for the first three days in Ibiza, leaving us without a nappy or sunhat between us. You can see now how there are occasions when as new, or even pro parents, we ask each other whether it wouldn't be easier just to stay at home.

Mother knows best

'I confess, for the first two years after having my twins we went no further than my mum's home in Devon. The thought of packing all those kids' clothes, toys, sterilisers, Cheerios and favourite comforters just seemed like my idea of hell. Once they reached two, I realised I couldn't hide away in Hendon forever. We discovered some great family-friendly hotels on the Net and refused to pack any more than a few outfits and toys for each child. Although all those other kids around the pool take some getting used to, it's nice to see the sun again!'

Full-time mum of twins

Coping with Rainy Holiday Boredom

Before I go on to encourage you to holiday abroad, I thought it only fair to deal with the prospect of a 'holiday' at home first. For most families I know, a two-week summer break (and possibly the odd weekend here and there) just about sums up their yearly holiday quota. Of course I know families who head to the Maldives at the first whiff of a week off school, and others who spend a month at a time at their Tuscan retreat; however, they really are the exception. The reality for most mums I know is that for two weeks over the school summer holidays they are free to enjoy sun, sangria and the prospect of baring their stretch marks to all. For the remaining time (if they're not chained to a sweaty office) they're climbing the walls trying to entertain three bored kids, while the summer rain beats against the windowpane!

Take this year's summer holiday, which as I write is just a few weeks away. I can tell it's all about to reach a crescendo, because a week doesn't go by at the moment without a summer fair, teddy bear picnic, end-of-year quiz night, sports day or cake sale at the children's school. Just as they are busy every moment of every day for the next few weeks (dashing from the egg and spoon race, to an after-school picnic, to a PTA-run barbecue and bouncy castle extravaganza), they will shortly have zero, nada, zilch to do from morning to night! You see, this year I am ploughing through the book (as well as undertaking various other freelance writing jobs), my husband is knee-deep in over-time as he takes over a new company, and the children, well, they'll just have to keep themselves busy! Although we've booked our annual two-week break in Ibiza at the very end of August (yes, after five years with kids we have perfected the boho family break!), that leaves exactly forty-nine days to kill when the kids won't be at school and more than likely it will rain!

'Heeeeeeeeeeeeeeeelp!' I hear you cry, even if it's just in sympathy for my plight! Looking on the bright side, at least I have a holiday in sight; I know plenty of families who only have three days at Center Parcs in late October to get them through. No one can deny that having a long, possibly wet and certainly challenging summer stretch without the opportunity of boarding an easyJet flight to look forward to can be tricky to say the very least! Tricky, yes. Impossible without inflicting manslaughter or joining AA by the end? I hope not. With my own forty-nine days in mind – Did I already tell you that? Sorry, it's somewhat in my thoughts – I have come up with an essential hit list for conquering holiday boredom at home.

Break the weeks up

I'd say the first essential tip is to break the weeks up. If you look at your calendar and see eight empty weeks staring back at you, you're bound to be tearing your hair out by week two. However, if you look at the holiday week by week making tiny treats or adventures within each seven-day period, you'll have pockets of excitement to look forward to at every turn. I've already started to pencil in the odd activity, excursion or playdate/sleepover for each week and it means that the empty days in between seem far more manageable.

I've reached my maximum overdraft limit this week and I wish I could confess that it was for some much-needed maternity jeans by Citizens of Humanity or a naughty splurge on voluminous tops at Whistles, but in actual fact it's been spent solely on craft material! Oh yes, the joys of the Yellow Moon catalogue! Just this morning the postman delivered a box almost bigger than my front door, stuffed with beads, feathers, clay, fabric pens, blank masks, acrylic sticky letters, make-your-own hand puppet sets and far more stick-on goggle eyes than I've seen in my life. Still to come are an array of seeds from the garden centre, a mini-shovel and pot plant set, and a blow-up goal and football!

The point of all this? Well, for my two, making puppets and then performing *The Wizard of Oz* for me (even while I'm trying to finish interviewing my travel guru), or beading necklaces and then setting up a stall at the end of the front path (to sell to the unsuspecting neighbours for twenty-five pence a pop) is a perfect way to spend an overcast summer's day. It also means that the amount of times the words 'I'm bored' will be uttered is unlikely to rise into double figures, therefore preserving my sanity, for another day at least!

Parks and woodland

All hail the great British outdoors! Whether it's your local park or the miles of woodland at the end of your county lane that does it for you, outdoor space is a life-saver for bored kids and stressed-out mums, and it's free! Once the rain has cleared and the puppet-making has driven you to distraction (come on, we're not screen testing for Blue Peter here!), a good day out at the park can work wonders to lift one's spirits. Pack a picnic, some sun cream, a football and an old bucket and spade and head to your local park for a good session of sandpit/goal-scoring/99-eating fun! (If you're feeling energetic you could even take bikes, a kite if it's windy or a bag of old crusts to feed the ducks.)

Day trips

Researching and organising day-trip options is well worth the effort as it's very effective in killing time over a long school break and provides goalposts to look forward to as the weeks tick by. When we're out and about over the course of the year I try to remember to pick up leaflets advertising activities and places of interest. You could go online and do a UK search by keying in words like 'museums', 'theme parks', 'steam railways' or 'lidos' – you never know what ideas this might inspire. You can also be guaranteed to find a whole array of good day-trip listings in magazines such as *Junior*; just look out for their pre-summer holiday issues. I must confess, I'm not a big fan of going to theme parks in the thick of summer, largely because the queues are horrendous and you seem to be lining up with hordes of other hot Brits, instead of enjoying any real fun. Having said that, if you research all the options you could think slightly outside this box and go to a local castle, city farm or adventure playground, where queuing isn't such an issue.

While overdoing the socialising in term-time is not a good idea, regularly arranging playdates for the summer holidays is a good way to keep your kids happy. Now I don't mean following in the footsteps of some mums I've encountered, who have a different friend to play every single day of the week for the entire break, but having a new dynamic in the house once every so often can really help break up the week. I'm lucky in that my two kids play brilliantly together, so often having a friend for one to play with totally disrupts the balance, but if you can bear to have one friend for each child, it can stave off boredom for one extra day and gives the kids something to look forward to. Also, when the favour is returned you can be lucky enough to have a few hours' peace yourself!

Mini-breaks

Even though I can't spend the whole summer in the Algarve (or better still, in the Caribbean with a kids' club and in-house nanny included in the break-the-bank package), it doesn't mean we can't leave London for the odd night or two. I've made sure this year to plan quite a few 'away' treats, so even if I'm not packing a Pucci bikini, I can still get the weekend bag out of the loft! To give you an idea of what these include, I'll give you my summer mini-break rundown: a night on a barge boat courtesy of my lovely dad, three nights camping in Cornwall with the children and my old buddy Clare (read on to find out how this went . . .), a long weekend staying in Gloucestershire at my close friend Katie's house and, if I can persuade my husband, a trip to some hotel within two-hour driving distance from London, where I can squeeze in a morsel of 'me time' in the spa!

Even if your budget is tight, you could explore doing a house-swap with friends for a night or two a cheap and cheerful seaside B&B, or a few days camping.

Teach the kids an extra skill

Now don't take this too literally and schedule in Kumon maths, Italian lessons and cuisine courses care of Raymond Blanc, all in the space of the Easter break! This is supposed to be a 'holiday' for the kids, after all. Having said that, booking up a summer-long session of weekly swimming or horse riding lessons can be well worth the extra cash. The kids will love learning something new and exciting and it's a good way to break up a long eight-week stint at home.

Summer camps

I must confess, I haven't yet resorted to summer activity camps, but that doesn't mean I never will. I suppose for working parents of slightly older kids the thought of weekly care which includes everything from tennis to archery could sound very enticing! I've listed a whole host of schemes and organisations in the back of the book that you may want to look into if summer camps appeal to you and your little ones. Even if it's only a week, it's a good way for them to mix with other kids and try out things like canoeing, climbing and hours of messy play that are just impossible for you to offer at home.

The only thing I'd advise against is using these camps as a source of childcare. You run the risk of overstimulating the kids when they may just be longing for a lazy day watching TV and playing in the paddling pool at home, and you can also miss out on some wonderful summer fun with them yourself!

Don't go to the other extreme and become a holiday rep!

After offering all these useful tips, I have to add a final word of caution. Just because the school day and the endless timetable of after-school activities has been eliminated from your diary, that doesn't mean you should morph into a Butlins holiday rep! Sure, stock up on craft activities, pinch a few easy recipes from *Junior*, book the odd swimming lesson and invite your daughter's best pal for a sleepover. Be brave and whisk the kids off to Thorpe Park or camping in the Lake District when the weather looks good. But, and this is a big but, don't feel you should fill every day with new and exciting activities and experiences; you'll only be utterly exhausted (and broke) by the end of the first week. I know that my two kids are shattered after a demanding school year and for a lot of the time will be happiest left playing 'shop' or trashing my flowerbeds in their culinary development of mud pies! We all know that too much unscheduled time will end up with your offspring clawing each other's eyes out, but on the other hand, a mass of over-scheduled time will leave them unable to devise their own fun. Trying to strike a manageable balance between organised activities and free time to play is key to surviving the summer hols, for both you and the kids.

Mother knows best

'As a family we decided to go and visit my in-laws in New Zealand at Christmas, so a summer holiday abroad was out this year. The thought of eight weeks without a trip away admittedly seemed daunting at first! In the end I gave each of my kids something to look forward to each week. They could all choose one friend to play, one day trip (taking it in turns each week) and one activity or skill they wanted to learn over the whole summer. My eldest boys chose football lessons once a week and my daughter chose a five-day intensive swimming course. The day trips ranged from Alton Towers to a day on Brighton beach. In between all of this I made it clear that I needed my own 'treats', so in the mix came a few rainy DVD pyjama days, where they got square eyes and I got on with some work, and admittedly I added two trips to the Tate Modern and one to Oxford Street to buy myself some summer shoes!'

Part-time working mum of three

The UK Rocks!

At some point almost every family will find travelling abroad impossible. Whether it be the financial burden, the guilt of all those non-environmentally friendly air-miles totting up or the impending arrival of a new baby, sometimes the thought of boarding easyJet at six a.m. with two toddlers and a six-week-old seems more trouble than it's worth. Take my pal Jennie, who's just one week off delivering her second child. Within the past six months she's given up full-time work and her husband has been busting a gut to make his niche art gallery a success. The impending arrival of number two in the middle of summer, and the ensuing months adjusting to life with a newborn and a jealous toddler, mean a summer jaunt is the last thing on their mind this year. For different reasons my pal Rena has decided to stay put too. Every summer for the past five years she's upped and left with her three children to her sister's house in Spain. This year she's having an extension built on her house, her children are taking music exams and quite simply she wants to stay within the borders of the UK.

I must confess that when I spend a sunny weekend at my father's home in rural Oxfordshire, or my pal Katie's family home in Gloucestershire, I wonder why I ever bother breaking the bank to head abroad at all. It takes minimum planning and involves maximum relaxation. As long as there's a garden, a few animals to play with and some woodland to make a camp in then I barely seem to see them until they're ready for supper. The added beauty of all this? You can take the car or hop on the train, in just a few hours you're there, and there's absolutely no jet lag!

Often, with a newborn in tow or a tight year-on-year budget, the thought of a remote rental cottage in Norfolk or a B&B near the picturesque Cornish coastline seems the perfect solution for everyone (the bank manager included). One way to start planning a one to two-week UK break is to think about where you want to go and what sort of accommodation you're after. If it's a full-on-fun-activity-packed break you fancy, you might veer towards somewhere like Center Parcs. However, if it's something less 'busy' you desire, you may want to start investigating campsites across the UK or even staying in a B&B on a working farm. Having said that, maybe it's a home-from-home you're after, in which case a cottage with fitted kitchen, DVD player and in-house cot could be perfect, or how about a little bit of luxury with a few days at a family hotel, where the children can play happily in the kids' club or the games room while you enjoy a deep tissue massage and a romantic meal with a good bottle of Merlot?

You may even want to do what I'm doing this year and mix and match a little bit of everything. I don't know about you, but the thought of camping for a full two weeks makes me break out in a hot sweat. Equally, the idea of entertaining the children for ten days straight at a beautiful but remote (and, dare I say it, by day four, 'booooooooooooooring') cottage in the Lake District, makes me reach for the luxury European brochures in an instant. The solution I've found that can work well is to book a cross-section of UK experiences over a few months. As I mentioned earlier, our summer plans include a weekend on a longboat floating down the Oxford Canal, a Bank Holiday camping in Cornwall, a four-day stay at a friend's county cottage and two mega-treat nights at a blow-the-budget family hotel in Somerset. All of these adventures pose something exciting to plan for and look forward to and when the total cost is added together they still come in well below the average cost of a fortnight in Tuscany.

Granted, the kids haven't learned to scuba dive, they haven't sampled the daily delights of Turkish cuisine, they haven't come close to getting sunburnt shoulders and I haven't spent one full day on a sunbed reading the latest Zadie Smith novel from beginning to end, but we've experienced all sorts of other fun. Take our three nights camping on the Cornish coastline: because I haven't seen much of my husband these past few months (I think he's actually sleeping in his work suit!), I decided to plan this mini-break with my old buddy, Clare. The beauty of our friendship is that we have an effort-less bond that means even if it's been three months without a phone call, we'll slip straight back into the easy banter of friends who see each other every day. The fact that she hasn't (as yet!) got her own kids also means that as godmum to my two, she is the all-singing, dancing, mask-making, joke-telling entertainment my children need for a successful camping adventure.

It's true that we got drenched on day one, my daughter got eaten alive by mosquitoes on day two and my son's favourite puppet got swept out to sea on day three. However, it's also true that they learned to cook sausages on a camp-fire, climbed trees taller than any inner-London climbing frame, fetched eggs from the chicken hutch every morning for breakfast and sang each other to sleep, while Clare and I sat up late into the night burning marshmallows and remi-niscing over old times. No kids' club here, but still a whole collection of wonderful childhood memories.

My friend Katie had a similarly enchanting experience when she took her six-month-old son, Archie, to his first festival. Admittedly this was no wild, dancing-until-dawn, Glastonbury experience, but nevertheless it was a wonder-fully refreshing UK break. Although she had a checklist of things to remember longer than Archie himself ('defrost pureed butternut squash', 'take buggy raincover out of loft', 'pack breast pump'), she says it was all worth it for the chilled weekend that followed. The sun did come out, she did enjoy a few cold beers while Archie jigged about to the music on her husband's shoulders and they did get almost a full night's sleep in their little two-man tent. Sure, it's not the only adventure they'll have this year, but it certainly broke up the long summer weeks with something more exciting than the weaning process of a delightful six-month-old baby.

I must confess that Katie's festival experience with new babe in tow and my conversion from 'camping over my dead body' to 'pass me the tent pegs' have made me wonder why Ibiza held so much appeal in the first place. Holidays in the UK are cost-effective, more eco-friendly, offer easy-peasy planning and packing for mum, and can be so close to home you could even nip back to feed the cat and check your emails. So why bother surfing the Internet for a Kenyan safari break? Before you chuck your passport in the bin, remember a few crucial facts. The weather in the UK is temperamental to say the least (my friend Sophie vowed never, ever to venture up north again after her week-long stay in Edinburgh was marred by constant rain, sleet and snow – in May!), you miss out on all the cultural and culinary delights of a foreign county, and, let's face it, who doesn't want to put CBeebies and Sainsbury's supermarkets behind them to lie on a sandy beach in eighty-degree sunshine, while the waiter mixes you a cocktail and your kids get braids and beads plaited into their hair? This moves me perfectly on to my section on travelling abroad, because in all honesty, however fun UK hols can be, tell me truthfully if your toes don't curl in delight at the thought of two weeks in the South of France or on a Mediterranean island?

Mother knows best

'I admit it – we haven't been abroad for three years. We have four children and the thought of stumping up the money for six aeroplane tickets and three hotel rooms just doesn't bear thinking about. We've found that the perfect solution is to rent cottages along the British coastline. We've tried Devon, Cornwall and Suffolk so far, all of which have been brilliant. We always go in August, and touch wood, bar the odd overcast day, the weather's been on our side. The kids play on the beach like on any other European holiday, we enjoy plenty of scampi and chips and when the rainclouds threaten we head to local museums, indoor pools or cinemas. Until we can save for that dream ticket to Disneyland, Florida, it suits us just fine.'

Full-time mum of four

Travelling Abroad

I must confess, I start looking forward to holidays abroad at least six months in advance. It's not that I don't have a full and exciting life (OK, so the highlight of this week happens to be the quiz night at my daughter's school), it's just that the thought of the sun on my skin and the sight of my kids flinging themselves into a villa pool comes pretty close to my idea of heaven. Not only do these memories fill me with anticipation and excitement, but in some weird way the prospect of all that planning and packing poses a lot to look forward to. I know only too well that it's no longer just about getting my favourite Pucci sundress cleaned or heading to Topshop to pick up some oversized shades (it's more about making sure the kids have a new DVD to watch on the flight and the newborn has a passport, so we can leave the country in the first place!) but I still enjoy the ritual preparations.

Take this year's holiday to Ibiza as an example. Although we're not departing until late August, I've still got part of my brain working on what to arrange, pack and look forward to. You may think I'm bonkers, but as early as May I'd ordered a couple of dive toys for my kids to use in the pool and a new maternity tankini for myself. We're still only in late June and I've been emailing my girlfriend who'll be out there at the same time to find out what dates we overlap and who'll be booking the large table outside at our favourite restaurant, La Paloma. Occasionally, when I'm pulling on my jeans as I get up in the morning, I'll run my fingers along my boho summer skirts and imagine myself wearing them in my father's Ibiza garden as we eat olives at sunset. Whether you love or loathe the holiday preparations, as summer approaches I think we all feel some tingle of excitement at the thought of breaking up the daily routine of home life.

Whether it's a week at your in-laws' apartment in Spain or three luxurious weeks at a fancy villa in Bali, it's having the opportunity to get away from it all that makes it worthwhile. No commuting to work, no school runs, no strict homework-then-bedtime night-after-night routines, no work deadlines and no UK weather! For us mums especially it's often the perfect break from running the home and being tied to the office-cum-kitchen-sink from morning to night.

In short, it's time to reconnect with your family, away from the stresses and strains of busy life. For someone who loves to plan for my holiday (and endlessly fantasise about it as I write this chapter and the June rain comes down heavy and fast outside), what can I offer you as tips to achieving a successful break abroad?

Destination and travel arrangements

Choosing the right destination and travel plan to suit your family is a key starting point. If you hate flying for long periods and are lost without a supermarket then opting for a trip to the Kenyan outback for your family of five may feel rather more challenging than relaxing. Alternatively, if like me you can't stand big resort hotels (more than six people round a pool makes me feel I'm crowded!) then a Club Med resort in central Spain could have you cutting your holiday short and returning to the tranquillity of home in no time!

Remembering to make your stay age-appropriate to your kids is also crucial to making or breaking a holiday. Long haul might be OK for a sleepy newborn or teenager, but it's not ideal for active toddlers (who get bored sitting still during a drive across town to see Grandma!). Likewise a tranquil hotel in the middle of nowhere might fit the bill for you and your bookworm ten-year-old, but would be a total nightmare for a crawling baby who is getting used to the sound of his own voice, and loudly! You may be used to the searing heat in mid-August, but will it suit your ten-week-old? On the other hand, skiing is great in the long term, but far from ideal for a toddler who's not yet walking unaided. The plus side of having pre-school kids is you can go on holiday out of term-time, making it cheaper and far less busy. Take note of this and maximise the potential!

The main trick to finding a destination, time of year and travel schedule to suit you is to make a mental list of what in your mind constitutes a 'great family holiday'. Obviously this changes from year to year as your kids grow up and new ones arrive. This year, for our unit of two grown-ups (one with bump) and a four and a five-year-old, the list of requirements goes something like this:

- Easy access (or direct flight!)
- Sun
- Villa with pool
- Quiet local beaches (that aren't overrun with sunburnt football supporters)
- Beautiful countryside to explore
- Reliable, trustworthy babysitter (for the odd evening out without the children)
- Cosy, friendly places to eat
- Fab boutiques and local shops
- The independence and freedom to explore the surrounding areas.

Luckily for us the kids play wonderfully together so having hordes of other kids isn't a top priority and, believe it or not, cooking the odd meal for the family while abroad has become more pleasure than chore, so all-inclusive holidays don't rank highly either. The simple fact is a European villa holiday ticks all these boxes and so far has been the perfect family break for us every year. (Having said that, as the kids have got older the 'easy access' has become less of an issue, as long-haul or broken-up travel has become a billion times easier, although this year with my bump in tow the shorter the flight the better as far as I'm concerned!)

Ask my sister-in-law Jo what makes her perfect holiday wish list and it would be completely different. With three kids close in age, who fight when they're at home for more than six seconds together, a kids' club and therefore a range of new 'friends' to play with is essential. Likewise, she cooks for Britain while she's at home, so the last thing she wants is to be making lunch every day in a villa. No, the inclusion of a full no-holds-barred buffet is non-negotiable when booking their holiday hotel. Both villas and hotels are far too close to the home experience for my dear friend Katie who won't settle for anything less than a Moroccan road trip for Archie's first travel experience: *Hideous Kinky* here we come . . . ! Whatever formula works for you make sure you think about it well in advance; this way you can try to please everyone, thereby giving you the least hassle and stress.

Choose your accommodation wisely

Although I have a weakness for villa holidays (I think it's the fact that I can sit beside a private pool while the kids splash around, not worrying for a second if they're too noisy, and I can drink Pimms and eat cheesy crisps without paying fifty pounds for it!), I admit they're not perfect for everyone. Many parents thrive on the fact that entertainment is laid on for the children by a hotel; others find villas too much hard work or too dangerous. (For example, if you're taking children who can't swim you must ensure that the villa pool is gated off. The last thing you want is to be paranoid all holiday that a child might find its way to the pool at midnight and drown.)

Whichever you choose, make sure that the accommodation comes via a reputable agency; better still one that comes with a personal recommendation as well. There's nothing worse than turning up to a building site or a cockroach-infested kitchen, especially when the brochure showed an infinity pool and glossy marble breakfast bar! Similarly, don't play it too safe; just because the hotel looks reliable don't forget to ask yourself if you'll go stir crazy if it's in the middle of nowhere, or worse still, surrounded by English-style bars. It's always worth looking into the local area and finding out what's on offer, before signing up to that all-inclusive safe Brit package.

It also helps to make a checklist of what you regard as essential criteria for the hotel, villa or apartment you'd like to stay in. Do you need interconnecting rooms? Is a ground floor apartment essential (with crawling babies and pushchairs it often is)? Do you require baby equipment (cots, bottle warmers, monitor)? And don't forget your own grown-up needs (evening babysitters, an adults-only restaurant or even a health spa).

Think about extras

Wherever you're off to, don't forget (in your last-minute rush to get immunisations or swimming goggles) that advance preparation is the key to a stress-free holiday. Ask yourself if you'll need a car on arrival (either as a taxi to your accommodation or as a car-hire to give you freedom throughout your stay). Check whether you need to hire baby or kids' car seats separately and what the local government regulations are on what kind of seat is required. What type and how much currency will you need? Ask yourself as well what you'll need immediately on arrival and therefore may want to carry in your hand luggage. (You may have left the UK in mid-winter wearing jeans and a sweater, only to be desperate for your sundress and flip-flops the moment you arrive.) Something else I find worth considering is what we will need for the first twenty-four hours. For example, if you're arriving late at night to a villa you'll need to take a few late-night snacks and something for brekkie to save you hunting for that twenty-four-hour garage after an exhausting trip!

If you're staying in a villa or somewhere far from home, you may want to consider taking a few useful toys, games and books for the kids, even a portable DVD player, which can be ideal for flying and occasional entertainment while you're there. I always choose a couple of new toys that I hide away and bring out when we arrive, to give the kids something exciting to play with over the two-week stay (even if these are small and cheap, it will help keep them occupied, and you always have the option of leaving them behind when you go home).

Read up

Whether it's Florida, France or Fiji you're headed to, it's wise to read up on the area first. It'll get you all in the mood for adventure (include the kids by showing them the brochure or pictures in the guide book) and help you plan excursions and meals out once you get there. Even if it's a pretty remote part of the world, you'll be surprised how many little boat trips, butterfly sanctuaries or beachside shellfish taverns you can read about in travel guides and magazines, online and in the travel sections of the weekend newspapers. If adventure or local culture isn't your thing, the process of 'reading up' may come with the added bonus of forcing you to see beyond the Mark Warner resort and to a few worthwhile finds a few miles away from the manicured gardens of the hotel grounds!

Pack with thought

It's much harder once you have kids just to throw bikinis in your luggage at the last minute and buy the mozzie spray at the airports. (After my friend Florence's son pulled a handful of Clarins products off the duty-free shelves, incurring the cost of £120 without even the joy of a designer face cream, Molly vowed never to shop for anything at the airport again!) For this reason, packing with care and thought is essential. I've gone from being a large bumper suitcase kind of gal (who confesses to taking a different bikini for every day of my honeymoon. Don't ask; it was a tradition among us newlywed *Elle* girls), to someone who takes the minimum for all. When you've got a son who insists that all fifteen pop-up books are essential and a daughter who cannot leave home without an array of floral sundresses (one for each day; where does she get it from I wonder?) you really have no choice but to be ruthless.

This year my kids will take a pair of Crocs each as their only form of footwear (perfect for beach, pool, sight-seeing, flights), a small selection of summer clothes (let's face it, they're in the pool/sea all day, so wear very little other than a cossie and a big smile), swimwear, a sunhat each, a few books, some felt pens, two DVDs each and my secret stash of toys. Likewise, I'll limit myself (it's true) to some Haviana flip-flops for the day, a nice pair of jewelled sandals for the evening, a few bikinis, sundresses and sarongs and a large supply of reading material!

After 'mislaying' my luggage one year in Ibiza for a full three days I also pack a change of clothes and a swimsuit in my hand luggage; believe me it's got to be better than sitting around in hot jeans and Converse trainers for three days, praying my vintage sundresses haven't been lost for life!

If you're taking a young baby it's worth planning this with an extra bit of thought. You may well need to take sterilising equipment, a travel cot (if they don't supply one in your hotel or you're on the move a lot), a light-weight buggy (with sunshade?), a mosquito net, a baby water float and a few pots (non-glass ones for ease of travel) of babyfood to get you through the first day or so. With slightly older kids you may want to remember their favourite teddy or comforter, the specific SPF that doesn't bring them out in a rash, a box of cornflakes to ease them into the local cuisine and some armbands for non-swimmers. I also always pack a small medical kit for emergencies, including plasters, Nurofen, Calpol, mosquito repellent and Piriton.

The joys of flying

Whether it's a two-hour or a ten-hour flight, try to remember the following:

Try to find a flight that leaves at a reasonable hour. Whenever we go to Ibiza we're stuck with two dud choices: six a.m., which means getting up almost before you've gone to bed, or ten p.m., meaning you fly with the late-night clubbers and don't hit the sack in your destination bed until way past midnight. I don't recommend either, so think hard before you opt for that cheaper flight and resort; there's always a reason it's cheaper and it's usually the flight time.

If possible book seats in advance. Maximum leg room and seats all together, please!

Check your passports and tickets. Obvious I know, but have you remembered to check your passport expiry date? (I'd suggest doing this at least six months in advance, leaving plenty of time to deal with the red tape if you need to renew it.) And have you remembered to get a passport for your new bundle of joy? (Even newborns need one now!)

Food. Milk for babies (getting them to suck during take off and landing will help ease the pressure in the ears) and snacks for others (I never get on a plane without a stash of crunchy apples, rice cakes, oat cakes, dried fruit and some lollies for landing, take-off or bribery to 'sit still!').

Socks. For all the family to keep those toes warm in-flight (but please, please don't wear them under sandals before you board!).

Entertainment. Never mind you (the latest issue of *Grazia* should do it anyway); just make sure the kids are happy! A good idea for those aged three-plus is to get them to pack a few toys, a portable DVD player with DVDs, books and colouring pens and activity books in their own little flight back-pack. I always keep a few small extras in my hand luggage for long flights, just in case World War Three breaks out in aisle ten! Staggering these activities is also a good tip. I always insist DVDs are watched during the last few sleepy/most bored hours, therefore saving the best for last!

Change of clothes. If it's sun you're headed to you could pack some light-weight clothes for you and the kids to change into before landing (likewise, if you're going somewhere cold, make sure you have a sweater or fleece in the flight bag). If it's a night flight, you may want to pack pyjamas and a teddy for the kids in the hope it will induce that sleepy feeling! (I've seen some families who board with their kids already in their night clothes.) I find that a pashmina (which can double-up as a blanket) and possibly a travel pillow for long flights are also useful (as are lip balm and face cream for a pre-landing refresher for mum).

Water, water, water. Call me obsessive but I always take excess drinking water on flights (remember, you'll need to buy this once you've been through security). I aim to drink 1.5 litres myself (even on shorter flights) and make sure the kids drink lots too. I admit it's a pain for the person sitting next to me when I'm hopping up and down to the toilet every five minutes (that's why I try to secure an aisle seat) but it's important to keep hydrated (remember, flying is very dehydrating) as this helps with jet lag and flight lethargy.

Last, but not least, patience! Try to remember that it will be boring and tedious and the kids will drive you up the wall with their incessant, 'Are we nearly there yet?' Take a slurp of Rescue Remedy (or an in-flight double vodka) and try to keep your cool!

I know this all seems rather a lot to remember, but in the long run it will help ensure a super-relaxing holiday abroad. You really don't need to pack the kitchen sink; you just need to be organised enough to sort out a few outfits per person that will work whatever the excursion. You certainly don't have to take the contents of M&S but the odd favourite snack or pot of Marmite might work a treat when you arrive hungry at a villa empty of the kids' favourite foods. Similarly, don't feel you have to book the most English-themed hotel you can find; you just need to do a little research and use this break as an excuse to push the boundaries and broaden your horizons (even if it's just learning to ski with your eight-year-old, or tasting locally cooked octopus with your toddler). Whatever your tastes and needs, at the very least I hope this chapter inspires you to surf the Internet for 'family holidays in Morocco' or get onto Thompson Holidays for a last-minute bargain!

Mother knows best

'We love holidaying abroad, but couldn't always stretch to a two-week stay at peak time. We now do a house swap every year with friends of friends who live in

Be Adventurous

It's hard to tell before you have children what kind of family traveller you'll be. Even the most free-spirited, around-the-world adventurer may tell you that once they'd dealt with wet wipes, tantrums and teething en route to Thailand, they vowed only to venture as far as Center Parcs from now on. I am your case in point. Never afraid to trek to the other side of the planet for a little cultural diversity, I have explored many of the world's fascinating corners in my time. Before undertaking a degree in Social Anthropology at Manchester University, I even spent a full year teaching English to children in a remote village in Southern China. No summer after that was complete without a road trip through Morocco, an overland budget exploration of Turkey, Israel and Egypt, or a month-long 'holiday' in some of Rajasthan's most beautiful desert villages. It seemed obvious to me that my newborn would come with us on new and exciting adventures (such as a boating holiday down the rivers of Kerala in India or climbing Mount Sinai at dawn).

It came as a surprise then that as my daughter reached

her seventh month (and we'd successfully braved our well-known Ibiza two months before) we opted for a rural Tuscan villa instead of a shack on a remote beach in Vietnam. As my own experience proves, you just can't gauge beforehand how much a babe will rock your world. No one can prepare you for how rapidly you learn to value every morsel of sleep you get, how the thought of lugging nappies and teething rings across the world seems far more hassle than adventure, and how you long for some lazy, hazy days drinking wine in the shade possibly more than you do the thought of seeing the sunrise over the Nile.

That's not to say my adventuring spirit has gone for good. No, now I'm onto my third, we're considering a few far-flung explorations before the little one can crawl and even the mud bath of the last Glastonbury hasn't put me off the idea of festival fun for the coming years. I suppose it's just the thought of living out of a backpack, going from one grotty youth hostel to another that no longer fills me with joy! Having said that, I haven't dashed out to book a Mark Warner break just yet! It's just made me look at adventure travel in a new light.

I know I'm not alone in my post-kids travel transformation. In fact, when looking around at fellow mums it seems that we fall into one of three categories when travelling *en famille*:

a) The ardent traveller

Thankfully there are a few ardent traveller mums in existence! Take my pal Danni as an example. Dan has never been the queen of western consumption and loves nothing more than heading to an outback village shack of a hotel that's only reachable by plane, train, boat and then foot. Having her first son, Ben, some eight years ago didn't mar her free spirit one bit. Ben in a back-sling, a few washable nappies in her hand luggage and off they went with a handful of return tickets to Thailand. As far as Dan is concerned it's a case of 'have baby, will travel' and, come what may, this has been the case ever since. To be honest, the words 'package holiday' seem about as alien to her as 'easyJet' (I think she presumes the latter is a plastic toy for boys).

I'm sure you all know a few parents like Danni: those we secretly envy for their reluctance to tame their travelling spirit, even with two kids in tow. Maybe it's their fetish for safaris, or their willingness to take their twins out of the reception year to trek around the Himalayas, or possibly even their ability to pack all their necessities into a 'Snow & Rock' medium-sized backpack. Whatever it is, there's something about their lack of fear or conformity which makes booking a villa in Europe seem almost as run of the mill as insisting your kids do their homework before supper-time.

b) The two-week-hotel/villa brigade

So, that would be me then? Me and half of Britain's middle-class families, I should think. Simply told, category Bs enjoy hot-footing it somewhere warm and marginally relaxing the moment the kids break up from school. We try to venture further than Europe every so often, but usually only when the holiday brochure offers kids' clubs, guaranteed sun and a spa for mums. OK, we sometimes stretch the boundaries and book a traditional B&B on a white sandy beach in Kenya or stay in a riad in Morocco (for a little 'cross-cultural experience' for the children) but little is left to chance and we *always* take Marmite for emergencies.

c) The home-from-home posse

This crew of parents wouldn't know where Bali was on the map, let alone what language to speak or currency to get on arrival. Posse C want a cheap and cheerful home-from-home holiday, where flights take no longer than two hours and you can eat steak and chips every night of your stay. The main aim is to get brown, drink and meet some other Brits (preferably so your teenagers can be kept busy around the crowded pool).

We may laugh (and blush slightly too) at how our thirst for travel has been squashed or reshaped by the arrival of children. Where we may once have sought out adventure and enlightenment, we now seek comfort and ease. Where we may have desired a complete change and diversity from normal life we now want normal life but with some sun and without the school run. So how do we go about being a little more adventurous with our travel plans? Obviously we don't hanker for ten weeks spent travelling between backstreet cockroach-infested youth hostels, but there may well be a small part of us that longs for our eyes to be opened a little by new experiences or diverse cultures.

One of the first things to remember is that you don't need to have a massive budget to go beyond the option of a three-star holiday in Malta. Some of my fabulous mum friends have started with the odd British jaunt to break the mould. My pal Florence, for example, is still treating the family to a holiday in Italy this year, but instead of making it two weeks they're going for one and attempting a following week walking in the Peak District armed with tents and a gas stove! My friend Luella has taken a leaf from Florence's book and has booked one week at a four-star hotel in Luxor, Egypt for her family (instead of their four-years-running favourite haunt in Southern Spain) with a three-day sailboat trip down the River Nile (stopping at villages to camp the night) and ending with a camel trek around the pyramids to round it all off. Both these alternatives cost less than their usual two-week standard holidays and come with the added bonus of camel rides and camping under a million stars (as opposed to just karaoke and Diet Coke on the hotel patio!).

Obviously if you fancy it and your budget allows for it you could go further afield than the Peak District or Egypt in your pursuit for change. My friend Nancy regularly packs herself and her kids off to a small family-run hotel in Goa (and we're not talking five-star beach front eyesore here) and my pal Esme thinks nothing of travelling around the South American outback with her daughter in a back-sling (sometimes for the whole summer). So Nancy and Esme seemed the perfect mums to help me brainstorm tips for surviving holidays that are off the beaten track. I hope the following helps you to feel more confident to stretch your family's wings:

- Plan your trip at a time of year when your chosen location is not too hot and not in the midst of a rainy season.
- It may be a good idea to get the kids to experiment

with the sort of local food they'll be eating beforehand, so they have a taste of things to come.

- Get a good guide book and plan your route and accommodation carefully beforehand. It's a good idea to have a few pre-booked pit stops where you can relax and the kids can swim and play freely for a few days.
- Encourage older kids to read up on the places you're visiting too (you could even devise a few projects like collecting shells, counting the number of wild birds and naming the exotic plants). The learning experience of the holiday should include everyone and it can start months before you leave.
- Check with your doctor about immunisations, the risks of Malaria and medication the family might need.
- Pack the absolute minimum. Clothes can be hand-washed or bought out there, so just take a few items each.
- Take a medical kit and in particular some Dioralyte, just in case of dehydration.
- Invest in some decent walking shoes for the whole family.

I certainly feel as my two eldest children grow up it may be time to stretch their imaginations a little on holiday. You only have to see the expressions of delight and awe on their faces when you show them a picture of the souks in Marrakech or the underwater wildlife of the Red Sea to get an inkling of how enriching a change of scene would be. If you can bear to go beyond the routine and safety of a farmhouse in Southern France or a caravan trip to Dorset, it is certain to be memorable at the very least!

Mother knows best

'We made a conscious decision not to upgrade our three-bedroom house but use our excess income to travel as much as possible. When you work as hard as we do, good adventure family holidays are what keep you going. We've been canoeing in Borneo, around Africa on safari, snorkelling in Mauritius, cheese-tasting in Southern France, yachting around the Greek islands and to meet Mickey and Minnie in Florida. The kids have such a broad sense of diverse cultures that it's worth every penny and sleepless night flight!'

Full-time working mum of two

Making 'Me Time' Overseas

I was having a conversation with an old friend recently about travelling with children. She told me that after a rather disastrous first-ever holiday with their newborn they'd written a list of 'golden rules' which they've followed for every subsequent family break since. Among these 'golden rules' was one that really stuck out for me: 'Never, ever expect any time to yourself on a family holiday.'

Now, I confess we all feel like this at times, and although I agree that holidays will never be the same again, surely the aim of every fabulous mum should be to carve out a morsel of 'me time', whether you're whiling away the Easter break in a two-bedroom flat in Kilburn or a luxury resort in the Bahamas?

The thing is, for many of us, having kids came after such a long period of being able to enjoy sunny, chilled-out, self-indulgent holidays that the moment you have to entertain a one-year-old around the pool you feel all 'me time' is lost for evermore. At the risk of sounding like a smug, know-it-all mum, I have a confession to make to my fellow 'golden rules' mums: I'm not denying that family holidays are bloody hard work, but what I will say is that I *have* experienced (gasp!) the odd moment of time to myself here and there.

I'm sure many of you with three kids under five (or even just the one who's close to turning two) are wondering how the hell this is possible. Do I rely on a fully staffed kids' club from morning until night? Do I take a nanny on every family mini-break I book? Or do I just plonk the kids in the hotel pool, set up a sunbed, order a glass of Pimms and hope for the best? The answer is actually none of the above but really stems from obeying one golden holiday rule of my own: Ensure that you have a balance of quality family time *with* the odd injection of 'me time'.

In my experience the best way to achieve this is to follow at least three of these six steps:

Share it out

My husband and I have a holiday rule of sharing out the childcare, which easily allows us both a little 'me time'. The hour-on hour-off method we adopt means that for an hour each, perhaps in the morning each day, one of you is 'on duty' with the kids, say at the pool or playing on the beach, while the other has time to relax (or have a lie-in!). This way we both find we're refreshed and full of fun when it's our turn 'on duty'. You could even try treating yourself to being 'off duty' for longer, say a whole morning then swapping over for the afternoon one day of the holiday.

Choose a hotel with a kids' club

Before you accuse me of contradicting myself let me confess first to the fact that both of my children *hate* kids' clubs. (I tried to leave my son at one in Mauritius last year and the staff called to tell me he was in tears and refused to 'ever, ever, ever come out from beneath the table'.) The fact that we usually stay in villas means the option is rarely there for us even if they did bound in without a backward glance. But for a whole heap of my mums I know finding a hotel with a kids' club is the perfect way to give their kids some structured fun with other children of a similar age, while they snooze in the shade/play tennis with a pal/finish a novel on the beach.

Keep boredom at bay

Even though we've never experienced the joys of regular time 'off' while the children make shell necklaces in a kids' club, by keeping boredom at bay you can be sure of at least an hour a day to chill (I'm talking post-toddler age here, of course). Whenever we go away we take a few games, books, bead kits or DVDs for the children so once they're exhausted by all the water play and late nights, they can play quietly with these inside or in the shade. We have a ritual in Ibiza of letting the children make a 'no grown-ups allowed' chill camp in the villa or garden. While they play in the camp before lunch I can enjoy a pre-lunch glass of rosé and finish reading an article on summer trends before laying out the food!

Nap times

If you have younger children who still nap in the day this can pose the perfect opportunity for a little time to yourself. When my daughter was seven months old and we holidayed at a friend's farmhouse in Tuscany, I vividly remember lazing by the pool, reading in the shade or doing a few laps in the water while she napped between midday and two o'clock. We were always close enough to hear her wake up, but had the freedom to be outside should we want to. Now the children are older we still encourage a family siesta after lunch, and even if the kids don't sleep I'll put on a short story CD or DVD so we can wind down before the afternoon.

Evenings 'off'

Even if you do seem to be running around after the children and wiping ice cream from sticky fingers from the moment you wake up, aiming for the occasional grown-up night should be within reach. Many of you will take your children from one tapas restaurant to another at night, but anyone who has kept their toddler up until eleven o'clock while they enjoy one last glass of vino will know that this can be pretty stressful for all. Sadly, we've all learned from the abduction of Madeleine McCann that leaving kids alone in a hotel room or villa (even very close by) is a risky business, so the only other option is to employ a babysitter, choose a hotel with baby monitoring services or tuck the kids up in bed and eat in on the terrace/balcony or by the villa pool.

When we go away we alternate evenings with the children. For one or two nights they'll stay up late and come and sample squid at the harbour restaurants with us. We'll then have a night where they go to bed before eight o'clock and we'll employ a trustworthy local babysitter (with recommendation and checked references from the hotel or villa owner) while we venture to somewhere more grown-up. If you are going to book a babysitter, try to get the same girl for each night that you'll need a carer, meet her first and introduce her to the kids. You may find that if you return year-on-year she could become a regular face for them. Failing this, we put the children to bed and cook one another a yummy meal to eat by candlelight in the garden, or order room service and eat it on the balcony overlooking the sea.

Friends and relatives

Our Ibiza breaks come with the added bonus of my father, who lives for part of the year in a remote Ibizan *finca*. Not only do I get to see far more of him than I do in the UK, but he has the wonderful ability of spotting (day four of the holiday, when we're tired and frazzled) when we need some grown-up time. He'll whisk the kids off to meet the local farmer while we snooze by the pool, or offer to look after them for the night while we eat paella beside the ocean. Even if you don't have a relative overseas, you may choose to holiday every so often with your extended family or a group of friends, which comes with the added bonus of occasional ready-made childcare services! My friend Jennie, for example, goes to Spain with her in-laws every few years and although most nights they'll all eat out together, they do offer to take Minnie out with them while Jennie and her husband explore somewhere as a couple for the evening.

I'm by no means saying dump your children with the kids' club carers/in-laws/Spanish babysitter at every opportunity, but what I am suggesting is working out tiny pockets of time in which you can enjoy some peaceful holiday time alone or with your partner. This doesn't mean you should neglect the possibility of a boat trip with your children, sharing the culinary delights of a late-night seafood jaunt with your five-year-old or even a mountain walk as a family; it just means that throughout your holiday you should attempt to carve out time for yourself as well. A holiday should mean time for all these things and if you bear in mind my suggestions you may just get to read a novel from beginning to end, after all!

Mother knows best

'I sometimes found holidays harder work than staying at home. The endless sun cream application, squabbling over beach toys and over-tired kids at the end of a day at the beach proved exhausting for us all. Last year I vowed to myself that the following year would be different. We've just returned from Sardinia and, true to

> my word, I managed to get up most mornings before breakfast and go for a run along the beach. Even if the kids were all in my bed eating dry Coco Pops when I returned, it was so refreshing to start the day with some time to myself. Certainly the perfect way to clear my head.'
>
> Full-time working mum of two

Sneaky Retreats Minus the Under-fives

I admit to knowing quite a few couples who regularly head for romantic mini-breaks minus their under-fives. One couple springs to mind whose tans are yet to fade from ten days in the Maldives at a kids-free beach paradise. How did they manage it? The open arms of their dream parents, who offered not only to move in for ten days, but to do the school run, food shop and nightly homework sessions as well! Another couple who live not too far from here are in transit from New York as I write, mixing business and pleasure while their twins are cared for by the live-in nanny. However, not many of us have parents who can turn up at the drop of a hat to play 'mum and dad' to their grandchildren, or a nanny who will move in for a week for the fee of a small vintage car!

Having said that, I really think if at all possible every parent, whether that be Mum and Dad alone or as a couple together, should attempt at least one sneaky retreat minus the kids before their 'little ones' leave for university! I will own up to my own grown-up mini-breaks before I go on. My daughter is six this year and in total, between my husband

and me, we've had five 'grown-up breaks'. The list reads
something like this:

1. Two nights at a boutique hotel in Bath (our babysitter
   held the fort).
2. One night at a friend's wedding in Somerset (my mother
   and stepfather babysat).
3. Four nights in Morocco (bliss, heaven, sheer ecstasy, all
   courtesy of my super-fab babysitter, again!).
4. Two nights at a friend's hen weekend (again, sheer
   wonderment, courtesy of my obliging husband).
5. A week cycling through the Grand Canyon for charity
   (this was my husband's sheer wonderment experience
   thanks to his super-obliging wife, aka me!).

In comparison to your own list this might seem positively
like flexi-parenting, but if you think about the two thousand, one hundred nights I've been a mum, nine nights 'off'
seems pretty humble!

The point I'm trying to make is that if at all possible we
parents should try to facilitate bursts of time away from home,
minus the kids. I'm not suggesting flying to Paris for a mini-
break every few weeks, merely recommending you attempt
to plan and actually carry through the odd night (or few
nights) every year or so, leaving the children in the care of
someone near and dear to you. For many of you this may
mean a fellow parent, a relative or great friend, or even a
paid carer who is happy and responsible enough to undertake overnight care. I know for my friend Lyn, her first
weekend away with her husband minus Riley was made
possible by a camp bed at her mum's home, and for my

sister-in-law Sue, a long weekend in Sardinia materialised by an offer of childcare courtesy of her sister, Jo. Even if you don't have family nearby, you may have a firm friendship with a fellow mum who could exchange a cheeky romantic break for you and your partner in Brighton (while she has your kids to stay) with a walking weekend in Spain (while you have hers).

It goes without saying that the benefits of a short break without your children are immense. I certainly found that the four nights we spent in Morocco last year strengthened my relationship with my husband and made us feel like a honeymoon couple all over again. Not only this, it was utterly relaxing in every way and wonderfully restorative to spend a full three days resting, eating, reading and sight-seeing, without always putting the children first. I know some parents find the thought of leaving their children, even for a night, impossibly heartbreaking and others have no network to rely on, making a break virtually impossible, but this doesn't mean you should give up on the idea. Even if you can't go away as a couple, you could attempt to do it alone. Take my examples in the above list. As well as three romantic mini-breaks, my husband and I have both managed time away on our own. My husband spent months organ-ising a charity bike ride in the States with some male friends (which included a good knees-up in Las Vegas after all the hard work!) and I enjoyed two nights drinking cocktails with twenty girls at a country house in Gloucestershire just before one of my best friends, Ros, got married. For many mums this may be the only way of making a night away once in a blue moon viable. Take my neighbour Mel: she has no family nearby and after having two kids in quick succession was desperate for some time away. After sharing her desire with some other local mums they all plotted and planned for a 'stressed-out mums' night away' the following month. After sweet-talking their other halves, they booked a small county hotel with a spa for a night of manicures, martinis and man-talk! I'm sure the men coped fine without them, but I'm even surer they'll be booking in a golfing weekend or night of pub-crawling in Glasgow very soon! The brilliant thing is, it allows you to put yourself first, indulge your 'old self' and enjoy some time alone, with good friends, talking over old times, sleeping until midday and, above all, missing those kids like mad. (It's amazing how much you'll look forward to seeing them again, even after only one night!)

Whether it's a night at a friend's house out of town or three nights abroad with your partner, in my mind it's worth attempting it once a year. However much we adore our kids, love the time we spend with them and revel in our role as 'mum', it isn't a crime to admit to wanting a 'holiday' away from them every now and then. As long as you are confident of the care while you're away, leave a good set of emergency numbers, write down details of food, bedtime routines, etc. and talk with your children about where you're going and when you'll be back, there's no reason it shouldn't go smoothly. Sure, there may be more than one occasion you have to cancel because your youngest gets chicken pox or your husband is called away on a last-moment business trip (and he was supposed to be babysitting!), but don't give up hope . . . Sneaky treats take a lot of planning, but boy are they worth it!

Mother knows best

'My best friend was always going away, leaving her kids with her mum or brother, but I just didn't think my nerves would take it. I missed them on a night out for my birthday so I'd never manage a weekend away! Last summer my husband and I went through a rough patch and we never seemed to find the time to sit down and talk things through, let alone eat a meal in peace then go to bed for some intimacy! My neighbour and great friend kept offering to look after the children and after six months of putting her off, I decided to take up the offer. I booked just one night on the coast and surprised my husband with it. It was very cheap and cheerful but it was a wonderful tonic for our relationship. I'd recommend it to everyone!'

Full-time mum of two

Top ten travel tips

1. Admittedly travelling with kids is a totally different experience to travelling solo. However, don't be put off, you will leave home again and it will be a (mostly) enjoyable experience!

2. Having a vast stash of games, crafts, playdates and day-trip options at hand (and an even bigger stash of imagination and enthusiasm) will help you survive holidays at home.

3. Booking a few cheap, cheerful mini-breaks can be a great way to manage those long summer holidays (and give you all some variety to look forward to).

4. Don't overlook the UK when booking your hols. It can be a cheap, easy alternative to going abroad, plus it's a brilliant way of being more eco-friendly by cutting back on those air-miles.

5. When booking a holiday abroad think about the age and interests of your kids.

6. Choose your accommodation wisely, wherever in the world you're heading.

7. Try not to leave planning and packing until the last minute. A little extra thought well in advance of a trip can save a lot of stress and hassle later on (especially when it comes to that long-haul flight).

8. Having kids doesn't mean you have to say goodbye to adventure travel for good. Variety, diversity and a little adventure can be a wonderful tonic for the whole family.

9. Don't forget to make time for yourself when you're on holiday (even if it's just that early morning swim in the sea while the kids eat a pain au chocolat with Dad).

10. If at all possible aim to have the occasional sneaky break with your partner or a group of good friends – no kids permitted!

Grace's Guru: Amanda Morison

Amanda Morison got the travel bug when she moved from Dartmoor to Swaziland as a child. As the travel editor of *Red* magazine, she gets to check out some gorgeous hotels around the world. She takes her sons, aged two and a half and one, as often as she can. Both boys have already visited seven countries, and adore airports and planes. Their current favourite destination is Morocco where they waved their arms energetically at horses, donkeys and shopkeepers in candle-lit souks. Amanda believes that having a family opens up, rather than limits, travel possibilities because children provide a fantastic way of meeting people and crossing language barriers. However, she does apologise if you end up sitting next to her and the boys on a plane.

What are your main travel tips for the following mums?

A mum who wants to travel abroad with a newborn
In my experience, newborns are fairly easy to travel with – it's the terrible toddlers who cause the problems! If you're breastfeeding, keep the teeny one happy by plugging him or her on every time they start getting fractious; this worked brilliantly for me on a twelve-hour flight with a six-month-old. If you're not breastfeeding, take more cartons of ready-made formula than you think you'll need. In the weeks before you go, encourage your newborn to drink the formula at room temperature if possible – it makes life so much easier if you're not constantly having to wait for milk to warm up or cool down.

Always have a papoose or sling to hand (you can cart children aged up to four years with the range at www. littlepossums.co.uk) because it makes life much easier on the plane, and on arrival. If your baby is small enough, you can lull them to sleep easily in a papoose, and older ones will love being walked around. Then, when you land, you'll have your hands free to grab your luggage – or any older children you've got running amok.

Other essentials to take for a newborn are squashable toys that rattle, squeak or have sparkly bits, and the ones that clip on are especially good at helping save parents' sanity. Muslins and wipes are two things you also can't take enough of.

Air pressure in planes is much better than it used to be, but it can still affect baby's ears. Take a dummy so they've something to suck when you take off and land. Sucking helps regulate the pressure in their ears and minimise the pain. Some airlines now let you take your car seat on board, which is fantastic because it gives the newborn a safe and familiar environment. It does also help to take your own car seat if you're hiring a car from a lesser-known rental company so that you can be sure you have a reliable, safe car seat for your newborn.

A mum who wants to travel abroad with a family of two-plus children For safety reasons, the rule on all airlines is that one adult must accompany one child under the age of two. For anyone travelling with children, no matter how many, safety is the primary consideration. A sling or papoose for the baby is essential, and consider lead reins or an arm harness for a toddler. Make sure they're used to being restrained in this way before you try it out though – tantrum meltdown in the airport isn't fun. Take a light-weight buggy and buggy board, and invest in a carry cover for it. I've lost two buggies to baggage handlers, so trust me, it's worth spending the extra money.

To keep the teenie entertained, here are a few ideas: Older

children love being given a bag pre-flight to pack with all their favourite things (you might want to check this doesn't include too many things like marbles; it's not worth the stress of them all rolling under the seat). Fuzzy Felt is always a winner, as are books; the babies like the pictures and the older ones the stories. Once children are aged two-plus, wrapped presents work well. Get a selection of cheap, travel-friendly goods (colouring book, Mr Men story, hair clips for girls), wrap them up and distribute as treats throughout the journey.

Snacks are essential. Take plenty of boxes of raisins, Tupperware pots filled with Cheerios and plastic bags filled with apple quarters and carrot sticks. (So the children don't turn hyperactive once airborne, avoid anything with a high sugar content.)

A mum looking for interesting ideas for a summer holiday in the UK Camping is suddenly chic, but it's a far cry from the mildew-infested tents I remember from my youth. Feather Down Farms (www.featherdownfarm.co.uk), the new tented cottage concept from the entrepreneur behind Center Parcs, are fantastic. I've done two, with my children (from six months) and friends' and family's children aged up to twelve. All loved it. You stay on working farms, and get involved with the animals if you want. Tented cottages (no electricity, but running cold water and flushing loos, plus proper beds) are dotted around a field with a chicken pen in the middle. Staying in a yurt is also totally trendy; some of the best include www.adventurecornwall.co.uk and www.yurt-holidays.co.uk.

Self-catering tends to win for me over hotels most times.

Use a reputable company (Rural Retreats, Classic Cottages, English Country Cottages) and put their knowledge to the test by giving them a call – don't just leave it to chance by going online because you might miss a real family-friendly gem. Ask questions like how many child-friendly adventures are available nearby, from swimming pools to petting zoos, how safe the garden is, and whether there are any specifically child-friendly things included in the house (this could be anything from a box of toys to the friendly owner taking teenies for a trip round the grounds in a tractor).

The Luxury Family Hotel group (www.luxuryfamily hotels.co.uk) is where to go for some relaxing. This group of hotels, across the UK, all provide fantastic childcare and seriously grown-up time for parents. Crèches are all Ofsted-approved, and there are adult-only dinner sessions, as well as child-focused teas, made using organic ingredients.

A mum looking to take her family on an adventurous holiday There's no reason you can't carry on being adventurous, but as you'd never forgive yourself if something awful happened, it's worth planning ahead. Check out all the relevant jabs you'll need and information on EHIC (European Health Insurance cards) at www.dh.gov.uk/travellers. Keep children hydrated (always pack water-purifying tablets), covered with sunblock (Liz Earle does a good chemical-free one) and smothered with anti-insect spray (Alfresco's non-chemical one is great – (www.alfresco.uk.com). It's worth bearing in mind that most companies specialising in family adventures don't really cater for babies. Take a look at www.exodus.co.uk, www.explore.co.uk, www.adventure

company.co.uk, www.familydiving.co.uk and www.esprit-holidays.co.uk. You can also check out the options following the links at www.responsibletravel.com. Alternatively, check into a family-friendly resort that offers all kinds of activities (www.neilson.co.uk, www.clubmed.com and www.powderbyrne.com), leave teenies in the crèche then climb every mountain, waterski every wave and ski every piste with the older children.

A mum looking for essential tips for long-haul travel
Standard travel wisdom is to reset your clock on the plane to your final destination. This isn't always practical with children, and my advice is, if they want to sleep, let them get on with it. Children tend to settle into a new time zone much quicker than adults anyway. Children aged six or older will probably enjoy the flight, as long as you let them fiddle with the seat-back TV and you have a few treats stowed to dish out to keep them going. Most parents I know take portable DVDs for long journeys, preloaded with as many films as they have memory for.

With younger children, try and wear them out before they get on the plane. This is when not to take advantage of early boarding because you've got children. Use those last minutes for an energetic game of chase. If you're going on a really long flight, say the UK to Sydney, think about building in a stop-over. Even one night will give you a break, and two twelve-hour flights is somehow a lot less daunting than one twenty-four-hour one.

A mum looking for a romantic mini-break, minus the kids There's not much to say about this, apart from

'Enjoy!' My favourite source of breaks for two is Mr & Mrs Smith (www.mrandmrssmith.com), a collection of hotels around the world that are perfect for romance. Even just a weekend a year away from the children will give you space to be yourselves, instead of just parents (and try to talk about something other than the children). It goes without saying that if you're happy with whoever is looking after the children, you'll be happy while away, so try and draft in your parents or siblings – a break away isn't going to be relaxing if you think the children aren't being well looked after.

What are the key dos and don'ts for the mum seeking the ultimate stress-free holiday?

Do

- Keep a printout of what you're expecting to find at your destination. If your pre-booked interconnecting rooms, a cot or ground-floor accommodation don't materialise, you'll have some comeback.
- Get your hair cut/highlighted, your legs waxed and your toenails sorted before you go. Finding the time might seem impossible, but if you even manage just one of them you'll feel more relaxed and in holiday mode.
- Take pac-a-mac raincoats and at least one warm garment per child. If the weather disappoints, at least you'll still be able to get out and about.
- Charge your digital camera batteries before you go!
- Allow plenty of time. Arriving at the gate with seconds to spare doesn't work with children in tow.

Don't

- Don't get too strung up on packing lists. Wet wipes, snacks, nappies and milk (if relevant) are all you really need to travel with; anything else crucial you can buy when you arrive.

- Don't think everyone on the plane is looking at you and thinking, 'what brats'. Planes are noisy places, and most people have their headphones plugged in anyway. If anyone is silly enough to have a problem, remind yourself that you're in a public space and not their private jet.

- Don't wear uncomfortable clothes, but make sure you're dressed fabulously (cotton trousers, secret support vest, linen shirt, gorgeous sandals). If mum looks great and feels comfortable, the rest of the family will feel happy too.

- Don't expect too much from your children – try and let them enjoy the holiday in their own way.

> **Amanda's fabulous mum's travel mantra:**
> **'Look at the world through your children's eyes**
> **– it's the best holiday you'll ever have.'**

The Fashion-savvy Mum

Pregnancy Dressing, Round Two

I feel in the perfect position to offer advice on this right now, as I write this chapter while three months pregnant. My swollen belly, humongous bust and puffy ankles are all part and parcel of any pregnancy and we mums often find we need a little more imagination to dress than normal! So, being on pregnancy number three, I come to this chapter with a wealth of experience and an even bigger bank of empathy.

For my first pregnancy I conceived as a stick-thin twenty-something fashion journalist, who spent a vast proportion of my life in twenty-six-inch jeans and skinny-ribbed white vests. By the time I twigged that my pot-belly was not in fact an over indulgence of Granola bars on a recent work trip to New York, but a little baby-bean growing in my womb, I was already racing towards the end of the first trimester. The next six and a half months were a blur of sampling every Häagen-Dazs flavour in the range and eating rich, creamy moussaka each night until I gave birth. The result was a healthy, happy, bonny daughter and an array of photos in which I appear to wear the same maternity trousers, have six chins, and two and a half stone of extra weight bulking up my once bean-pole frame.

My second pregnancy was a totally different story. Only eighteen months on from my last encounter with stretchy maternity tops I found (to my surprise) that this time I didn't even need them. My bump was as cute as a Teletubby hill and didn't even show itself until well into the fifth month (my nickname at work was actually 'Mrs No-bump', such was the anticipated arrival of some sort of bulge). I still devoured delicious food but this time it wasn't cream cakes and pecan-toffee ice cream I fancied so much as fresh wok-seared greens and avocados.

Whatever the reason for my small, but perfectly formed bump, it didn't matter; my son's birth weight was pretty much the same as my daughter's. I, however, was confronted with a whole catalogue of different fashion dilemmas from the first time round. With the second pregnancy I wanted floaty tops to go over my old, slightly bigger and baggier jeans; the first time I wanted any reasonably stylish bottoms I could slip over my ever-expanding thighs and tops that covered the incredible wobble of my upper arms.

So what does pregnancy number three hold in store? All I can tell you is this: the moment the thin blue line appeared on my pregnancy test, the top button popped open on my jeans. I'm lucky to find any bottom-halves I can squeeze into, and forget my bras, they fit like nipple-warmers they are now so small! All this and I'm only three months in. Heeeeeeeeeelp! In terms of comparing the three pregnancies, I'd say the way my body is exploding in every direction feels almost identical to my first pregnancy (and my craving for moussaka certainly still stands), so only time will tell if this is the way I carry girls . . . (Since writing this I have given birth to a beautiful, bonny nine-pound boy so my theory about pregnancy shape and a baby's gender is obviously way off the mark!)

The point of all this intimate size talk is simply to illustrate how diverse pregnant bodies can be (even for the same woman during different pregnancies). With these changes in body shape and baby-bump size come a huge array of style challenges that can start any time from day one, and go all the way through to the day you give birth and beyond. Embracing these changes is part of enveloping yourself in motherhood, but that doesn't mean they don't come with their own hiccups and traumas. Just because our bodies are expanding beyond our control it doesn't mean we want to give up on our innate sense of style, or freedom to express ourselves through our clothes, now, does it?

The style challenges for women going through their subsequent pregnancies can seem even greater than the first time around. Although you may well have sussed what basics will carry you through and what little tricks help you to feel lovely (even on days when you can't see your toes), this time around you don't have the same luxury of time that you most likely had with your first pregnancy. Take the time my friend Gayle fell pregnant with her twins. She is a self-employed fashion stylist, so not only did she have pockets of time each week to devote to herself, but she also has the professional know-how for how to look fabulous in whatever she throws together. I remember bumping into her in a local high-street store, her in week sixteen of her pregnancy, me flushed and hot, lugging a double buggy up the stairs. While I rushed through, chucking any long vests I could spot into a basket hanging from my double Maclaren (this being my three-minute window to shop), Gayle leisurely browsed through the rails, holding up to her bump floral empire-line sundresses and attempting to customise with a scarf here, a pair of over-sized shades there or a pretty vintage-look shrug. While she had hours to complete a super-stylish pregnancy look, I was so manic with a newborn and a toddler I could barely leave the house in anything but pyjamas.

By the time you're onto pregnancy two or more, stylish dressing just doesn't feel like a priority. You may well still be carrying some of your extra weight from the first time around and your main concern is your existing child, not looking like (dare I say it?) a 'yummy mummy'. You're so bound up with combating nausea and tiredness with a toddler (or more) in tow, skipping your lunch break at work so you can skid home just in time for bath time, working out how to decorate your three-year-old's bedroom so she doesn't feel disgruntled at having to share it with the new arrival, and budgeting for the most economical childcare route, the last thing on your mind is maternity fashion! Well, stop right there! I am with you in this remember? (Do you really think I have time to be sorting out stylish pregnancy looks for myself when I'm busy helping to teach my son to read, making innovative packed lunches for my daughter and writing this chapter?) But I know deep down that if I put a little effort and thought in now, I'll feel tons better in the long run. Whatever your feeling on fashion, no mum can deny that clothes equate to confidence at some level and feeling good as a pregnant mum helps you to step out into the world with pride (well with a small smile at least!).

So while I'm figuring out how best to dress my third-time pregnant, glowing self (we must be kind to ourselves when we can!), I thought it the ideal time to share the journey with you. I figured one of the best places to start on how to be a stylish, bumpy mum would be to split pregnancy into the three trimesters. This way I work through specific challenges in turn, bearing in mind throughout that fabulous mums want style, ease and speed in one simple formula. So here goes . . .

First trimester (weeks 0–12)

You might imagine that the first three months would be the easiest in terms of pregnancy dressing, and in many ways you'd be right. You don't have to think of imaginative ways to cover a bump that feels as big as a hippopotamus and your ankles haven't yet had time to swell up to the size of tree trunks. But the first three months can be a time when you're feeling rather bulky and bloated, while you attempt to hide your little paunch from friends or work colleagues. For most mums it's also a period of battling with nausea, exhaustion and sickness. In reality you're far too busy trying not to chuck up your breakfast on the bus to consider how to hide your expanding tum. So let me make it easier for you with this little style checklist.

Good, supportive underwear. My breasts are always agony in the first trimester, and even the lightest touch would have me wincing (let alone the full-scale embrace of my three-year-old!). Wearing a good, supportive, non-wired bra will ease this immeasurably. A quick thought about the knickers side of things too (and when I use the term 'support-ive' knickers I use it 'loosely', because that's exactly what pregnancy calls for: ease and comfort!). I wouldn't suggest buying a whole array of granny-style hip-hugging panties (this will make you feel truly frumpy) but putting your itsy-bitsy G-strings and snug satin pants to the back of the drawer and replacing them with some cute cotton knickers always helps me feel more comfortable during pregnancy.

Voluminous tops. A good selection of voluminous tops will stand you in great stead throughout your pregnancy and months of breastfeeding. Luckily for me smock tops are totally 'on trend' this season, so not only will I look stylish and in keeping with *Vogue*'s latest 'must have' list, I'll also be able to find tons of cheap styles on the high street. (Don't you love it when that happens?) The great thing about smock tops is that they are fluid and comfortable, can be worn well with slim jeans (so as not to make yourself look too tent-like) and will hide any bump, small or large, until you're ready to tell the world your news. (If your working envi-ronment requires more of a suit look you could just go for a more man-sized white shirt with rolled up cuffs and wear it sexy with an open neckline.)

A little bit of DIY. I know this sounds silly but many women don't want to resort to maternity jeans or trousers in their first few months (even if, like me, you feel you have no choice!), so a little DIY comes in handy. I've found that if I sew two buttons either side of the fastening of my jeans I can then use a piece of elastic (with slits or holes every few centimetres) to join the buttons together. This works as long as I wear long tops to cover my amateur attempt at DIY. I can still wear all my wonderful skinny Sass & Bide jeans without actually having to fasten them properly at the top!

Second trimester (weeks 13–26)

I always find the middle three months the most enjoyable. Most women I know feel the same. Usually the sickness has faded, the news is 'out' and you can enjoy showing off your growing bump a little more. By three months in I feel safe to plan some faithful outfits that will see me through the coming trimester and hopefully beyond. At this point you'll have a good idea of how rapidly your body may change (and, as I mentioned before, this varies vastly between women as well as between a woman's different pregnancies). It's also worth bearing in mind what seasons you'll be dressing for as your pregnancy progresses. So, here are a few basics tips that will carry you through the second trimester, whether you're a working or full-time mum.

Layering. The art of layering is a worthwhile trick to master in pregnancy. Investing in a selection of cheap high-street vests to wear under your existing tops will really save you time, effort and cash. The trick is to make sure they are *long*; this way they'll cover your whole bump even if your pretty pre-pregnancy-bought top is riding slightly higher than normal. You could even be adventurous with colour and wear a bright pink vest under a pale blue T-shirt or an aqua one under a sky blue kaftan top. In the summer you can just layer two vest tops, allowing you to keep cool and look stylish. They are also mega-useful to wear under any favourite cardigans or frock coats, meaning you'll still get to enjoy them even if only the top two buttons do up!

The perfect jeans.   I still stand by my ethos that a good pair of maternity jeans is essential in pregnancy. If you're like our fortunate fashion guru, Lucie McCullin, you'll still be wearing your man-cut Levi's to week thirty-five, but for most mums comfort and ease comes with an elastic waistband! Scores of designer labels, high-street stores and maternity brands offer maternity jeans in various styles and cuts, so look around and find the perfect pair for you. If you're lucky you'll be able to wear them to work; if not it may be worth buying them for weekends and getting some maternity suit trousers for the office.

Show off the good bits.   My friend and fashion hero, Gayle, vows that the middle trimester is a time to elegantly cover your bump while still showing off the parts of your body that remain the same. Gayle's bump bore twin girls so believe me, it wasn't petite, but she dressed it perfectly with long strapless dresses and tops (which showed off her still-slim arms) and knee-length leggings under babydoll dresses (which gave a glimpse of lower calf and ankle that for many don't puff up until the last trimester). Even if your upper arms and ankles have given up on glamour you could try wearing tops cut off at the elbow to show a slim wrist or a plunging neckline to show off a hint of bosom and an elegant collarbone and neck.

Leggings.   I know not everyone can (or should) wear leggings. You admittedly run the risk of looking like Dawn

French on a bad day. (I have to confess I fall into this category and have vowed never to go near leggings despite the fact that some of my favourite designers have managed to make them look glamorous.) Having said that, for some women, they are a life-saver during pregnancy. Take my friend Jennie. She's carved a wonderful pregnancy 'look' for herself second time around using leggings as a basis of this. She wears good-quality black cotton leggings with jersey dresses, A-line tent mini-dresses or long punk T-shirts belted below the bump, all teamed with flat pumps or gladiator sandals. I don't know how many pairs of leggings she owns (it must be ten at least!) but they've allowed her versatility and grace without the fear of flashing her legs to the world (especially after a long winter hidden under jeans).

Third trimester (weeks 27–40 +)

These final months can really and truly be the hardest. Up until now you may have got away with wearing your existing floaty chiffon tops, summer kaftans, long fitted roll-necks, baggy jeans and layered vests, but now your bump is getting bigger you really need some fashion imagination before you leave the house in anything more than a tracksuit. By all means if you want to 'stuff it' and resort to your partner's oversized Nike tracksuit bottoms, than don't let me stop you, but remember, you run the risk of feeling just about as attractive as Wayne Rooney after a long game on the pitch. Having said that, most of us rarely want to feel like a glamour-goddess every day; we just want to feel comfy and stylish all in one neat(-ish) package.

Low-waisted bottoms. This is a time to really explore low-waisted trousers, jeans and skirts. Any with a low, elasticised or drawstring waist are ideal to experiment with. In my first pregnancy I lived in a low-slung gypsy skirt that fell nicely below my bump, some cashmere drawstring trousers (or linen for summer) and a pair of jeans that had pre-pregnancy seemed far too low on the hip, but now seemed a perfect fit for my obliterated waistline. All you need are long tops (or those faithful long vests again!) to meet the top of your bottom half and you're away!

Flats. If you haven't explored the wonderful world of flat shoes up until now then here is your chance! Now by 'flats' I don't mean your stinky work-out trainers. I mean something slightly more elegant and versatile! I'm a huge fan of ballet pumps and if you invest in some now you'll more than likely use them well into the coming years. Other good ideas for summer are: Birkenstock sandals, thong sandals or Haviana style flip-flops (which are dirt cheap on the high street so you could get them in an array of colours to match different outfits). And for winter: warm 'Ugg'-style boots and Converse trainers (again, you could get a few pairs in different shades if you're feeling flush).

Black. There's no denying that black is slimming. I found that by the last few months of my first pregnancy (and in the dark days of December) black stretchy tops, polo-necks (with a charcoal grey vest peeping out the bottom) and a faithful pair of maternity trousers formed the basis of my working wardrobe. I'd sling over the top a large, long colourful set of beads or funky pendant, but I was so huge that black felt a safe and easy way of slimming out the effect of a huge baby bump and a few stone in excess body-weight.

Open coats.   You may have resorted to black as your staple wardrobe shade, but that doesn't mean your old coats (worn open) won't still come in handy. Any good sheepskin coats, funky summer frock coats or chic belted macs can still be worn to make you feel more in touch with the old you.

Accessorise.   This last stretch is an ideal time to maximise on your accessories. I don't mean chucking them all on at once in the style of Jimmy Savile or Mr T from the A-Team, but a few well-thought-out accessories can really lift a plain outfit. Try, as I mentioned above, beads and pendants, or a corsage on an open cardigan can help distract the eye from your big bulge. Other good ideas could be dangly earrings, a brooch or a fab handbag, all nice touches that don't affect comfort but do enhance style.

Obviously the idea is to mix and match any of the above pieces of advice to suit you and your ever-expanding bump (and body). You may find you need the advice from trimester three well before you hit six-months.

Even if none of the above appeals to you please, please, please remember these two thoughts:

1. Stay true to your own sense of style. If you wouldn't wear an item or 'look' pre-pregnancy, why feel you must now?
2. Try to think about your pregnancy wardrobe ahead of time. This way you have a better chance of feeling good

about your changing shape, instead of wishing this time over.

Mother knows best

'I never know what to wear during pregnancy so all Grace's tips are invaluable. I'm on my fourth pregnancy, so any formula that lays it out like this suits me! I'm nearly always pregnant during summer so I swear by low-slung gypsy skirts, long vests and tight T-shirts, a good pair of flip-flops, a basket bag and some huge shades. Well and truly sorted!'

Full-time mum of three

Breastfeeding Dilemma

Hopefully this section will find you safely tucked up on the sofa, newborn in your arms and the toddler playing with their Brio train set at your feet. You'll have managed somehow to feel (sort of) stylish throughout your pregnancy and now, while navigating your way through sleepless nights, breastfeeding and adjusting your first-born to the concept of 'sharing', you've got to work out what you can sensibly wear during breast-feeding. Not much to do in the coming weeks then, eh?!

Let's start by saying firstly that no new mum should expect (or in my mind *want*) to make this precious time a fashion parade. Any multi-tasking mum who aims to get out and about in six-inch heels, a £1,000 buggy and a flat tum is another breed altogether. OK, you may have a baby blessing, christening or even family occasion looming where you want to look on the right side of glam, but for the majority of the time in these early weeks 'fabulous' implies 'functional': end of story.

With this ethos in mind, the first thing I did this morning was to invite good old Earth Mum (and, I have to say, admirably stylish) Amy over for a cuppa and a digestive. Amy has breastfed her three children well into their second year, and always seems to do it while remaining effortlessly cool, calm and chic. I can honestly say I've never seen her fighting with bra straps, exposing two bare boobs for the whole of the Thursday morning playgroup or grappling with flying breast pads and leaky patches. I too have breastfed my kids (admittedly not until their second birthdays but both to seven months exclusively) and hope that I've managed it with (close to the same) grace.

Earl Grey brewing in the pot, digestives diminishing from the plate, children announcing 'War!' in the garden, we put our heads together and came up with these simple answers to the dilemma of dressing while breastfeeding:

Do go for:

A good feeding bra. Pretty obvious advice, I know, but totally necessary just the same.

Layering. (Yes, it's that good old concept again!) By wearing a vest, or long-sleeved T-shirt underneath whatever top you choose (a kaftan, a gypsy top, a blouse, a vest, a jumper: anything goes with layers!) you can lift your over-garment, place your baby on the breast to feed and just pull down the under-vest. This prevents revealing any bare tum or second breast while you're feeding.

Cardigans/button-down tops.   Offer easy access at all times.

Floaty tops.   Worn with a vest or long-sleeved T-shirt underneath, these will look pretty and not too clingy.

Pashminas, pretty scarves and muslin squares.   Ideal for covering your exposed bust and giving the baby some shelter.

Don't wear any of the following (or at least wear with caution):

Tops designed specifically for breastfeeding.   I don't know about you, but I've yet to discover one that is anything but horrific.

Long dresses.   Unless they open at the front or can pull down easily over one breast.

White shirts or tops.   That will reveal your breast pads and/or leaking milk.

Black tops.   Unless you have a good supply of muslin squares. (I only say this because that's all I wore when breast-feeding my daughter and I ended up with patches of white-milk sick all down my black back for most of the day!)

Satin blouses. Any spilt milk will really show up and be hard to shift.

Single–layered top. (Unless you've lost all your baby weight.) Tops worn alone with the aim of lifting them up to feed will just expose your bare waist to the world; often the last thing you want six days after giving birth.

Lots of dangly necklaces. You'll only regret it when you bash them into the feeding head of your newborn (or when they're slightly older and can grab them unexpectedly, throttling you in the process!).

Garments that are dry clean or hand wash only. It goes without saying that this creates extra fuss, hassle and expense.

Amy and I both agreed that ultimately breastfeeding mums want ease and comfort. The last thing you want is to be struggling with an awkward top, mopping up leaky milk from your very finest silk chiffon designer blouse or revealing two big breast pads through a white T-shirt. My friend Florence agreed when she arrived mid-Earl Grey break. She remembers vividly her sister's wedding seven weeks after giving birth. She was so wrapped up in deciding what to wear to cover her bulging post-baby tummy that she totally forgot that she'd need to breastfeed during the church service. She arrived in a gorgeous 1950s floral tea dress and high wedge sandals, complete with cute baby smiling for the pictures. It wasn't until mid-way through the vows, when her son started screeching for his feed, that she realised she had absolutely no access to her bust. Florence resorted to racing to the nearby pub, taking her son to the toilets, lifting her whole dress up to her neck and feeding him on the toilet seat! A mistake she's unlikely to make again in a hurry.

That Six-minute Dressing Window

Indulge me in a little reminiscing if you will, for old time's sake at least. There was a time, not too many moons ago (well five and a half years, the age of my first child, to be precise) when my 'dressing window' looked something like this:

I would wake up for work at around seven-thirty. Before leaping out of bed I'd lie there for a short while, thinking about the day ahead. More than likely it would be a smooth motion of dressing, eating a light breakfast, taking the Tube to London's West End, where I'd have my morning swim at my gym before emerging at nine-fifty-five ready to saunter into my office in the hubbub of central Soho. The day would then be a combination of fashion launches, copy deadlines, meetings with my fashion director, viewings of some latest designer collection or other (over champagne of course) before a skip and a jump home for supper (often out locally with friends). So at seven-thirty-one, what I'd lie in bed thinking about would be what wonderful fashionable creation would carry me through a day like this. Often depending on the weather it would be anything from skinny jeans, a wafty chiffon designer top and three-inch stilettos, to a printed wrap dress and a pair of Mary-Janes.

Being a child-free girl about town I could either a) plan the outfit, slip it on and head to the kitchen for my bowl of Special K or b) leisurely try on each and every item until I found the 'perfect' look (before grabbing a latte as a substitute breakfast). Of course I was always safe in the knowledge that if the outfit didn't feel right halfway through the day, or I had a sudden fancy launch after work, I could make a call to a fashion PR and request to 'borrow' any number of exquisite masterpieces.

Fast-forward to today: the likelihood is the day will start well before seven-thirty (in fact this would be considered something of a lie-in). At something more realistically like six-thirty, my son (followed shortly by my daughter) will pile into our bed. After a sleepy cuddle-session, mayhem will ensue and the next hour will be a blur of helping the kids to get dressed, making breakfast for us all, brushing teeth, gathering the library books/homework bags/maths project folder/packed lunch/£1.50 for the school trip to Chinatown, before bundling everyone out the door and off on our long walk to school.

You'll probably notice that I have omitted dressing myself from this little scenario. Well, that's because it has to happen so quickly that if you blink you'll surely miss it. And here we have the daily dressing nightmare for most modern mums: you have what feels like six seconds in which to do it, and if you haven't managed to find matching socks, a top to accompany your bottoms, a pair of jeans to fit, well then you'll just have to go to work or do the school run in your odd socks, pyjama top and jeans that are two sizes too small. Not ideal, I'm sure you'll agree.

The simple fact is, to avoid stressful dressing and emerge with a semblance of style-savvy, you need to plan ahead. Now I'm not saying you should become one of those super-organised women you read about in *Vogue* (who plan their monthly wardrobe in a Smythson notebook on the first of each month); I'm merely suggesting a small amount of forward planning. Having a vague idea of what your day involves the night before will help you to think about what clothes will work best for the upcoming day. If, for example, you've got a full-on day including rounds of playgroups, nursery drop-offs, supermarket shopping and a session in the sandpit then some good jeans, a pair of Converse trainers and a vintage logo T-shirt should cover all the above perfectly. If, on the other hand, a key business meeting followed by a parents' evening is on the agenda, then a pressed suit and subtle skinny roll-neck with some court shoes should do the trick. Just by thinking for a split second the night before about what the day has on offer, you've taken most of the stress away. If, for example, you need to check if the suit needs an iron, surely it's best to do this the night before, saving you a mad cursing session with an iron 'that doesn't bloody work anyway'? Similarly, if you're planning to walk the school run and rain is forecast, fishing out your wellies and belted trench could save you the hassle of scrabbling around at the back of the cupboard while trying to get the family out the front door.

Believe me, I see so many mums who dart from their cars to the school gates and back again in under ten seconds, because they are barely out of their dressing gown. Sure, some will have the time to return home and spend a chunk of the morning applying make-up and sifting through their wardrobes (or some may well stay in their dressing gowns and go back to bed), but surely it would be better to feel half-decent when you leave the house and then be footloose and fancy-free to tackle the day ahead? I'm by no means suggesting creating whole catwalk looks for a normal day as supermum (you'll *never* see me in wedges for the school run!), but a half-decent, practical yet effortlessly cool collection of clothes is surely within the reach of any fabulous mum?

Mother knows best

'I've always been totally disorganised when it comes to dressing in the morning. My bedroom tends to be heaped up with clothes and resembles more of a jumble sale than a place of rest. All that had to change when I had my triplets. Admittedly the first six months I wore nothing but two velour tracksuits in endless rotation but after this I wanted to emerge as some sort of sane person in the adult world. Clothes helped me to do this. All I did was blitz my wardrobe, getting rid of heaps of junk and working out five good outfits I could wear for summer and five for winter. It makes life so easy and means I don't have to think about what to wear each and every day.'

Full-time mum of triplets

Wardrobe Essentials

It's very hard to compile a 'must have' list of clothes for all mums, simply because taste, lifestyle and body shape vary so much between us all. It's unfair to say 'suits are a big no-no', for example, when many women work in offices where suits and blouses are obligatory. Just as unrealistic would be the goal to not give up on trends when you're a mum, as anyone who's experimented with leggings/skinny jeans/shorts will know that they can look utterly ridiculous on women with anything less than supermodel legs. I also know some women who are utterly content to wear comfy joggers and a plain white T-shirt day in, day out. For these same women the thought of strutting their stuff in a belted trench or pleated denim skirt would seem about as appealing as doing the school run nude.

Having started with this note of caution on generalised fashion advice, I must now be honest about the feedback I have had from fellow mums on my style suggestions. Since writing my first book, *The Fabulous Mum's Handbook*, I've been bombarded with letters, cards, emails, face-to-face exchanges (and even the occasional bunch of tulips) from fellow mums who have been delighted with the easy-going, straightforward fashion tips I offer readers. Two particular women spring to mind. The first: Eleanor, a mother of three under-fives, who trekked through the snow to my book-signing at Waterstone's to let me know in person how her wardrobe overhaul and refocus on style-identity had boosted her confidence and self-esteem 'immeasurably' (so much so she'd decided to look into starting her own maternity clothing business, something she'd dreamed of doing for years). The second: Sandra, who, recognising me from a feature in a glossy magazine she read, strode up to me at my local branch of Tesco and described how she felt like a 'new woman' after following the advice in *The Fabulous Mum's Handbook* fashion chapter.

These are just two examples of a multitude of voices all singing the same tune, and it goes something like this: we are busy, multi-tasking mums who still want to look and feel good. A few easy-peasy tips on what to wear (and what not to wear!) that embrace various styles, shapes and ages are just what we need to step out with style. So, here I am again trying hard to give busy mums just this. Of course there is no blanket formula to suit all women (what size-eight, twenty-three-year-old mum from Manchester will want the same wardrobe basics as a size eighteen, forty-something mum-of-three living in Surrey, and vice versa?). However, there are still a few wardrobe essentials that I feel will carry most women through their day-to-day lives, still leaving room for innovation, personal expression and your own fashion flair (to whatever degree you wish to take it). So here we have it, a shopping list of basics (obviously depending on your job you may have to add 'fitted suit' or 'tailored trousers/pencil skirt' to the mix):

Basics for summer

Bootleg jeans. Forget skinny, cropped, mannish and high-waisted; if you buy one pair of jeans to carry you through summer and winter make these bootleg. Of course, experiment with other shapes if you fancy it, but a pair of good, denim jeans with a slight boot-cut (and remember I didn't say flare!) will carry you through the whole year (every year, no matter the current trend). Wear with Converse trainers, plimsolls, flat sandals, wedge heels or ballet pumps in summer and round toe boots or stilettos (for a night out) in winter.

Knee-length skirts. I have 'issues' with my legs so I'll always stick with long 'maxi skirts', but almost all the mums I know swear by a floaty knee-length number of some sort (gypsy, denim, floral chiffon, prom).

A maxi-sundress or tea dress. Again, the less said about my legs the better, but put it this way, a maxi-sundress is a godsend for me every summer! Strapless and floor-skimming worn with thong sandals is my usual summer uniform (accessorised with long beads or an antique brooch). If you prefer something shorter but equally versatile, go for a chiffon or cotton tea dress (possibly in a floral pattern to incorporate some colour and life into your wardrobe staples) and wear with sandals or white lace-up plimsolls. You could wear it loose and floaty if that's your style or belt it to highlight your waist. Team with a great bag or summer basket and you're away!

Vests, vests, and more vests! Yes it's that 'v'-word again! Summer isn't complete without a good selection of white, black and coloured vests to layer up, wear alone or slip underneath a kaftan or floaty number.

Floaty top or kaftan. Whichever suits you best, but both are ideal for covering self-conscious areas (tummies, the tops of arms or a breastfeeding bust) while keeping you cool and stylish. Team with jeans or a cut-off denim skirt (a mini is fine if you feel you can carry it off and feel confident).

A crisp white shirt. This is one of my must-have fashion basics as it looks so clean and fresh tucked into jeans, with a thin plaited belt and flat pumps.

A light jacket. A denim jacket (if you're feeling retro), trench coat, white cotton fitted jacket or printed summer coat are all great for cool spring mornings or the odd August rain shower!

Thong sandals, Birkenstocks, plimsolls, wedges. Take your pick – they're all incredibly versatile!

A great bag! A designer or high-street maxi-bag in a striking colour (or white) or a basket bag (possibly adorned with beads or lined with a printed cotton) are stylish yet practical for the mum who has to carry everything for all eventualities.

A few last accessories. Long beads, the odd vintage brooch, some super oversized shades or a selection of dangly gypsy earrings. All of the above can be thrown on to suit your mood.

Basics for winter

Jeans. See above

A warm winter coat. More likely than not you'll spend most of the winter months wearing a coat (at the school gate, watching your youngest play football, commuting to work) so it's worth investing in a quality one that will last you at least one season. Sheepskins are snug and stylish (but costly) so equally good is a fitted wool coat or a funky green military parka (also waterproof so very handy for British winters!). Think about buying a coat with a hood as it comes in very handy, especially when you're caught in the rain pushing a buggy with no spare hand for the brolly that last mile home from Tesco!

Knits. Obvious, I know, but by investing in some (or a couple of) wool or cashmere-mix roll-necks, chunky knits, belted cardigans or low V-necks, fitted or oversized, you'll save yourself endless time wondering what to wear on a cold and blustery day. If you're looking for a safe style to suit all I'd suggest going for plain colours (black, charcoal, cream, pale grey or, if you're feeling brave, a bright colour like fuchsia pink or cobalt blue) instead of stripes, spots or prints as for a lot of women these can unintentionally draw attention to areas you're trying to hide.

Long-sleeved T-shirts. I love to wear these (in either black or a bright colour) under some of my more fluid chiffon spring/summer tops. They'll keep you warm but still allow you a dash of colour or print in your winter wardrobe.

Something in tweed. An item in tweed can make a nice contrast to all the black wool and denim we tend to favour in winter. You could try some wide-leg tweed trousers, a tweed pencil skirt or a tweed fitted jacket to dress up jeans and a plain roll-neck.

Kitten-heeled black boots, some sheepskin lined boots, Wellington boots and Converse trainers. Any or all of these will offer practicality and style in the cold.

A maxi-bag. In black or camel (or even winter white if you don't mind giving it the occasional clean).

Thick, black opaque tights. Team with pencil skirts, maxi-dresses, jumper dresses, your tweed skirt, a denim mini (if you have the legs for it) or even your silver sequin Christmas party frock. Versatility encapsulated!

It's those final accessories again. A great chunky scarf, some leather gloves, a crochet corsage brooch or long beads (worn over a jumper dress or high-neck sweater) all work well in winter.

It goes without saying that you can (and, I hope, will) mix and match these ideas with your own existing wardrobe. My friend Paula, for example, will always wear winter tweed to work but tends to team it with a fitted white shirt, a bunch of pearls (all different lengths) and some killer heels. On the other hand my pal Rainbow loves her cashmere knits but chooses high-waisted ultra-long vintage jeans (in a pale 1970s blue) to accompany them (and so she should, with her hour-glass figure!). Whether you throw a bright orange 1970s vintage coat into your winter mix or a Topshop mini-sundress into your summer selection, the point is to formulate some key basics that will carry you through the year. Having these hung at the front of your wardrobe will save you hours of stress and bother first thing in the morning and guarantee you ease and confidence throughout the day.

To add a little inspiration here I thought I'd ask five of the most fabulous mums I know what four items they couldn't live without in their wardrobes. This way you'll see what bits and bobs can be added to your basics to mark your own stamp on them.

Rosie, magazine beauty director, seven months pregnant and mum to Arthur (two) A smart coat; fabulous, well-fitting underwear; a black polo-neck; and a selection of long, sleeveless vests.

Rena, full-time mum to Jemma (twelve), Sol (ten) and Miel (five) Sheepskin winter boots; a selection of boho jewellery; a good investment handbag; and a pair of well-fitting jeans.

Paula, senior fashion booker and mum to Toby (six) and twins Daisy and Phoebe (four) Navy blue, cashmere, round-neck cardigan; stone-coloured, slim, fitted trench coat; a good quality handbag; and ballet slippers.

Sonia, full-time mum to Joshua (five) and Mia (two) Skinny black jeans; a black, cotton round-neck; ruffled shirt; a classic padded black handbag; and a classy pair of black leather round-toe stilettos.

Ros, talent executive and four months pregnant A stone-coloured pashmina; a fantastic pair of big round shades; a long necklace; and a fabulous empire-line coat.

Whether it's sorting through your existing clothes, working on how to accessorise your favourite items or shopping for a few extras, make a little time for your wardrobe and you'll look and feel better, I promise.

Mother knows best

'I'm not one for trends or fad fashion but I was really struggling to find new things I wanted to wear each week. In the end I went for boot-cut jeans and twin-sets in a variety of colours for cold days and a vintage

Shopping Made Easy

Many of you will remember from *The Fabulous Mum's Handbook* my hilarious account of shopping with two toddlers in tow (believe me, smeared rusks, an 'ickle accident' and the disgruntled faces of other shoppers haven't left my memory in a hurry!). Here we are some years on and I'll bet you're wondering if shopping gets any easier with two school-children and a baby bump coming along for the ride. The answer is simple: logistically, shopping *en famille* is easier now (no double buggy, no bucking eighteen-month-old determined to get out from his straps 'Noooooooooooooooooow!' and no huge changing bag full of nappies/wipes/snacks/rattles and the kitchen sink!). However, any mum who's tried to accomplish a day's clothes shopping with two bored and whiny four/five-year-olds moping at her heels will know 'easy', 'relaxing', 'inspiring' or 'full of joy' aren't exactly the terms they'd use to describe it!

It's true, go to any shopping centre in Britain at the weekend and you'll find hordes of families traipsing around, Dad looking bored outside a fitting room while the kids decapitate themselves with hangers. It seems like a pretty 'normal' way to spend a family weekend. An iPod for your partner, a new frock for you, some pyjamas for Adam and a first training bra for Ella – follow this with a spot of lunch (burgers all round) and you have summed up an all-too-familiar Saturday for families across Britain. Fortunately (at least that's how I like to see it), my husband works in retail so he works every Saturday. This makes Saturday shopping as a single mum with two kids (and hordes of other 2.4-children families) about as appealing as stabbing myself in the eye with a needle. I really can't think of anything I'd rather do less than join the masses for till queues and burgers on my day 'off'.

Yes, there are times when the hole in my son's school shoes just won't disappear and my daughter's raincoat cannot legitimately pass as a winter coat any longer and I'm forced into doing a military dash to the local high street, children in tow, but believe me if I can possibly avoid it, I do. The thought of actually going shopping *en masse* for pleasure, well that's a really mean feat! How many of you have actually come away with a bag full of 'perfect' purchases as your children make faces in your fitting room mirror or pull endless packs of G-strings off the racks? You get my point. So how does one busy mum shop with ease to buy those all-important bootleg jeans and dream summer maxi-dress *and* keep the kids happy?

*Successful strategies for shopping (*en masse*)*

Isolate your target, aim, fire.   For me, knowing what I need before I go shopping is integral to a successful outing. Making a 'hit list' will target exactly what you're looking for and save hours of ambling around the wrong shops, ending up with a spandex boob tube (because it had seventy-five per cent off) instead of a pair of summer Birkenstocks in silver. If you've jotted down what it is you need (everything from 'new top for your thirty-fifth birthday' to 'glitter-pens for the craft box') you can work out exactly which shops you'll need to go to, and in what order.

Once you've isolated your target and aimed your shopping basket it's now time to fire! (Sorry, I know this isn't a military operation but we all admit it can sometimes feel like it!) If it's a pair of flat pumps you need then head straight to the shoe department; if you just amble through a store you'll all end up exhausted and distracted by the time you reach the footwear. If you've got all day to shop alone, then it's great to mooch, but if you're accompanied by your kids (and their twenty-minute window of patience) it's much better to be focused.

Doing your homework can make the difference between a wasted shopping trip and a successful one. You could try sourcing items you need via the women's glossies (the beginning of each season is a good time to do this). By tearing out pictures from the likes of *Grazia* and *Red* (or *Vogue* and *Heat* if these fashion pages tick the right boxes) you could start a small folder or pile of items on your wish-list. If you call the store in question beforehand to check they have the style and size for you in stock you could save hours of hassle and disappointment. Alternatively, spend half an hour one evening surfing the websites of your favourite store. My friend Elaine did this last night in her search for the perfect pair of jeans. She isolated three potential winners from GAP, wrote down the store-codes and headed to her nearest branch the next day to try them all on. With her kids safely munching muesli bars in the fitting rooms she managed to find the ultimate in skinny-fit jeans and spent the rest of the afternoon watching *Shrek the Third* at the movies with a big smile on her face (as opposed to dragging the kids around yet another high-street store getting more and more irate as she did it!).

Feeding rooms. If you're shopping with a baby you may find it easier and more convenient to shop in stores with feeding rooms. My pal Catherine and I spent a large part of our first-borns' babyhood charting London's feeding rooms from A–Z. Although nipping to Selfridges for the afternoon was a rarity, knowing they had one of London's best feeding rooms (rocking chairs, super hygienic changing area, TVs for the feeding mum, bottle warmers, cold mineral water and all on the same floor as the shoes!) made it even more appealing to the new mum. Having a private and relaxing pit-stop for feeding your baby certainly induces a more relaxed shopping experience than darting around the high street looking for a bench to breastfeed your little one! (You could try John Lewis for good feeding rooms too.)

Shopping with an ally. It always helps to think safety in numbers. This applies only too well to shopping *en masse*. Now by numbers I don't mean ask your six-year-old to bring a few friends along for the ride, oh no. I mean see if you have a willing partner, pal, sister or mum who fancies coming along to shop and help. I bought one of my favourite silver glitter party frocks while my sister Fleur treated the children to two scoops each from the ice-cream parlour next door.

Obviously your ally will want to do their fair share of shopping too, but by sharing the day it will make it much more fun for all.

Involve the kids.   Involving the children in the shopping experience will make it far more fun and engaging for them. While you're trying on a pair of flip-flops ask them to fetch you a pair in another colour or, while you're browsing over roll-necks, why not ask them to select their favourite item for you to try on? Taking the odd reading or colouring book can also help keep them busy.

A treat incentive.   Offering a reward at the end of a shopping trip (when the children have behaved well and been super-helpful of course!) always seems to work for us. I don't endlessly drag the kids around Topshop while I stock up on vests, but on the occasions that we do all go shopping together, offering a bunch of stickers, a balloon or a book each from the book shop usually helps keep enthusiasm high.

Go on, give me a break!   If at all possible carve out a window to shop alone! There must be a few hours here and there when you can dart to the high street to replace that moth-eaten cardigan? How about when the children are at school or nursery? In your lunch break from work or even on a Sunday while the in-laws pop over for a play? Even if it's only a few times a year it will give you the sanity to select some key pieces for your wardrobe.

Lazy shopping.   If all else fails there is always the shopping by Internet option. Almost all leading clothes and interior stores give customers the choice to shop online and you can do this in peace and at your leisure. Check out my 'Useful Addresses' section for some great website ideas.

Kids' Fashion, or 'I Won't Wear That!'

Kids' fashion is a sensitive subject, not least because for some mums out there dressing their children with the utmost care and thought represents *exactly* the image they want to project of about their happy, stylish, 'perfect' family. I'm sure there are mums who obsess about being the first to get the new hot-off-the-press tweed waistcoat with gold-plated buttons (designed by none other than an international pop phenomenon), and will make special trips up to the West End to queue for designer logo shoes in a limited edition shade of fuchsia. When you see their children they will be starched, dressed and groomed as if they're about to smile for a Burberry campaign and God forbid they get chocolate cake down that velvet, hand-smocked and beaded party dress!

Even if keeping your offspring up to date with the latest must-haves isn't your thing, there are still many crazed mums out there who seem to lose all their common sense when dressing their children. How else can you explain dressing your four-year-old daughter in a silver appliqué 'sex kitten' T-shirt, or a miniskirt almost revealing her knickers? Why on earth would any sane woman kit her son out in a suit at the age of three with a waistcoat, tie and flat cap to match? I mean, for goodness' sake, has the clothes industry lost its senses?

My motto when choosing clothes for my kids is, 'Make them comfy yet fun, pretty yet childlike'. I'm not a big fan (well, that's putting it mildly) of cartoon or Disney motifs so when I say 'fun' I don't mean a tracksuit covered in Bob the Builder. What I mean is letting children enjoy colour and patterns and exploring things like large floral print dresses, spotty leggings or fun logo T-shirts; all things we tend to grow out of (or wouldn't dream of wearing) later in life. I rarely spend a fortune on their clothes; what's the point when they grow out of it in six seconds or ruin it in the sandpit? However I do invest in occasional special pieces, such as a party dress or a gorgeous wool coat for winter; I just make sure they have room to grow in them.

As with my own wardrobe, I try to plan what they're going to need before I buy their basic clothes for each year. Of course, this is a personal choice and many mums love to splurge on their kids (come on, we're all guilty of it!) but it can feel just too extravagant to buy a complete mix-and-match wardrobe every season for a three-year-old! Never mind once they have a school uniform and only wear their clothes for two days a week.

My favourites are H&M Kids for basics (coloured vests,

long-sleeved T-shirts and great wool tights), Boden Kids for their funky tops and dresses and GAP for kids' denim. I'll throw in some eco-friendly pieces along with the odd designer item (my daughter has worn the same Ugg boots for the past two winters, for example). I am a fan of Converse trainers and Kickers for both sexes (although they are a pain to do up if your child hasn't mastered laces yet!) and Birkenstocks and/or Crocs for summer. (My daughter always seems to have a much-loved pair of pretty Accessorize flip-flops every summer, but these are usually care of her doting aunty and not an over-indulgent mum!)

This advice will suit many mums, but for some I know it will make little impact. Designer, supermarket brand, eco-friendly, cashmere, even with flashing lights and luminous zips, some children won't want to wear *anything* you choose for them. Take my pal Gayle, whose twin daughter Sienna refuses point blank to go out in anything other than a pink tutu and silver glitter pumps (even if it's a wet walk to the Post Office). Being a fashion stylist, Gayle has a whole array of cute outfits for Sienna to wear, but oh no, Sienna is a little fashionista in her own right and under no circumstances will she be told what to wear each morning. If Gayle dares to force her into a pair of jeans and some wellies one of two things happens: 1) After much bargaining Sienna will wear the jeans, but only under the tutu, 2) Sienna will scream and kick so much that the wellies will be left by the front porch, where Gayle found them!

For many kids (and Gayle is hoping this is the case with her adorable but iron-willed Sienna), making strong statements about what they wear is a passing fad. As soon as they insist on wearing only *that* Spiderman outfit they'll decide it has to be *that* red pair of OshKosh dungarees, and so the new phase will begin. In this instance you have little choice but to go with it. More than likely it's a sign that your child (often toddler) wants to gain control of their world and wants you to know they have 'rights'. Obviously, if it's December and a bikini your three-year-old has decided they will not be parted from, you may need to work on that bargaining technique, otherwise I'd suggest letting them be Spiderman/Angelina Ballerina/The Gruffalo as much as possible until they get it out of their system.

Occasionally this fashion fad is here to stay and refusal to dress in the clothes you choose (or get dressed, full stop) becomes a part of everyday life. My friend Catherine experienced this with her son Tom when he flew into a rage every time he got dressed in the morning. He'd sulk right through his cornflakes and all the way to the nursery gates until Cat was in total despair. At first she tried to ignore it but when he refused to get out of his pyjamas she realised she'd need to tackle this 'phase' head on. The first thing she did was to insist that Tom learned to dress himself. By giving him that control back he then felt a little more empowered by his choices (even if it did mean he wore shorts over jeans and a sweater inside out and back to front!). She then bargained with him and said that if he dressed himself without a fuss each day for the whole week she'd take him shopping and he could choose two tops and two bottoms that *he* liked. This seemed to work a treat and although during this part of Tom's life I only remember him in an orange, long-sleeved T-shirt and blue cords, he was happy and felt very grown-up!

My daughter's own choice of clothes has luckily been slightly broader, but I've learned not to choose things without showing her first. It seems whatever I select without her approval is far too 'spotty', 'scratchy', 'hot', 'purple' or, God forbid, 'boyish'! Even if it's just asking her to select one of three dresses in a catalogue, getting her approving nod will mean she's likely to wear it or, as a last resort, give me the justification to tell her, 'Well, you chose it yourself!' She's going through a phase at the moment of coming home from school, stripping off her clothes and changing at least five times before bedtime (hopefully this form of self-expression will pass once she starts her new non-uniform school in September). I've now had to put a cap on this and allow her three changes max. I don't want to stunt her freedom of style; however, I don't want to be clearing up a fancy dress carnage every night!

I think the trick to dressing your kids is to keep it simple and easy. Don't fret too much if all they want to wear is a pair of gingham printed shorts and a luminous T-shirt (they'll only pay you back and go goth in later in life). But at the same time try not to let them have complete free rein (I'm a firm believer in age-appropriate clothes). Give your children choices and involve them in what they like to wear. Remember whatever they end up wearing will get covered in paint/sand/pasta sauce sooner or later, so let them enjoy themselves and wear what they feel most comfortable in.

Mother knows best

'I just haven't got the time or cash to make what my kids wear into a fashion parade. I just stick to jeans for both my boy and girl and an array of long-sleeved coloured T-shirts to go on top. If they get a fairy dress or Batman top from friends or relatives then great, but at home we've all got far more to think about than what tights match what frock!'

Part-time working mum of two

Top ten fashion and style tips

1. Dressing with ease, confidence and style during pregnancy is a challenge but not impossible. Dedicate some time and energy into getting it right and you'll feel the benefits. (I've found it definitely makes me feel more confident and outgoing, not to mention rather proud of my 'radiant' new figure!)
2. You don't need to spend a fortune on maternity clothes but by investing in some good supportive underwear, a pair of well-cut maternity jeans and some extra-long, ultra-stretchy high-street vests you'll have the basis of a stylish, versatile nine-month (and beyond) wardrobe.
3. Throughout pregnancy and breastfeeding stay true to your own sense of style. (This might not be the best time to experiment with punk or embrace everything pink, floral and traditionally mumsy.)
4. Pre-plan those winning wardrobe essentials each season, even if you're rotating a handful of stylish outfits, you'll feel confident that they work well and flatter your body shape.
5. Having a good selection of bags, shoes and accessories to choose from can be the making of even the plainest outfit.

6. Try and give your outfit a moment's thought the night before. (You'll never dress well with the clock ticking, your youngest pouring cornflakes on his head and your eldest torturing your middle child over who brushes their teeth first!)
7. Try and make clothes shopping easy (follow my S.S.S. tips). You may find it becomes a bi-annual pleasure as opposed to an almost weekly *nightmare*!
8. Utilise catalogues and the Internet for quick-fix basics.
9. Don't stress about kids' fashion. Involve them in their choices and try to allow them creative freedom in what they want to wear (as long as this doesn't involve pants on their heads and pyjamas for a Sunday brunch with freinds!)
10. Just because you're a mum it doesn't mean you can't take pleasure and pride in looking and feeling good in clothes (it just means you have far less time and energy in which to do it!).

Grace's Guru: Lucie McCullin

Lucie McCullin is the Senior Fashion Editor at *Elle* magazine and has contributed to a vast array of top-end publications such as *US Elle*, the *Sunday Times Style* magazine, the *Independent*, the *Guardian* and the *Evening Standard*. Her job at *Elle* entails styling leading fashion shoots (everywhere from Bali to Brighton) as well as celebrity cover stars, meaning a 'normal' day for Lucie can entail mingling with celebrities such as Jennifer Anniston, Kylie, Paris Hilton, Catherine Zeta Jones and Gwyneth Paltrow!

Lucie also attends the international fashion shows on the catwalks of New York, Milan, Paris and London and works with some of the world's leading fashion photographers (such as Norman Jean Roy, Gilles Bensimmon and Pamela Hanson). On top of all this she somehow manages to run her company Fashion-Edit which plays the role of personal stylist to many well-known private clients too!

When Lucie isn't spearheading the country's trends or making A-listers look immaculately groomed, she'll be savouring some family time at home (on the coast in Deal) with her husband Alex and one-year-old daughter, Lila Skye.

What are your main fashion and style tips for the following mums?

A pregnant mum With a bit of thought you can easily adapt your pre-pregnancy wardrobe to fit your growing bump. First things first, blitz your wardrobe and dig out all smock tops, tunics, flared shirts, cardigans and anything stretchy (denim is worth keeping out for the first half of pregnancy too). Secondly, store in boxes anything you know will not fit during your pregnancy and while you are breastfeeding – it will only depress you having these lurking in your wardrobe!

H&M and American Apparel do really useful cotton stretch waistbands in lots of different colours that you can wear over your regular jeans, hiding open buttons and covering your expanding bump. Even better, go online to Blossom's denim bar where you can buy your favourite denim brands like Seven and James which are customised with their own

Blossom Band – a stretchy panel stitched on. Alternatively, you can just stretch a hair band through your trouser button-hole and over the button so they won't fall down. I also found the current trend for wide-leg boyfriend cut jeans perfect for pregnancy. These can be worn under your bump, whatever your size. Just loosen your belt as the months go by. Plus when your thighs thicken at around three or four months there is still plenty of room! The best pair I found was a pair of Levi cinch-back jeans that lasted my whole pregnancy.

The easiest option by far is to invest in five or six great dresses and wear them in rotation. For variation wear them layered over colourful cotton vests or under cardigans. Empire lines, pleat front, tunics and long sleeves are all good shapes for the bump. Go for stretch jersey then you can wear the same dress from beginning to end and after. It also looks nice if you tie a sash or a thin belt under your bust for more shape. If it's cold, just pull on a pair of cosy woollen tights and a pair of flat boots and if it's hot, a cute pair of ballet pumps or a Haviana flip-flop (which come in a million different colours). Steer clear of anything with laces or buckles as it's impossible to bend down by six months. This way you will have no dramas getting dressed in the morning – life should be stress free and with a dress you have a whole outfit in one go.

In terms of what shades and patterns to go for, I'd suggest dark colours and prints. Also, remember a crucial tip, which is to layer your tops – wearing an open cardi over a vest immediately makes the bump less round.

Shoes are a great way to enjoy diversity and creativity

without being too limited by the expanding bump. As long as your fetish isn't for sky-high heels you can still have fun with footwear, even if you feel like a hippo! I swore by low-heel wedge shoes and found they worked really well with a bump – it's solid and still gives you that little bit of glamour. When my baby bump became heavier I opted for any flat shoes that slip or zip on. Why not buy two or three pairs of colourful ballerina pumps? (Pretty Ballerina, French Sole, Chanel and Office do great designs.) It'll be worth every penny and you'll definitely get the wear out of them both during pregnancy and beyond. Pretty flip-flops are perfect for summer when it gets too hot for those cute silver ballet pumps and for winter I'd invest in one great pair of flat leather boots or Uggs (which offer extra room, ideal if your feet are puffy and swollen).

If I were to give you my ultimate clothes wish-list for pregnancy it would go something like this:

Lucie's ultimate wish-list for pregnancy clothes
- Lux big knits – wrap around and belted are ideal.
- A belted cape.
- Empire-line dresses – prints are great for distracting away from the size of your tummy.
- Pleat-front tops.
- Floaty bias-cut chiffon tops and dresses.
- Neat trench coat – wear open or belt over bump.
- Pregnancy tights – (I found H&M did the best wool ones.)
- Men's style vests – Topshop and American Apparel do great ones – the longer length is perfect to keep your bump cosy.

- Pashmina to wrap around your bump.
- Kaftans for summer.
- Belts to wear under your bust or around your hips (or you may look like a tent!).
- Great underwear – go for bigger size knickers than usual – silky or stretch cotton hipsters. You can buy really pretty maternity bras from Elle MacPherson and Petal at Blossom. (Please just promise me you'll avoid G-strings and thongs, which are just too unsupportive and sore after around month six!)

And her ultimate shops for pregnancy clobber
- Elias and Grace
- Blossom
- GAP
- Topshop maternity

A breastfeeding mum   The first thing to remember is to *keep your clothes practical and simple.* You'll have so much on your mind in those first few months the last thing you need is a complicated wardrobe. I'd suggest a few of the following items for an easy, stress-free breastfeeding wardrobe:

- Wrap cardigans and tops – the easiest way to get the boob out!
- Anything button-down is perfect.
- Borrow a couple of your husband's shirts – grandad style is also good.
- Oversize smocks – you can put the baby underneath while feeding – GAP and Primark have fabulous ones.

- Cool capes and ponchos – also perfect as you can be completely covered.
- Diane Von Furstenberg wrap dresses (and obviously all the great high-street copies if you are on a budget).
- Pretty feeding bras – again Elle MacPherson does great styles that are really pretty and use good colour pallets (they are quite sexy too, which can make a pleasant change after a nine-month pregnancy wearing faded white sports bras!). Do try to remember that even though you're often tired (and sometimes feel rather like a milking machine!) it's still important to feel girly and feminine.
- I loved the Kari Me wrap-around baby slings because you can breastfeed without taking the baby out – there's a good choice of colours too.
- I'd also recommend having a selection of pashminas on hand at all times (or if it's very hot some large cotton scarves). When you are breastfeeding in public you will need something to drape over your shoulder while you undo clothes and it's simply impossible to hold a baby, unbutton your top and latch the baby on without exposing yourself to the world (and going beetroot red at the same time!). Muslin squares will do but a scarf is much bigger and prettier (plus they can double up as baby blankets). It goes without saying that you will need one fabulous, oversized bag to hold everything – go for a canvas tote or soft slouchy leather maxi-bag. Instead of the usual changing bag with all the compartments you can easily use pretty zip-up wash bags to kit out your tote – Cath Kidston do lovely printed ones. Remember to include a small one for breast pads and nipple cream.

I learned the hard way what to avoid wearing while breast-feeding (as many of my new-mum girlfriends have too). Let me share with you then, some of the fashion no-nos when dressing for successful breastfeeding.

Turn your back on the following during breastfeeding
- Dark fabrics – shows up milk, dribble and vomit!
- Silk – shows up anything wet.
- Wide belts that dig in when the baby is feeding.
- Fiddly tops.
- Dresses that don't button down.
- All jumpers/roll-necks unless you can comfortably fit baby underneath.
- Fluffy mohair or wool is not great for burping baby as they end up with fur balls!
- Dainty necklaces – your baby may well break them.
- Chunky bracelets/watches – will just get in the way.

A mum with a large family and little time to shop or dress I always feel that whatever your family size or clothes budget it's important that a mum can just throw on an outfit, wear it all day and still feel great. This is where my top tip for the five or six dresses in rotation can work well again (see my advice on pregnancy dressing). If dresses aren't your thing then why not aim to have five key outfits that can be interchanged with different tops/shoes, etc. depending on your mood, the occasion and the weather? To give you an idea of how this can work, here are my key essentials for a successful winter wardrobe:

Essential garments for a successful winter wardrobe

- A pair of black or blue jeans – one great pair of jeans is better than ten pairs that don't fit brilliantly.
- A cashmere jumper (you can buy brilliant quality cashmere so cheaply on the high street these days).
- Two jackets – such as a wool or tweed man's style and a more feminine crop style. These can be worn over a million different tops/jumpers/dresses.
- Simple shirts.
- A sheepskin gilet.

If time is a huge issue (and getting a full day of clothes shopping in hand is almost as impossible as flying to the moon and back before bedtime!) then maybe you should consider a personal shopper who can do all the hard work for you. (Big department stores often offer this free of charge.) It may take only a few hours to source some key looks that will last. The next best alternative is to shop online. Consider the following:

- Net-a-Porter – designer goodies (which may be pricey but good for a treat) who deliver the same day or definitely by the next day.
- Matches – Like Net-a-Porter items here aren't cheap but if you're planning to buy something designer this is a brilliant place to start.
- Topshop
- ASOS
- And of course eBay for fabulous designer bargains, vintage clothes and great original accessories.
- (Go to my 'Useful Addresses' section for more information.)

Once you've got the basics in your wardrobe sorted out accessories are the best way to personalise your look with speed and efficiency. Even if you have little time to shop, just spending an hour buying a few favourite accessories (or an hour online) can change every outfit you wear for the next six months. You don't need to go mad, but a few of the following my help make an outfit not just a collection of items but a winning personalised look!

Accessories to consider
- If you have any money to spare invest in one great designer or top-end high-street bag and use until it falls apart. Just remember, it needs to be big enough to fit your life.
- A wristful of pretty bangles.
- Long silk scarves will add colour to a simple outfit.
- Ugg boots.
- Leather boots.
- Colourful Converse trainers.
- Pretty sandals.

I know it sounds laborious, but if you can set aside a small chunk of time to work out around ten easy but stylish outfits that suit you well you'll find dressing so much easier. I always recommend my photo system for women who have little time to shop and dress (yet still want functional looks that work day in day out). In short you photograph a handful of winning outfits hanging up along with the accessories that match, or work with the outfit. If you stick these Polaroids to your wardrobe door it's so much easier to dress with speed in the morning. If this sounds like far too much hassle why not just try to leave out your clothes the night before?

Two other tips to remember (in those six seconds you have to think about clothes!): be wary of high-street prints or the popular mail order ones – you don't want to look like every other mum at the school gates! And remember my key busy mum's motto: keep it classic, simple and practical. Don't attempt to be too trendy – you don't have the time!

A busy mum looking for key wardrobe essentials (whatever her shape and size) Women come in so many different shapes and sizes that it's hard to dictate a 'look' or formula that will suit everyone. Above all I'd say the key is to know what works for you and don't try to be too adventurous when every new trend or craze comes along. Often simple designs that flatter your specific body shape and make you feel lovely work far better than the latest 'must-have' skinny jeans/logo T-shirt/wrap dress. The point about dressing well (especially as a busy mum with a growing family and a million and one jobs to do each day!) is to feel confident in your clothes.

I've given this question a lot of thought and drawing on my experiences, the clients I've worked with (who believe it or not aren't all size zero stick insects!), the fashion shows I've attended and the personal clothes crisis I've encountered with a new baby of my own, I think this hit list of wardrobe essentials works for most women.

Wardrobe essentials to suit the working mum (from a size zero all the way up to the size twenties!)
- A trouser suit – the jacket and trousers can also be worn separately (make sure the trousers fit really well).

- Classic cotton shirts.
- Modern tops (which incorporate interesting details such as pleating or draping).
- One smart coat in navy or beige.
- Straight cut denim – this can be worn with the jacket from the suit.
- Boy cut tailored trousers – very sexy with a simple camisole or shirt.
- Classic high court shoes.
- Big sunglasses.
- High leather boots.
- A luxury bag.
- A statement designer watch (or good copy!).

A mum looking for innovative ways to dress her children I feel it's important to keep your baby looking like a baby for as long as possible. I just can't understand the desire for dressing babies like mini-adults (in frills and frock coats with matching shoes). I loved dressing baby Lila in all-in-ones and they made life so much easier. (I'd just layer up with a vest underneath and a lovely knit cardigan when it was cold.) My favourite brand was American Apparel (they have a huge range of colours with the added bonus of mail order).

I never really bought into the whole girl equals pink thing either. Lila looks gorgeous in pale blues and aqua and even brown was utterly divine as the winter months drew in. Look in the boys' department for plain trousers or cords and plain knits – the colours are much nicer. For example, a pair of chocolate brown cords looks cute with purple tights underneath and sheepskin bootees. And a chunky khaki cardigan looks adorable over a floral Babygro. Another reason I would recommend buying unisex colours is in case you have another baby. Many sweet Babygros or cardigans (in greens, purples, browns, blues, reds and coppers) can be used for either sex and will last well for subsequent babies or as hand-me-downs to your friend's children. (Dressing kids is expensive so this will save money and time in the long run.)

The high street is great for buying children's clothes (especially when they grow out of things in the blink of an eye). Do remember, however, to avoid obvious high-street prints as every other child will be wearing them. High-street stores are great for plain wool, stripes and polka dots which you can buy lots of and then add in the occasional prints from slightly more expensive places too. (My hot favourites are Bonpoint/Caramel/Quincy/Igloo/Couverture.) I've found that dressing children in summer is so much simpler than in winter. (Lila lives in dresses all summer, which couldn't be easier!) Winter often hurls more problems into the equation but I've found with a little imagination, keeping kids warm and stylish during a cold snap is possible! Why not consider some of the following:

- Invest in a woollen pram coat and pair of leggings – get two sizes up so arms and legs can always be rolled up. (Nuture by Nature do a great pram coat that is reversible and although it's expensive your baby will live in it.)
- Let your toddler choose a colourful fleecy snug suit.

- Recycle your own holey cashmere or wool sweaters. Cut them into little scarves and stitch ends or boil an old wool jumper you don't wear any more to shrink down to kid-size.
- Invest in some kids' leather moccasins, plain or fur trimmed – you can buy these from Jesse Western.
- Ask a generous godparent to buy a cashmere bonnet from Brora as they are the perfect investment and stretch for longer use.
- Use baby socks as mittens – they are longer so stay on better and come in much more fun colours.

What are your top accessories for the fashion-savvy mum?

1. A Clements Ribeiro baby bag from Blossom.
2. Large pashminas in any colour – so useful for breast-feeding, baby blanket, scarf, etc.
3. A transitional oversized bag that holds everything – (Chloe, Mulberry, J&M Davidson and Luella for designer or Whistles, Topshop, River Island for a cheaper alternative.)
4. A pair of fabulous shades.
5. A Smythson leather photograph holder (or similar) for showing off the baby pics.
6. A pretty locket with pictures of your husband and kids or a charm necklace with their initials.

What are your key style dos and don'ts for the ultimate
fabulous mum?

Do

- Blitz your wardrobe and store away anything you won't be using for the next year, i.e. skimpy skirts and high heels.
- Get your outfit ready the night before.
- Make an effort to get dressed in the morning, i.e. not by mid-afternoon.
- Treat yourself to a manicure or pedicure once in a blue moon.
- Ditch the maternity pants and buy some well-fitting sexy lingerie.
- Wear an under-wired bra once you have stopped breast-feeding.
- Invest in a gorgeous bag and flat shoes.

Don't

- Don't wear old tracksuit bottoms all day – your partner will despair!
- Don't wear baggy T-shirts without a bra.
- Don't stay in all your maternity clothes after you've had the baby (unless they were transitional pieces to start with). Opt instead for your baggier jeans, low-slung waist-bands, long vests and voluminous tops.
- Don't revert back to your old wardrobe too soon. You will probably carry some baby weight for a few months so opt for items in your existing wardrobe that are more fluid and allow room to breathe out! (Any favourite well-fitting items will cling in all the wrong places for a good few months post-birth.)

- Don't go for trends – stick to classic, simple pieces and accessorise.

Lucie's fabulous mum's style mantra:
'Treat yourself and your curves!'

Feeding the Five Thousand

The Meal Machine

Let me reminisce for a moment: there was once a time when Sundays meant little more than my partner doing the 'bagel run' at midday. He'd return with hot, fluffy, white bagels already stuffed with smoked salmon and cream cheese, we'd eat, read the papers and then snooze. This would take us safely through to the early evening where supper would be a choice of a) Chinese takeaway, b) Pizza Express, or c) Kettle Chips, hummus and a good slushy movie.

Now, let me do a quick calculation of the food I've prepared today and please bear in mind it's only six o'clock in the evening . . .

- 2 x breakfasts for the kids (my son insisted on Cheerios, dry of course, followed by Marmite toast cut into soldiers; my daughter 'pleeeeeeeased' her way to a smoothie of blended banana and strawberries and two bowls of home-made muesli).
- 1 x breakfast for me (green tea, a bowl of muesli and the remaining slurp of smoothie).

- A 'healthy' sandwich for my daughter's packed lunch, plus some chopped cucumber, and a handful of washed and halved grapes (I have no idea if she'll swap them with her neighbouring lunch partner's Organix crisps and dried apricots).
- 1 x tray of fruity flapjacks (admittedly with the 'help' of my three-year-old).
- 8 x portions of pasta bolognese, grated cheese, broccoli, peas, carrots and cucumber for my son and his pals (who have come for a pre-nursery lunch and a 'let's wreck the house!' session; and a huge bowl full of chopped strawberries and the bulk of the still-warm flapjacks.
- 3 x salmon salsa and fruity couscous (for the mums who stayed for a gossip).
- 2 x bags of after-school snacks (cut-up apple, carrot sticks and the very last slices of the flapjack).
- 1 x large pot of chicken soup (for tomorrow's Friday night supper).
- 2 x plates of roast chicken, peas, broccoli and potatoes for worn-out, hungry children. Ice cream in cones for pudding (because I'm a softie!).
- 2 x oatcakes with manuka honey and a large cup of tea for Mum (by heck, I need it!).

Before I hit the sack, you'll also be able to add these to the equation:

- 2 x slices of Marmite on toast (for the children to munch while they watch a pre-bath DVD of *The Little Mermaid*).
- 2 x plates of the left-over roast chicken, some roasted

vegetables and a large batch of sweet potato crush (some to be saved for tomorrow night's dinner party).

Altogether, by the time the day draws to an end I'll have made twenty-six meals and snacks, largely for other people. For most of you fellow mums this will come as no surprise whatsoever. My sister-in-law Jo, for example, operates what most of the time feels like an 'open house policy'. I was at her home just yesterday and it seemed to me there were more children around her table at kids' supper-time than in the whole of my daughter's reception class! Bearing in mind the catastrophic leap our lives have taken from Sunday bagel heaven to dinner lady reality, it's no wonder we feel like meal machines for most of each day.

Don't get me wrong, I'm the first to invite friends for supper/mums and their toddlers for lunch/my family for Sunday brunch, creating a whole bank of happy kitchen memories. There's no doubt that if I were in an office all day choosing between a limited array of limp egg mayo/tuna sweetcorn baps and a melted Kit Kat, I'd look fondly on my time as multi-tasking writer/mum/chef. Having said that, there is a very fine line between making 'the food of love' and the conveyor belt of meals that seems to be an integral part of many modern mums' lives. With this thought in mind I set myself the task of investigating how to make food fun again.

Mother knows best

'I'd simply had enough of cooking my way to an early grave. I now insist on shutting up shop two evenings a

269

week. If the family wants feeding, the husband or kids must cook a meal for us all or dial for a take-away. This new rule isn't up for discussion, I'm afraid, and lo and behold my thirteen-year-old has mastered a very fine macaroni cheese recipe!'

Full-time mum of two

Making Food Fun Again . . . and Meals More Manageable

The words 'food' and 'fun' said together evoke the kind of playful images of kids' meals that I hate. Cheese muffins with vegetable appliquéd smiley faces or mini-chicken pies made into the shape of boats sailing on a sea of peas under a potato sun; all very cute and accessible in the photographic pages of Annabel Karmel's bestselling cookbooks, but a bloody nightmare for busy mums who barely have time to think beyond fish fingers, let alone making a meal fit for the Turner Prize! Maybe with this in mind I should take 'fun' out of the title for this sub-chapter altogether? Anyway, the idea remains the same: to offer a few tricks and tips to make the endless rounds of family cooking a little easier.

I spent a while looking at my working week and the dawning realisation that making food for myself, my family and friends counted for a large proportion of each day (believe it or not, even the days I lock myself away to write seem underpinned by a cycle of dirty dishes and rounds of Marmite toast). I spoke to my mum friends (a mixture of full-time mums and mums who go out to work) and got an idea of how much they cooked and what pleasure/pain they gained from the daily cycle of being responsible for the nutrition of their family unit (with the exception of my sister-in-law, Jo, who it seems is responsible for the nutrition of the whole extended family and all of North London's under-eights). Bar a small handful of mums who have partners who undertake the childcare and household responsibilities, I'd say ninety per cent of all the women I spoke to do almost all the cooking within the home.

For many of these mums, cooking breakfast and supper for five, making packed lunches for three, hosting Sunday lunch for twelve and a children's birthday party for twenty-six is all on top of working hellish hours in full or part-time jobs. OK, some may have a child carer who unloads the dishwasher now and then, but how many working women do you know who come in from a long day's graft in the office to well-fed kids, faces immaculate and homework done, a pot-roast in the oven and a glass of red wine poured and waiting on the kitchen table? My point exactly!

After accumulating a multitude of mums' voices (and boy, can we mums talk when it comes to discussing feeding the five thousand), I've devised a hit list of ideas that may help ease the burden and, dare I say it, make food 'fun' again. (Please, do me a favour and think of 'fun' and cooking in terms of a messy Jamie Oliver family-style kitchen not an immaculate picture of perfection in the vein of a *Vogue* food shoot!)

Eat supper as a family at least once or twice a week.
I started to realise very early on in my research (if picking
the brains of fellow mums over tea and a digestive biscuit
can be labelled 'research'), that cooking one supper for your
children at five o'clock and another for you and your partner
after the kids have gone to bed often fed our lethargy with
food (excuse the pun!). I know it's hard when you have very
young kids, but once your children are four-plus you could
try eating all together as a family (or just with one parent
if the other works late) a couple of times a week. I find that
on weekdays this is harder, mainly because the children are
starving when they leave school and need to eat almost as
soon as they step through the front door. However, at weekends eating together is definitely worth a try. This serves two
worthwhile purposes: the first that whoever is cooking the
meal only cooks it once; the second that the kids are much
more likely to experiment with new foods, learn good table
manners (as long as yours are up to scratch thereby setting
a good example!) and engage in some good family chit-chat.

Admittedly, it's not as relaxing as tucking into supper safe
in the knowledge the children are in bed, leaving you free
to totally unwind (hurled ketchup, demands for juice, cries
of 'He got more pudding than meeee!' spring to mind), but
slurp a good glass of wine and keep your cool and you'll be
amazed at how easy it can be! Or make lunchtime the main
meal of the day so you can still maintain your evening's
peace. The big Sunday roast is the perfect tradition for bringing
the family together, if you can face the extra work!

Take turns to socialise. In every social group, pack of school mums or posse of old university pals there are one or two mums who do more than their fair share of entertaining. I've talked about my sister-in-law Jo as one such mum. Another is Nicky, a fellow school mum, who rain or shine has half of my son's nursery class back to hers for lunch after the Wednesday morning drama group. I also do my fair share of coffee mornings, mums' lunches, free-for-all teas and grown-up boozy supper parties.

I'm the first to admit I often love a full house and compliments on my batch of hot muffins, but it's also important to share out the socialising in order to prevent catching the 'I feel like a dinner lady' bug. It's virtually impossible to invite yourself to other people's homes, but you could suggest a picnic or an 'each mum bring a dish' rule to help share out the workload (and cost). This may even prompt another mother or carer to open up their home.

Picnics. I don't know about you, but it's often not so much the cooking I mind, but the clearing and washing up afterwards. (You know the scene, peas scattered the length of the kitchen, chicken ground into the chair seat and mashed potato smeared across the French windows.) To avoid being the cleaning lady as well as the dinner lady for much of the day, as soon the weather is nice enough I try to incorporate picnics into our day-to-day life whenever possible. I use 'picnic' as a loose term because this can mean anything from a 'proper' picnic at Highgate woods before my son's afternoon nursery session (yes, I even include paper cups and napkins) to a 'home picnic' where I plate the kids' supper, lay a rug in the garden and they eat al fresco (meaning the stray peas roll into the flowerbeds and not between the slate tiles where they have to be cautiously prised out).

Often in the summer a cold supper of an open ham, cheese and tomato sandwich, some carrot sticks, a few low-salt crisps, a yogurt and a piece of fruit (followed by a Magnum from the ice-cream van, of course!) is all the children need.

Helping hands. A key rule I applied to both my children almost as soon as they could walk was to help around the house. This often starts with the kitchen. Everything from laying the table and fetching ketchup, butter or chopped salad from the fridge to filling their plastic water cups from the tap saves me time. These sorts of helpful chores can lead on to jobs like stirring the pasta/grating cheese/chopping salad (for the elder children and always under my watchful eye), to washing the vegetables and plating the salmon fish cakes. The children always feel super-helpful and in this situation more hands make less work.

Make food to last. I've listed a whole host of recipes at the back of the book that will help busy mums make food to last. I hope my meal ideas will also suit the whole family (preventing you having to cook one thing for the children and another for the adults). The idea is to offer up some easy-peasy, delicious recipes that you can cook at your leisure and will last you a few days (and, if frozen, even longer). Things like pasta sauces, roasted vegetables, couscous, fish pie and roast chicken are ideal for this and mean you can make it in bulk once and sit back while it's enjoyed for a few meals at the very least.

Have your limits.   At the end of the day you are many things to many people but you're not a slave to the kitchen! Sometimes at six o'clock in the evening when my children call in unison for a snack, faces firmly glued to a DVD, I can't help myself from walking in to turn off the TV and nicely but firmly telling them that if they want anything more from the kitchen they must walk their little legs into the next-door room and get it for themselves! I have a dry-foods cupboard within easy reach which contains nothing but oatcakes, rice cakes, unsalted nuts, dry fruits and muesli bars. At this point in the day both kids know it's time to get off their bottoms, fetch their own oat cake snacks and keep their mouths firmly shut! (Bless them for learning so quickly . . .)

Mother knows best

'I absolutely insist my partner shares the cooking each night; it was almost a pre-nup! We both work and I come home to cook the kids' tea after school so every other night it's absolutely fair that Tom makes dinner for the two of us. He's always enjoyed cooking so I'm lucky there, but even if he didn't, a simple pasta dish or some grilled fish would do, I just want a few nights off from the oven, that's all.'

Full-time working mum of twins

Nutrition Secrets for Fabulous Kids

Ironic, I know: on the one hand you're trying to make your work in the kitchen less, on the other you're trying to get your little cherubs to eat super-healthy nutritious meals for breakfast, lunch (even if that's packed) and supper. Cooking wholesome, delicious, enticing food is at the fore of many a mum's parenting mantra. And so it should be; we can hardly harp on about our healthy-eating regimes as mothers and our desire to have calm, happy kids if we feed them junk morning, noon and night.

I won't go on and on about the benefits of giving your children a varied diet. There can't be a mum out there who hasn't read at least one children's nutrition book, watched a 'you are what you eat'-type horror show illustrating the monstrous beast your child will become if he/she continues to eat junk, or been witness to the ripples of the Jamie Oliver school dinners campaign across the nation. This aside, the desire to feed and nurture our offspring well is a core maternal instinct in many women I know; it's just that time restrictions, lack of imagination or finances get in the way of all this. The simple question is this: how do you formulate a well-balanced diet for your kids and how do you manage it with ease, speed and efficiency?

Inspire from early on

It sounds pretty obvious doesn't it? But if you try to inspire your baby with food from early on she's likely to respond with an interest in food well into childhood. Letting your baby join in at meal times (even if she does little more than bash her highchair with a spoon and cover her hair with mashed papaya), having an array of colourful finger foods (chopped banana, carrots, raspberries) on offer, and letting her experiment with mouthfuls of safe adult food will all evoke an interest in and love of food.

Obviously, baby food in jars and packet snacks are fine as long as they're used with caution (my kids have always loved the Peter Rabbit brand with no added salt, sugar or preservatives). By this I mean use them when you're out and about on the go or possibly at a restaurant/friend's house for lunch, but not for every meal, every day of the week. Giving your baby jars or ready-made baby food can be a slippery slope of ease and convenience while limiting the child's diversity of flavours and textures. My daughter, for instance, was very partial to a jar of Organix pasta bolognese. It came in handy whenever we were out for the day or I was having to spoon-feed her from the passenger seat of the car on long journeys. However, she became so used to the specific flavour and texture that it took months of spitting out, refusal to open her mouth and raging tantrums before she reluctantly tried my home-made version of the same meal. Needless to say she's five now and will eat mum's homemade bolognese pasta by the truck-load!

Food is fuel

I'm constantly amazed at the amount of energy my children have. My son in particular has been renamed 'Sky Rocket' due to the speed and enthusiasm with which he embraces life! From the moment his eyes ping open in the morning to the time I coax him into slumber at night, he's go-go-go! I find that the best way to sustain this energy (and there's a difference between a constant zest for the day's activity and a hyperactive maniac!) has been to maintain food routines to structure his day.

Breakfast

I am a true believer in breakfast for the whole family. My daughter, who is at school for the whole day, needs a good breakfast to fuel her for work and play. She'll have a piece of fruit mid-morning and then a light, packed lunch at noon, so it's a priority to ensure she's got a full stomach to start the day. Luckily she's like me and loves breakfast, so getting her to sit down for a large glass of fruit smoothie (it was apple and blackcurrant this morning), some muesli or toast with sugar-free jam or peanut butter, is no problem whatsoever.

My son is slightly trickier as he's far more likely to want to entertain us with a puppet show during breakfast than actually eat anything himself! Having said that, I'll always manage to get him to gobble at least one live, fruit yogurt with some raisins and cashews sprinkled on top and on a good day he'll let me persuade him to have some wholemeal bread toasted Marmite soldiers as well. If all this fails (which I'd say at least once a week it does), I'll be left with no option but the 'Cheerios-and-fruit-on-the-go' one. This means simply throwing some dried Cheerios into a small Tupperware pot, adding a sliced banana on top so he can eat it in the car while we take my daughter to school. Not ideal I know, but a familiar scenario for many mums, I'm sure!

Lunch and supper

Along with breakfast I always try to ensure my children have a good lunch and an equally nutritious supper. I try to make sure both meals have a good chunk of carbohydrates (usually in the form of wholemeal pasta or sweet potato), protein (I won't lie here and suggest this takes the shape of tuna steaks, king prawns or veal. It is far more likely to be roast chicken, a chunky, meaty bolognese sauce or some salmon), and vegetables (luckily my children love broccoli, so this accompanies every meal along with carrots/peas/cucumber/sweetcorn). I have a rule that every meal is finished off with fresh fruit or yogurt (alternating for lunch/supper, or if the kids are hungry they have both). After supper, if they've done well and eaten a good proportion of their meal and pudding they are allowed a 'treat'. By 'treat' I mean a chocolate finger, a home-made iced lolly (just frozen fruit juice), cookie or something similar. Now I know a lot of families insist on just fruit as pudding but I remember enjoying the odd treat as a child and I see nothing wrong with a taste of something small and sugary if they've been good and eaten a well-balanced diet throughout the day.

Healthy snacks

My friend's daughter, Minnie, eats three large meals a day and never snacks. Her mum, Jennie, says when Minnie comes to spend the day in our house, her eyes light up with the knowledge that snacks will be available throughout the day! I've always found that my kids need little snacks mid-morning and mid-afternoon to give them an energy boost.

My daughter for example is like a grumpy Gruffalo if she doesn't have a few oatcakes or a banana between school pick-up and suppertime. Be careful not to overload your kids with snacks (this may put them off their main meals), but a few little nibbles here and there always work a treat in our house.

Snacks I recommend are: raisins, oatcakes, rice cakes, some cubes of cheese, carrot sticks, any fruit and sometimes, if we're out at friends or in a café, they'll be offered a croissant/mini-muffin/biscuit.

'Kids' food'

I'm the first to admit that my children are fans of the foods our culture have now labelled 'kids' foods' and which you see on children's menus everywhere. It would be silly for me to deny that chicken nuggets, fish fingers, sausages, chips and pasta, pasta and more pasta aren't part of my kids' diets. In fact, I know very few parents who don't have these somewhere in their kids' weekly eating plan. The trick is to try not to make this a basis for their whole diet. Sure, we'll have sausages, sweet potato mash and a heap of veg every few weeks (and fish fingers even more) but I'll mix this up with fresh fish, roast chicken and really simple things like cheese on toast. You can do home-made 'junk food' too that is actually perfectly healthy. I make my own chicken nuggets as much as possible (well, it's my friend Sara's recipe actually) to ensure I know exactly what type of chicken is going in the middle of the crumb!

Being imaginative with packed lunches

It's very hard when you're rushed off your feet in the morning to pack an imaginative lunch for your kids. In my fantasy world my child's packed lunch would be stuffed with an array of small pots containing couscous, pasta salads, cold meats and chopped baby tomatoes, accompanied by some nutritious, home-made flapjack cookies and a heap of fruit – all of which they'll eat gleefully (yeah, right!). The reality for many parents is to stuff a limp sandwich, a cheese straw, a ready-mixed drink and a packet of chocolate buttons into their lunchbox and send them on their way.

I think the problem is not just time-related but also competitive lunch envy (and that's between kids not mums). It's very hard to give your child carrot sticks and wholemeal bread if her best friend has crisps and chocolate mousse. For this reason alone I go down on bended knee in thanks to my daughter's school. The headmistress is almost as nutritionally aware as Jane Clarke, my guru for this chapter, and has from day one insisted on healthy packed lunches. So stringent is her ethos that there is a ban on any sweets, chocolate, cakes, biscuits and crisps and only water is permitted as a drink (and don't be fooled into thinking this isn't enforced: my daughter returned home with her Innocent smoothie last week telling me, 'Just water, remember, Mummy!'). To many of you this may sound ruthless but in actual fact it's forced us parents to be imaginative.

Having a fruit-only snack at school mid-morning also means that when my daughter sits down for her lunch she's hungry enough to eat pretty much what's packed. As a parent you're safe in the knowledge that your child won't baulk at her selection of healthy sandwiches just because Jack/Kara/George has an array of Quavers and Dairylea Dunkers!

A warning about salt, sugar and additives

The moment your child is active in the big, wide world it's very tricky to avoid their requests for what can only be described as rubbish food! Gone are the days when you can spoon-feed them organic vegetable hot-pot or stewed cod, sweet potato and orange segments. Oh no! They'll be lured by TV advertisements for multi-coloured, sugar-packed ice lollies and stretchy cheese, they'll be peering eagerly at the crisps aisle in Tesco and they'll be introduced to a whole array of junk food at kids' parties. Hey presto, before you know it, all that effort you made to keep their diets salt and additive free, will be undone by the latest gimmick which turns their tongue purple for two days or resembles a toy more than food. I've already confessed to giving my children a daily 'treat' (and I said 'giving', not being whined at for an hour until I 'give-in'). They often have a few plain biscuits, some organic low-salt crisps, and the odd bag of chocolate buttons. I confess that on a long-haul flight recently I took a stash of lollipops and chocolate delights for take-off and landing. So I'm no saint, believe me. Having said that, I do feel it's our right as parents to be responsible about our children's intake of salt, sugar and additives (and this means 'ham' slices in the shape of their favourite characters and plastic-like cheese are banned!). There are times when you have to, or even want to, bend the rules (come on, it's hardly fair to eat your way through a Twix and then insist your child has an organic apple!), but in general we all owe it to our little ones to try to give them healthy, balanced choices and to limit their intake of salt, sugar, additives and gimmicky food choices.

Don't ignore the liquids!

You might be virtuously giving your kids organic stews and fruit-only treats, but if you allow them ready-to-drink cartons or fruit-flavoured waters you may as well give them a bag of boiled sweets or a can of full-sugar fizzy pop. Even if you're giving them no/low-sugar drinks, the artificial sweeteners they're packed with carry their own risks. I'd like to say my kids only drink tap water and, although they don't mind it, the truth is that they opt for juice every time. In most cases I tend to do what I've done since they were babies and dilute some real fruit juice (not from concentrate) with water (around a quarter juice, the rest tap water).

The challenge of a fussy eater

It's actually unfair to call my daughter a 'fussy eater' because it's hard to know how much of her 'fuss' comes from severe allergies to egg and sesame that have underpinned her relationship with food since very early on. When she was eight months old I gave her hummus (which includes sesame, of course) as a dip for her pitta bread. What followed was a serious anaphylactic shock which involved her lip swelling to the size of a golf ball in the blink of an eye, her body breaking out head-to-toe with hives and her breathing slowing down to a terrifying rate. I have since had her tested for every food under the sun and carry both antihistamine and an EpiPen wherever we go. However, over the course of her five-year life she has had several re-occurring attacks (one was on holiday where she ate a sausage that had been bound with egg), which have shaped her relationship with and 'fear' of certain foods.

The result is a child who loves to eat, but has formed very strict meals and food groups she considers 'safe'. For example, as I mentioned she loves pasta bolognese but won't try other sauces, she adores cheese on toast, but it has to be dabbed with Marmite, she'll gobble up my home-made fish pie but daren't taste anyone else's. My son has his bouts of fussy eating, but a few offers of something new and he's usually swayed. My daughter, on the other hand, is scared of the effect a new food might have on her and the fear often over-rides her common-sense logic about trying something different. (Can you believe it was only this summer that we convinced her to try home-made chips!)

I have tried all sorts of approaches to get my daughter to experiment more with new foods (some of which have worked, others not). Here are a few tips you could try:

- **Stay calm:** Whatever you do, try not to get angry, uptight or stressed. Easier said than done I know, but if you turn on the pressure, your child will turn off the enthusiasm.
- **Eat together:** I find eating with my daughter makes her feel calmer and more involved with the meal. If we're trying something new together she's often more likely to ask for a small bite if I explain exactly what it is and enthusiastically eat it myself, rather than if it just appears on her plate with no explanation.

- **Give them a choice:** If I want my daughter to try something new I often give her a choice of a few things at once. By saying 'Do you want to try tuna, goats' cheese or marinated courgette?' for example, I'm handing the power back to her.
- **Start small:** Try not to overload the child's plate with a new food, it will really put them off. Start small and build it up. (I've even once started with just one pea!) But if they just put that tiny morsel of food in their mouth you're halfway there.
- **Decoys are OK:** It's not a habit I want to repeat every meal but sometimes if I read to my kids over supper this takes the emphasis away from the 'new' food and helps eliminate any potential stress. (It's amazing how much a good princess tale helped when introducing white fish!)
- **Reward, reward, reward:** A chocolate treat, a sticker chart or, for a really big achievement, a visit to the toy shop, are wonderful incentives for fussy eaters. For my daughter in particular, trying a new dish can be a huge hurdle and rewarding her courage is paramount.
- **Involve them:** Asking kids to help with the shopping and cooking takes away a lot of their fear of food; it also empowers them to choose items. You never know, they may well find something you didn't even think about selecting. My daughter, for example, asked to try a yam when she spotted it on a shopping trip in Waitrose – I had to raid the recipe books for ideas on cooking dinner that evening!
- **Try, try and try again:** My husband swears it takes a child ten times or more to try a new food they're wary

of. (He probably read this in the Sunday papers back in the days when we had time to read the papers.) I do know from experience that offering food once, twice or even three times is rarely enough; you have to keep on offering it, with unwavering enthusiasm, until you see the tide might be about to turn.

Manners matter

Am I really old-fashioned to expect good manners at the meal table? I'm not saying using a knife and fork from the age of one, but for school-age kids this should surely be encouraged? Sitting nicely at the table, waiting for the other children to finish before leaving the table and asking the golden question 'Please may I get down?' are all obligatory in our kitchen. It may seem outdated but I'm afraid these rules are here to stay!

Believe me, it's not that I want to create some sort of stuffy restaurant environment around the kitchen table, it's just that I really believe good table manners encourage calmer mealtimes and respect for the food we eat. I daren't hope for immaculate manners for the duration of every single meal (my son's annoying habit of trying to eat with his fingers and squeezing vast amounts of ketchup on everything ensures this is an impossibility anyway!) but aiming for good manners most of the time is a good start.

Set a good example

The only sure-fire way to get your children to eat well and value nutrition is to live by example. If you tend to eat fish and chips while watching your favourite soap opera you can hardly expect your nippers to request a green salad and beansprouts! Make eating well a family affair and you'll all benefit, I promise.

Nutrition Secrets for a Fabulous (but Busy) Mum

I confess the more children I have the harder it is to maintain the nutritional habits and body shape I'm happy with. When I had my daughter I was in my mid-twenties and I just had to think about losing weight and my body obeyed.

I could skip supper one night and drop a dress size the next morning (at least that's how it felt). I seemed to live off green salads for lunch without feeling hungry and floated from one fashion launch to the next nibbling canapés and keeping my arm readily outstretched for the next passing glass of champagne. I don't remember shopping with a particularly alert nutritional conscience, either. OK, I made sure my trolley was filled with fresh fruit and vegetables, but in went with the Kettle Chips and Snickers bars too. Weight concerns or energy dips just weren't part of my vocabulary.

A lot of women I know feel the same. For example, Sexy Samantha (sorry, this nickname seems to have stuck – let's just call her 'Sam' from now on), was always a size eight. We met just after university and I always remember hooking up with her in bars, where heads would turn as she arrived in skintight leggings, black sky-high court shoes and a figure-hugging jersey dress (the obligatory red lipstick firmly applied to those famous plump lips). Sam would wolf down the bar snacks along with her martinis and then at midnight as we caught the last tube home, she'd gobble a burger or kebab, managing somehow to keep her red lips intact. At her desk she'd eat jelly beans and Jaffa Cakes and never, ever tipped the scales past nine stone.

Sam is the first to confess that now she has kids, life is a different story. A curvaceous size twelve, she really has to work at her weight. She eats Special K with skimmed milk for breakfast, goes to the gym most days before work and limits herself to sushi or a chicken salad (with a light dressing) for lunch. Come the evening it's a virtuous steamed this or that and only a small dollop of her husband's cheddar cheese mash. If she's feeling very good she does confess to doing an extra fifteen minutes on her resident exercise bike before allowing herself a fat-free yogurt while watching her favourite show, *Ugly Betty*. Sam swears that the moment she hit thirty it became much much harder to stay trim and feel good about herself. (Childbirth, breastfeeding and a decade drinking booze like a fish I'm sure contributed to this too.) No doubt many of you will sympathise with her sentiments. I know I certainly do.

It's not only that it becomes harder to achieve your ideal weight, but it's true that your body shape alters after childbirth (stretch marks, saggy boobs, that extra roll of tummy that won't shift even with a million sit-ups every morning). A multitude of women I spoke to agreed that they hardly recognised their twenty-year-old bodies in comparison to their post-kids bodies. I know there are mums out there who come hell or high water will stay super-svelte and skinny into their late-thirties and beyond. Let's be honest though, this is often due to a large amount of dosh spent on personal trainers, nutritionists, beauty treatments and cosmetic surgeons. Most women I know just don't have the money, time or desire to go through all that in the pursuit of the body beautiful.

Combined with your changing body shape comes a shift in your lifestyle. Whereas once you may have been in the throes of first passion (far too love-sick to eat), rushing around in a new job (working all the hours God sent to get that promotion) and possibly even managing to squeeze in that all important spinning class after work, you're now cooking endless rounds of fish pie with apple crumble for afters and nesting at home with a tub of vanilla ice cream, which is more than well deserved now the children are in bed and the ironing is done. Often you're so busy keeping up with the nutritional demands of your offspring (organic this, freshly pureed that and a colour pallet on the plate that makes it look like a Van Gogh print) that your own nutritional needs fall well below anything else on your 'to-do' list. Let's be honest, you're more likely to grab a ham sandwich or a bag of crisps than steam yourself some seabass for lunch, true?

It doesn't take a genius to figure out that a compromised body shape and adjustment to your new size fourteen jeans (the size ten pair went to the Cancer Research shop some years ago!), combined with a lack of zest for cooking for yourself, equals one very grumpy, frumpy mum! I know, I've been there. Just a few months before I fell pregnant for the third time I'd been totally frazzled by work deadlines. Suddenly my clothes were feeling just a little bit snug and I'd fallen into the habit of eating pizza take-aways, Marks & Spencer's ready-meals and quick-fix energy hits (in the form of anything beginning and ending in chocolate) that could be gobbled late into the night at my desk.

It's very hard to keep up with the demands of being a busy mum and not let something slip. More often than not that 'something' happens to be our nutritional know-how, needs and motivation. To stop beating myself up about the unwashed mound of clothes I could no longer pull over my thighs and the pile of empty pizza boxes that filled my recycle bin outside, I needed to correct my own nutritional shortfalls and pinpoint some good areas to tackle. You see, for most bright, modern mums the knowledge is there – we just need a little prompting every now and then to get us back on the right track (or as Sam says 'give us a kick up the bottom when we need it!'). If you're in need of a light shift in focus then take note and begin today!

Start with a good breakfast

I know how hard it can be to start the day with a wholesome breakfast, but the same rule I set for the kids has to apply to me too. I fully empathise with the fact that some mornings you're so pleased to cling on to that last five minutes in bed that you sacrifice that fresh smoothie for a much quicker croissant-and-latte-on-the-run. Equally, you're more than likely to be so busy doing everything you can to get your little ones to eat a healthy, fortifying breakfast that you'll forfeit your own breakfast in the process. Heaps of mums I've chatted to about this agree: you're just so manic in the morning, spoon-feeding the youngest Weetabix, searching for your middle child's library book and screeching at your eldest to remember his PE kit that cooking yourself a scrambled egg to accompany some rye-toast is a joke!

All this crazed multi-tasking rings very true (I live it every morning), but that doesn't mean attempting a good brekkie isn't worth a try. As I've said before, I swear by my home-made muesli topped with fresh fruit and yogurt (or the rice alternative to milk, Rice Dream). All of these can be prepared in advance (the muesli weeks before and stored in an air-tight jar, the fruit the day before and kept in a sealed bowl or container in the fridge). On a cold day bunging some milk in the microwave before stirring in some organic oats, a handful of raisins, possibly a couple of chopped apricots and a small heap of almonds is as good a breakfast as any (often better, as oats will hold off hunger for longer than many other breakfast cereals).

I promise if you give yourself five minutes to sit down with a cup of tea (green or jasmine are my favourites) and a bowl of the above, you'll feel energised all morning. You'll also be much less likely to dive into Starbucks for a large cappuccino and walk out with a double chocolate muffin too!

Healthy snacks rule

Just like the busy kids who allow themselves a good hearty breakfast and don't need a snack to get them through to lunchtime, some mums are no different. My wonderful friend Ros, for example, who even at ten weeks pregnant (and a sure sign for me that hunger will strike like a ravenous beast, on the hour, every hour) can start the day with a heap of berries and seeds and not need a fill-up until her working lunch break. Sadly, I am not one of these mums. I am a snacker through and through and need a ten a.m. food break, not only for a nutritional boost but simply because the thought of a banana with my cup of Earl Grey or maybe even a large dollop of manuka honey on an oatcake lifts my spirits immeasurably.

If you're of the snacking type, then welcome! However, join with a word of caution; there are the 'good' snackers and the 'not-so-good' snackers. The first camp is the one I try my best to remain in for the majority of the time. 'Good' snacking includes a vast array of fruits and raw vegetables; oatcakes with a variety of 'healthy' toppings (banana with a spot of sugar-free peanut butter, almond paste, cream cheese and low-fat ham or cottage cheese); low-fat organic yogurts; and those biscuits that are on the virtuous side (Rich Tea and digestives are ideal). 'Not-so-good' snacking, on the other hand, includes muffins, cakes, chocolate, sweets, pastries and anything else laden with saturated fats and sugar. Of course I'll enjoy the occasional delicacy from above (just flick through my 'Tea-time Treats' recipes at the back of the book and you'll see) but to balance these treats, the healthy snack rule I like to follow is: for eighty-five per cent of snacking only eat good snacks, then for the remaining fifteen per cent you can indulge in chocolate covered HobNobs, Fabulous Mum's ginger cake, chocolate and banana 'monkey muffins' and cream teas. But remember, always snack in moderation, no matter what you're eating, otherwise you won't enjoy the benefits of your main meals.

Don't skip meals

For many of us skipping meals seems the easy way to stay trim. Often if you're in a busy job or rushing around with the kids it may not even be a conscious decision, but just one made in haste. Whatever the reason, skipping meals (and more often than not it's lunch which is forgone) means you'll have a real energy crash later on. It was only yesterday that I had some friends here for tea and one mum had been so busy sorting out the decorators in her new house, calling for carpet samples, arguing with her mobile phone company over a lost cheque, and picking up her daughter from school, that she'd bypassed lunch altogether. When she arrived here at four o'clock she dived into the cake tin and didn't re-emerge until home-time.

I always find that if I skip my lunch I'll do exactly the

same and end up scoffing a bag of crisps on my way to school pick-up. Not only this, I'll feel far more tired than usual and behave like a bear with a sore head when my husband returns home in the evening. As with children, you need to keep your sugar levels constant and your energy levels high throughout the day. The only way to do this is to eat three good, slow-burning meals at spaced-out intervals.

Try not to pick at the kids' food

If you eat your main meal once the kids are in bed then try not to gobble up all their five o'clock supper too! It can be hard not to swipe that roast chicken drumstick or left-over heap of cold fries but you'll soon pile on the pounds if you have two suppers every night! The temptation to pick at their food is strong I know, so I opt for a healthy snack to eat with my children at kids' tea-time. This could be anything from some fresh fruit and live yogurt to a small bowl of my breakfast muesli. Really it's just something to fill that hunger gap and stop me tucking into all the left-overs before stacking the plates in the dishwasher.

Wicked wine!

Sadly, wine, and just about every other alcoholic beverage we love, is bad for us too. When I'm not breeding or breast-feeding I easily find myself slipping into the habit of guzzling a glass (or three) of the sacred vino every night! The thing is, not only is it full of calories but I also find that if I drink a few glasses before dinner it just makes me want to snack on everything in the fridge and more, and that's before I even sit down for supper! My friend Elaine says the same. She'll be incredibly virtuous all day and then the moment she opens a bottle of plonk in the evening all her reasoning and good intention goes out the window. By saving the wine, or whatever your favourite tipple may be, for the weekend (and the odd weeknight treat) you'll find the week is less of a blur and that it's easier to stick to eating moderately and healthily. Not only will you enjoy it more at the weekend but you'll also find that family-sized bar of chocolate you've been hiding in the fridge will last all week!

Exercise and feel good

There's no point in eating well and taking your nutrition seriously if you don't combine this with a little exercise. I mean this for the whole family too. Walking the school run, going for a twice-weekly (or more if you can) run/swim/cycle/gym session/yoga class will help you burn off calories and release those all-important endorphins which help you feel energised. Added to this you'll boost your self-esteem enormously as any exercise you do, even if it's opting for the stairs at work over the lift, will help you get your body and your groove back.

Mother knows best

'I've always tried to eat a varied and balanced diet, but I'm a sucker for carbohydrates and can't resist pasta, noodles and bread. Especially now I have a child, I tend to live off rounds of toast and quick pasta dishes with ready-made sauces. The only problem with this is they tend to really bulk me up and I was starting to find my size sixteen clothes a squeeze. I've started to limit myself to toast in the morning and then one carb-heavy meal a day (usually lunch, so it releases energy slowly throughout the afternoon), and I try to stick to proteins and salads in the evening. It didn't take too long before my snug jeans were fitting perfectly again.'

Full-time working mum of one

Shopping *en masse*

I'm going to presume here that on most occasions the weekly food trip requires you towing your brood around the supermarket. Admittedly, I sometimes (and I stress sometimes) manage a quiet stroll around the supermarket, happy in the knowledge that my daughter is at school, my son is at a playdate and my editor isn't waiting for the imminent arrival of the first draft. These carefree shops for food are heaven in comparison to the crazed dart around the supermarket that is shopping *en masse*. I love browsing the aisles, carefully selecting the juiciest seasonal fruit, discovering exotic ingredients I've never heard of and browsing the wine shelves for a good deal.

However, the reality is the majority of my shopping trips end up feeling like crazed stopwatch hit-and-run raids. Having said that, I have discovered on my quest for making motherhood more fabulous, that there are ways of making shopping *en masse* a little easier for all, none of which involve allowing the kids to stand in the trolley, hurling abuse at fellow shoppers and eating unpaid-for crisps.

Pre-planning is essential. Make a list, preferably the night before you go, of all the things you'll need. This is key to a smooth, stress-free (well, almost!) shopping trip. If you're willing to go all-out on the organisation front, then why not plan some or all of the meals for the week ahead? That way you're more likely to remember all the ingredients and less likely to buy any unnecessary foods that may go to waste (a great money-saving device that my friend Jennie swears by).

For most families the only window for doing the food shop is at the weekend. Sadly, this is when all the other families are doing their shopping too, so if you can bear it, go early. Now I don't mean setting the alarm for the crack of dawn, but once you're all up I say get going and get it out of the way! But have breakfast first so you're not fending off the demands (and your own temptation) for freshly baked pastries. Once you're en route, I always find that reiterating some simple rules on how to behave while shopping helps to eliminate the tiresome need for telling the children off every five minutes once you're there. No one wants to be 'that' mum in the supermarket who's lost all control and can only resort to empty threats.

I find the key to a successful shop is not only knowing what you want before you get there, but involving the children in the selection process. It's great for their nutritional awareness to be involved in selecting fresh, healthy produce and as I said earlier it may also help picky eaters to feel involved in what they're being offered. If you have the energy you can even make little games as you go around. For some inexplicable reason my two squeal with excitement when I say, 'Who can select the biggest cucumber?' and my son in particular is obsessed with selecting the heaviest sweet potato from the pile. I also ask them to do things like counting out ten green apples or using the tongs to put four croissants into a bag. It sounds laborious but it keeps their enthusiasm-tank full and defuses any possible boredom.

Even Lotte finds supermarket shopping with the wonderfully behaved Ava a challenge. She says it all goes well until they hit the sweet aisles and then it all goes to pot. Any parent knows that these aisles are tantalising to say the least. You could avoid them altogether (but any child over the age of three will have that sussed immediately), *or* you could, and I can't believe I'm going to say this and risk a large sack of hate mail from the anti-sugar squad, let your children have one *small* treat to get the whole family around the supermarket intact and still sane. Let's be honest, a mini Mars bar won't kill anyone, will it, and in dire situations I feel we can be forgiven for succumbing, don't you?

It sounds ridiculous really, that I'm laying out how to shop successfully with kids in tow, but any mum who does it on a regular basis will know what a headache it can be. By far the worst part can be the queuing, the packing and the paying part. It's at the tillpoints that you often see siblings tearing large chunks of each other's hair out or a mum looking red-faced and harassed, as she piles yet another box of cereal onto the conveyor belt, her newborn's screams piercing the air. What I try to do is take a couple of children's books or magazines in my handbag, which I offer to the kids to read while I'm packing. We start with them helping me to unload the trolley – which lasts all of six seconds before they'll be looking for a new adventure. This is when I'll whip the reading material from my bag and ask them to sit and read it within my view. If this doesn't last the duration, a bribe of 'one ride on Thomas the Tank Engine' if they sit nicely (or, better still, continue to help unload the trolley), usually does the trick. Obligatory helping to unpack at the other end is part and parcel of the shopping *en masse* chore in our house, but once this is done it's usually still only mid-morning and the weekend can really begin. Phew!

Having deciphered a way of shopping *en masse* with some sort of sanity intact doesn't mean you shouldn't attempt a few pockets of solo food shopping every now and then. Even if it's not a sunny Saturday morning at Borough Market (while your in-laws entertain the children), a little time alone to shop in peace (away from the superstores) is essential for keeping your passion for food alive. It doesn't have to take up much time either. You could try nipping to a local organic store on your lunch break or taking a detour on your way back from dropping the kids at school to a local deli or food market.

Mother knows best

'I always shop once a week with my two kids and once a week alone. I get the basics with the children at the weekend and let them select their own yogurts, snacks,

> fruit and sandwich fillers and then I go one evening to a late-night supermarket, once the kids are in bed, to choose all the lovely things like wine, spices and exotic fruits that I hate to be rushed into deciding on. Thank goodness for twenty-four-hour shopping, eh?'
>
> Full-time working mum of two

Eating out – you must be joking!

Whatever happened to our vast choice of restaurants? Once upon a time eating out went something like this . . .

Me: 'Where do you fancy going for supper, darling?'
Boyfriend: 'Oh I don't know, maybe that nice gastro pub with a garden near the Heath?'
Me: 'Yes, that would be nice. Or shall we go there for a drink first and then stroll over to that cheeky little Italian for delicious antipasti, followed by seafood pasta?'
Boyf: 'Great, I'll just grab my jacket and we can go.'
I'd apply a little lip gloss and off we'd saunter.

Oh, the good old days eh? Now eating out goes something like this . . .

Me: 'Oh Christ! We have to meet so-and-so for Sunday lunch with the kids.'
The once-boyfriend-now-husband: 'Do we have to? Wouldn't

it be easier to eat at home and then meet them for an ice cream in the park later?'

Me: 'You're right, after last weekend's Sunday brunch that ended in full-scale chip war, two tantrums and an ice cream sundae sugar-rush that went on all afternoon, I'd rather walk over hot coals barefoot than eat out as a family on my day of rest.'

That settled I cook the fourth round of kids' fish fingers in a week and butter a bagel for the man and myself. We then stare blankly at our nutritionally invigorating Sunday lunch (not!).

The first hurdle is in actual fact not the potential chaos of eating out *en famille*. No, the problem is often not behavioural at all; rather it's the dire shortage of good family eateries on offer. 'But my local town/broadway/common/village is full of cafés offering kids' menus,' I hear you cry. A-ha, in this we have the real problem! Why is it when you go anywhere 'family-oriented' or 'kid-friendly', you are expected to leave all your nutritional standards at home with the goldfish. Silly, silly us! Why on earth would you equate a long day out with the kids with the need for healthy, nutritious food options? Just as Jamie Oliver highlighted the poor quality of school lunches in his school dinners campaign, leisure activities and kids' menus often fare no better at providing healthy and well-balanced meal options. We all know what a kids' menu entails in the majority of eating establishments. Here I have the standard menu, and I dare you to tell me different!

Kids' menu

Bangers and mash (with a handful of peas if you're lucky);
Chicken nuggets and fries (but dare we ask if this has ever really come in contact with the chicken in question?);
Fish and chips;
Burger and potato wedges (with a limp piece of tomato and lettuce, posing as one of the requisite 'five-a-day').
And to drink . . .
Apple juice (from concentrate, of course).
And to round the insipid feast off . . .
Ice cream – chocolate, strawberry or vanilla (of course the e-number-laden sauce and hundreds and thousands are colourful at least!).

Admittedly, I have been to a handful of restaurants where the choice is somewhat broader (our local branch of Giraffe is an very good example). There is always the option of ordering your kids a small portion of one of the 'grown-up dishes'; however, kids' menus are part of our family-eating culture and there's bound to be one kid in the group who is savvy to your offer of vegetable lasagne and will spy the bright gold kids' menu a mile off, making damn sure they flag the option to the others in a second! I'm not about to start a nationwide campaign for restaurants (and theme parks/indoor play areas/hotels) to re-do their whole approach to kids' food. However, choose carefully where you eat out. Even the nicest restaurants can fall short when it comes to children, so ask. I've even done some of the legwork for you and included a few gems in my 'Useful Addresses' section at the back of this book.

Once you've sussed the good, the bad and the ugly you may feel brave enough to tackle Sunday lunch with your best buddy and her brood. The question then is how do you keep everyone happy and well behaved while you guzzle a glass of house white and catch up on the latest gossip?

Eating out tricks and tips

Pack some healthy snacks for the kids. If you're anything like me, you probably won't make it to the restaurant until gone one o'clock and it may well take a full hour for the food to arrive once you've ordered. Some carrot sticks or cherry tomatoes will help keep hunger at bay and will also help matters if they order nothing but chicken and chips as their main course!

Take some colouring books and crayons. Although many restaurants have good kids' activity sheets, it may be wise to take a little something extra if you have time (especially if you've been brave and gone for a not specifically child-oriented restaurant). Sticker books are always a fun distraction too. (I would, however, limit activities to this. I recently arrived at a local gastro pub to see a couple of brothers glued to a portable DVD system; hardly the right way to evoke good manners or encourage social skills!)

After ordering, ask the children if they need to go to the toilet. This may help the usual stampede for the loo immediately as your food arrives and that second glass of wine is being poured! It's also good to encourage the practice of washing hands before mealtime.

Nine times out of ten, I find that if you do the above and take the time before you leave to remind your children how to behave in restaurants (i.e. sat at the table and not acting as trip hazards for the waiting staff), you should enjoy a pleasant, sociable lunch out with friends all with the added bonus of not having to wash up afterwards. Hurrah!

Mother knows best

'I'm so fed up with the limited choice of good kids' restaurants. You either have to sit in what feels like a soft-play free-for-all, eating shit food, or go somewhere fancy for rich dishes that the kids will then push around their plates. No thanks! Along with my close mummy friends we've decided that in winter we'll all take it in turns to host the weekend lunch, bringing a dish each time, and in summer we'll go *en masse* to the local park and take a picnic with minimum fuss and hassle. We've saved a fortune and I don't think I've seen chicken nuggets in the shape of the letters of the alphabet once this year!'

Full-time mum of two

Candle-lit dinners

For this chapter at least I've saved the best until last. I started this section with a good moan about being a 'meal machine', before moving on to grumble about shopping *en masse* and the trials of eating out with your ever-growing family. Joking aside, I have had many wonderful meals with my children and most of the time don't mind in the slightest slaving over a hot stove to give them yummy and nutritious meals. This doesn't, however, change the fact that the very best meals in the week are those spent with my husband, the children tucked up safe and sound in bed, the house returning to some semblance of a peaceful home (as opposed to an indoor play-fest!).

I make it my mission to have at least three quiet meals a week at home with my man. Although these rarely take the form of candle-lit dinners, flower petals strewn across the table, Moët chilling in the fridge and Frank Sinatra playing on the record player, they still form the basis of our grown-up relationship, distinct, for the length of that meal, from our roles as mum and dad.

If you look at your average week, I'm sure most fab mums would be lucky to find any other time in the day for some intimate conversation with your partner. From the crack of dawn until they collapse into bed, the children are either constantly present, or either one or both of you is at work or doing the household chores. Breakfast time is rarely a family affair. Most mums I know (myself included) get up with the kids to a house absent of father/partner (my husband leaves the house every morning at six-thirty). Many women, in fact, leave first to go to work (my neighbour Elaine escapes just before seven every morning, leaving her husband and daughter to breakfast together). Snatching lunch as a family, let alone just you and your partner, is about as likely to occur as going back to bed for a siesta mid-afternoon.

So you see the evening meal is often the only opportunity you have to sit down and catch up with your husband over some good food and possibly a glass of wine. I know every night is unlikely, but making a big effort to eat together a few times a week will benefit you both.

When my husband arrives home just before seven o'clock, I'm usually in the thick of reading practice/running the bath/tidying the house/preparing my daughter's packed lunch (always wise, as the morning seems far too rushed to be imaginative). The house is chaotic and it's all systems go for bath, stories, cuddles and bed, before my husband and I finally chill ourselves. The best way to do this in my mind is to share a bath (or have a shower each), slip on some comfy clothes and sit down to a good meal. If the phone rings leave it, you can always call them back, and try to resist the temptation (and that means both of you) to carry on working, check emails, do the ironing or fill out the PTA travel questionnaire that's been sitting on your desk for weeks. If you must do these things, wait until you've properly stopped for an hour at least. The days are so full and rushed surely you both deserve this down-time?

In terms of what to eat it doesn't need to be a three-course meal with white napkins and champagne flutes; any nutritious, simple dish will do. Our favourites include roast chicken with sweet potato mash and sugar snaps (often cooked earlier for the kids and reheated for us), salmon steaks wrapped in Parma ham with fruity cous-cous and a green salad, or my crusty lamb served with green beans and brown rice. (Check out some of my recipes at the back for more ideas.) Often these meals can be prepared in minutes while you're cooking the kids' tea, and kept in the fridge before bunging in the oven while you get the children ready for bed. If you have a willing husband you may want to take turns to cook so you both get time to chill with a novel or newspaper while the other person slaves over the hot stove, or do what we do and share out the workload (one cooks the other washes up).

I really and truly find it's over these suppers that we properly share news about our work, the day that's passed, the children's news and any other gossip that comes up. Without this window for re-connection I'm sure the days would turn into weeks and we'd fall out of step in no time. I know for some families where one partner works nights or stays at the office late almost every evening, this is a hard act to follow, but even if you don't manage a few times a week, whenever you physically can is important. It's just about making time for each other outside the realm of co-workers/parents/friends/daughters/sons and general multi-taskers!

Mother knows best

'Sam and I try to eat together most nights. If either of us is working late, the other one eats with the kids and then stays up and joins in with a piece of fruit or a cup of tea. It feels vital for both us that we talk at the end of each day or we just feel like passing ships in the night, or worse, flatmates!'

Full-time working mum of two

Top ten food and nutrition tips

1. Don't be surprised if as a busy mum of 2.4 kids you feel like a walking, talking meal machine for a large proportion of each day! However, do not be disheartened! Try and approach food and eating with fresh eyes, creating innovative and time-saving devises that help make food 'fun' again.

2. Be aware of your children's nutrition and make it a priority at home, school and at play. Healthy eating should be a way of life for you all.

3. Don't beat yourself up for not creating five-star meals every day. Learn off-pat some easy-peasy, yummy family recipes that you can rely on week in, week out for speed, satisfaction and nutrition (check out the dishes at the back of the book for ideas).

4. Aim to make time for family meals, ideally every day, and if not make it a priority at weekends (or whenever you, your husband and children can be together).

5. Keep everyone's energy levels high (and the desire to dive into a crisp and cake binge low!).

6. Try to tackle fussy eating head on. Slowly but surely you should be able to encourage a more open-minded approach to food.

7. Don't neglect your own nutritional needs; we all need exciting, delicious and nutritious meals to keep us going!

8. Aim to make your weekly shopping habits more pleasure than chore.

9. Don't give up on eating out as a family (it may just be a little harder work than it once was).

10. Re-ignite the romance by prioritising some grown-up

evening meals as a couple. Come on, you must have some candlesticks somewhere!

Grace's Guru: Jane Clarke

Jane Clarke BSc (Hons) SRD is Britain's leading nutritionist. For over ten years she has run a highly renowned private practice in Central London and has treated some of the world's top sports people and media personalities while continuing to maintain a special interest in the nutritional needs of young children and the elderly. As a successful writer she as written many books including the UK best-sellers *Bodyfoods for Life* and *Yummy*. She has a weekly page in the *Daily Mail*'s Tuesday health section and a two-page column in the food section of *Weekend Magazine*. She has been a regular contributor on ITV's *This Morning* programme and was the nutritional adviser on Jamie Oliver's *School Dinners*.

Jane lives in North London with her adorable five-year-old daughter, Maya.

What are your main nutrition tips for the following mums?

A mum who's trying to rekindle her love for food and cooking My advice to all busy, multi-tasking mums is to keep it simple. So many mums feel the pressure to provide a huge array of exotic vegetables, different sauces and varied carbohydrates and pulses at every meal. This excessive pressure for choice is totally unnecessary. Take pleasure from a few simple ingredients and make sure these basic foods are of high quality. Instead of getting stressed about the variety of green vegetables or specific pasta shapes Maya has on her plate I try to ensure she enjoys eating good quality, simple, easy dishes.

Come on mums, get off this awful treadmill that makes you feel that food must be complicated. I always find that kids prefer the simple meals anyway. An easy cheese on toast supper made with wholemeal bread and organic cheese is a winner in many homes. Other simple dishes could be eggs on toast, grated cheese on wholemeal pasta, risotto and peas or a lovely hot crispy jacket potato.

I certainly don't cook a five-star meal every night of the week. Like many of you, I'm sure, I'll be working hard all day and the last thing I need is the added stress of cooking a complex and taxing dish for Maya and me in the evening. I take inspiration from the Italians and make sure I have good quality ingredients in the fridge and larder and go back to basics with my weeknight cooking. Even if Maya and I just share some Heinz tomato soup, a chunk of good cheese and a few slices of crusty bread I know it will be nutritious, delicious and above all, easy to whip up. Of course the weekends can be different and a time to put my effort and energy into creating inspired and lengthy meals, but by taking the emphasis off this during the week it makes cooking at weekends a pleasure and not a chore.

The key here is to enjoy the meals that you eat together as a family. If you've been slaving over a hot stove for an hour (after a long day at work and an hour of kids' homework) you'll be ratty and harassed during the meal. Children pick up on this and it stresses them out too. I firmly believe that tension prevents a person from absorbing the nutrients they need. There was a study done in the 1950s on this theory of stress and absorption of nutrients and I think it's important to mention it here. Two groups of children in two different orphanages were given the same meals for a six-month period. One group were fed in a loving, happy dining environment, the other in a cold, stressful one. Although the meals were exactly the same, the children fed in the loving, happy environment thrived and were healthy while the others weren't. Obviously other factors can contribute to this but a key lesson here is to try to relax and enjoy cooking and eating as a family so it benefits you all in the long run. By going back to simple ingredients and recipes it's far easier to achieve this.

A mum who's looking for quick but enjoyable ways to food shop with kids in tow I tend to do most of my food shopping online. There really is little pleasure for either Maya or me in trawling around the supermarket every week for tinned soup, cling-film and toothpaste. Many families will do one big weekly shop together but this can be so stressful and really contributes to sapping the pleasure out of food shopping altogether.

While the Internet has become a life-saver for basic food shopping I still believe it's crucial to get other core ingredients and fresh produce at the weekend, with Maya if at all possible. We take great pleasure in mooching around the local butcher, Italian deli, cheese shop and fishmonger together, getting core ingredients for the fridge and larder. For starters the staff are very knowledgeable and responsive (and seem to enjoy the presence of children, especially in Italian delis) and will offer great advice about what is fresh, seasonal and full of flavours. Secondly it is far more relaxing selecting some good salmon or pasta in a calm environment without a list of one hundred other things to do and buy in that half an hour.

I'm a firm believer in using your local independent shops, not just because they deserve our support but also because they teach kids an immense amount about variety and quality. It's rare to find the same selection of cheese at your local supermarket as you would in a specialist cheese shop, for example, and it may well encourage children to try new varieties or choose a favourite for themselves.

Another tip you may want to consider is abandoning the idea that you have to plan each meal in advance, therefore shopping in strict lists. I find that Maya and I vary what we want to eat depending on mood and energy levels and it can be very restricting having to stick to a regimented meal plan each day. When shopping make sure you get the basics and have some good meats, fishes, cheeses, breads and pasta in the house, but don't make shopping so military that you feel you can't give in to your desire for hot soup or a fresh salad on a whim.

A mum who wants top tips for easy family meals
The main point I always stress is to cook just one family meal for each sitting. I have so many clients who come to me harassed and worn down by cooking three different meals at one supper-time because their three kids all want

different things. Don't do it! Try to avoid the conveyor belt system that forces you to offer endless choice at each and every breakfast/lunch/supper. Either work out what meal options you are prepared to make (say a pasta or a rice dish) or decide what it's going to be and cook the same for everyone. The crux of this is to be kind but stay firm. If a child doesn't want to eat what's on offer then I'm afraid they have to go without. You'll run yourself ragged cooking an array of complicated meals for each child in turn and find yourself into a position where this is expected.

I've been firm with Maya from the start and have avoided many of the fussy eating problems some of my peers have got themselves into. Some of the simple meals she enjoys are: risotto, pasta, rice, jacket potatoes and good local or organic sausages, all served with a vegetable or some easy salad. She tends to need some form of carbohydrate in the evening after a long busy day so these fit the bill perfectly. During the week she'll finish a meal off with a fruit pudding (compote or baked apple with yogurt) and at the weekend I'll have had time to make something like crumble, apple pie or chocolate cake.

Ideally the whole family should eat together but in reality this often isn't viable. I know that Maya is very hungry after a day at school and needs supper much earlier than me so it's just impossible to eat together most weeknights. But while she eats I always make sure I sit down with her and have a cup of tea, some fruit and a chat with her. This helps her relax and gives me an opportunity to stop too. At weekends we manage to eat together much more and this is a real joy. Either I'll take pleasure in cooking leisurely meals at home

313

(the leftovers from which may well last into the week) or we'll eat out, thereby giving Maya much more choice about what she wants.

A mum who wants healthy eating options when eating out with her brood   I'm a big fan of noodle bars because the kids' options tend to be both healthy and fun. Most children love to use chopsticks and there can't be many children who won't eat noodles! The options are good and your child can select from a simple noodle dish to something which is more soup-based.

Simple pizza joints where your child can have a fresh margarita and salad are also worth looking into as are good quality Italian restaurants (sadly chains tend not to be as great as many independent family-run places). I'm also a big fan of Lebanese restaurants and cafés where you can eat with your family relatively cheaply and healthily. Here you're bound to find delicious chicken skewers, good breads and dips which both you and the children can enjoy. Failing this, if you're stuck in a department store or eating on the go, opt for a soup and sandwich for the children if you can (instead of the chicken nuggets and chips so many places offer these days).

Lastly remember that you're the customer and in any restaurant you should feel free to ask for half portions of adult food or simplified dishes of more grown-up recipes.

A mum who wants nutritious yet delicious meal solutions when she's eating alone   Oooh, where do I start! There are so many easy, yummy dishes a mum can make for herself it's a shame so many of us resort to a bag of crisps and a cup of tea! It really is time mums prioritised themselves. Just because you're not feeding a Sunday lunch party of eight or a brood of hungry school kids that doesn't mean it's not worth putting some effort and thought into it. Remember food is fuel and it's so important you feel energised for a busy life.

Come hell or high water, I always make an enormous salad for myself in the evening. I'll use fresh leaves and then throw in anything from roasted root vegetables, asparagus, peas, broad beans, chickpeas and potatoes depending on my mood and hunger level. This will form the basis of my evening meal and I'll accompany it with some cold roast chicken, Parma ham or some fresh baked or steamed fish. On a cold night I may well make a risotto (with broad beans or a simple parmesan one) or even a dahl, a simple lentil dish, that can simmer away while I'm in the bath.

However tired I am I always give this evening meal (or lunch if I'm at home in the day) a little thought. I'll buy the ingredients on the way home from work or make sure I get the key foods at the weekend so when the time comes I have a selection of fresh, yummy things to put together. Think of it as something to look forward to when you're home alone.

A mum looking for exciting yet speedy romantic meal ideas My tip for romantic meals is to keep it light and herby. Too much stodgy food can make you feel tired and lethargic so you want to get the right balance of lovely aromas and good flavours instead. One dish I would recommend, which is easy to make yet looks enticing and tastes wonderful, is lamb cutlets. Simply grill with some olive oil and rosemary and serve with a watercress salad and it's done. Really delicious!

Another good alternative is to make a fish dish that is light yet appetising. I recommend a prawn stir-fry (you could even use good quality frozen prawns for this). Just add some seasoning, sesame oil, light soy sauce and some colourful vegetables, then serve with rice or noodles. Fresh fish wrapped in spinach is an easy yet tasty alternative. Lay out some raw spinach, season with dill, lemon and olive oil, then wrap the fish up in the spinach. Cover it with some foil and cook it for ten minutes. A really tasty meal without much fuss at all!

What are the key dos and don'ts for the mum wanting good nutrition for the whole family?

Do

- Keep cooking simple. Just remember that less is more.
- Eat with or accompany your child at meal times as much as you can.
- Use your freezer. Cook extra food at the weekend you can freeze and then use it up in the week.
- Spend more on quality meats and fish but try and make it go as far as possible.
- Feed your kids before their energy reserves get really low (especially after a long day at school).
- Make packed lunches and snacks as healthy as possible (dried fruit and oatcakes are ideal snacks).
- Buy as much local, seasonal produce as possible.
- Make shopping for food and eating out a pleasure.

Don't

- Don't put pressure on yourself to produce amazing, eclectic meals seven days a week.
- Don't feed you or your kids junk food.
- Don't give in to advertising or peer pressure on what to feed the family.
- Don't drink alcohol on an empty stomach.
- Don't give in to the whims of a fussy eater.
- Don't add too much salt.
- Don't get stressed by the shopping and cooking of food.
- Don't let you or the kids snack too much between meals.
- Don't resort to endless ready-meals.

> **Jane's fabulous mum's family nutrition mantra: 'Keep cooking simple and try to be consistent about what is nourishing and what is on offer!'**

Working Nine to Five

Do I Go Back?

Since the success of my first handbook, I seem to have coined the phrase 'the bubble' in describing maternity leave after having one's first child. For almost all the working mums I know this has become something of a catchphrase. Like me, my posse of working girlfriends (all aged between twenty and forty-something) had enjoyed flourishing careers or odd jobs that gave them the freedom modern women have fought for (namely to travel to South America for New Year and take a week 'off' to prepare and recover from Glastonbury festival!). Whether these pals have been high-flying business women or fly-by-the-seat-of-your-pants workers they've all described heading towards the maternity 'break' of their first child as entering a kind of bubble. Here you nest, feed, change and grab snooze whenever possible (and for an odd few, answer a handful of emails from the office). By and large this is a hazy time of getting to know your newborn away from office politics, copy deadlines, demands from Hong Kong distributors and conference calls.

After giving birth to my first-born this bubble lasted almost seven months. I breastfed her exclusively (until at six months, twenty pounds and having no distinction between the upper thigh, knee and ankle, I gave in to the dreaded baby rice and hours of pureeing butternut squash), she slept peacefully in our bed and I hadn't seen a pub for so long I'd almost forgotten what a glass of chilled white wine looked like. Although I wept at the thought of leaving her with a blonde, bubbly carer who seemed to have swallowed a nursery rhyme CD, there was never any doubt in my mind that I'd eventually wean her off my mammoth bust and struggle back into my skintight jeans, ready and raring to write up the season's trends for *Elle* magazine. Being a working mum was, without question, my new role.

The same applied for the large majority of my fellow first-time mum friends. We'd all busted our guts at university or as interns and worked all the hours God sent to get where we were today. None of us had any doubt that a new addition to the family would not stop us from continuing to enjoy this. Take my friend, Lyn. She didn't sleep for what seemed like a year while she built her events organising company from a back room of her West London flat. This was the kind of determination that made head-hunters fall at her feet and landed her the role of events organiser for one of Britain's hippest companies. A job that entailed excitement, glamour and a good wage wasn't about to be lost after the birth of her bonny son. A little sacrifice here and there, but giving it up was never an option.

My other good friend, Jennie, felt similarly about her career as a charity fundraiser. Although glamorous parties and champers weren't her thing, raising vast amounts of dosh for worthy causes and publicly speaking about her charity's plight was a job she'd worked hard for all her life. Even though she maximised her maternity leave, as the final sixth month approached she was preparing for her return to office life with military precision. Whenever Jennie, Lyn and I met for our Saturday sandpit session or the odd girlie natter over a bottle of Sauvignon Blanc, I rarely remember any discussions about giving it all up for full-time motherhood. Admittedly, we'd offer each other tips for negotiating flexi-time options, or ways to get home before bathtime, but the thought of ditching the briefcase and attaching a pinny for good never crossed our minds.

Press the fast-forward button on the Fab Mum film and we find ourselves in a very different scene. It was only last weekend that the sandpit session was abandoned because it had rained solidly for the whole week and the drinks night out was postponed because Jennie, Lyn and I are all pregnant (me with my third and Jennie and Lyn with their second). The third best option was lunch at my house. As the children dismantled my daughter's bedroom and dressed in every garment from the fancy dress box, we took this opportunity to discuss our morning sickness, swollen breasts and maternity dressing tips before moving on to more pressing issues: do we go back to work?

For me the decision was made some three years earlier when I left my job at *Elle* to write freelance and fulfil my dreams of becoming an author. Undeniably, this brave move was spurred on by my desire to spend more time with my two children (both still under two). Somehow, having a second child tipped the scales in favour of more flexibility and more 'home time' than it had done when I had only one child. As I approach having my third child the question

'Do I go back to work?' is now redundant, because my work is inextricably intertwined with my home life (and for this I feel truly blessed).

For Jennie and Lyn the transition of going from one child to two seems to have tipped their scales too. Suddenly the long commute to work, the over-time, the 'glamorous' trips abroad, the calls from the boss on their day 'off' seem just slightly too high a price to pay as one child becomes two. For Jennie it seems that as her daughter Minnie grew up she was missing out on more and more, so having a second would just double this anguish. Although she's got a long-term game plan to partner up with her husband in his contemporary art firm, for her the pre-school nurturing of her growing family has become paramount. Lyn shares these concerns but also raises the valuable issue of finances. With one child already at nursery, paying for childcare for a second doubles this cost. You either incur nursery or childminder fees for two kids or change tack and employ a nanny (which for a full-time working mum would cost a minimum of £20,000 a year). In reality you have to be earning a pretty top wage to even consider this extra burden.

I back any scheme attempting to gain better childcare solutions for working mums. In my mind, women should be fully paid for far longer than the statutory first few months of maternity leave (a year would be much more humane) to enable them to do the first year of childcare themselves. I also feel that childcare options beyond the family unit should be far better than they are at present in order to entice women back to the workplace. (You only have to open a newspaper to read headlines such as NURSERIES ARE DAMAGING OUR BABIES AND LEADING TO A SOCIETY OF ANTI-SOCIAL

ADULTS, but what other viable and economical choices do many working parents have?) Until the government improves childcare options for us career mothers, many women I know who are embarking on their second or third child are left with the same predicament. It's not 'Do I go back to work?' but simply, 'I can't afford to go back'.

The combination of financial restraints and an emotional shift (which makes many women desire more time caring for their children) means that for a large proportion of mums I know, having another child means readdressing their work/life balance.

I know I certainly felt that having a second child made my responsibility to both children feel far more powerful than it had been before. That's not to say I didn't feel guilt at leaving my daughter to return to work; I just found that once it was two snotty faces at the door my heartstrings twanged just that little bit harder. I'd find myself sitting on the Tube thinking, 'Is this job really satisfying all my dreams?' or I'd be at some fancy fashion launch while my husband read bedtime stories, thinking, 'Is this really making me happy?' I remember writing a feature on a new underwear launch and struggling to muster a thousand exciting words to sum it up. I sat staring out of the window and saw a mum giggling playfully with her baby in its buggy. I clearly recall wondering, 'Will I still be writing about knickers in ten years' time, while my kids are teenagers and I've missed every sports day?' My growing family meant a definite shift in my priorities and raised a whole host of questions about what I wanted from life.

Of course, many women keep working full-time as their brood grows (one friend who is a mother of three young kids and works immensely hard as a TV big-wig; another, Danni, has continued to run her fashion retail business throughout her children's childhood), but I shouldn't think that there are any mums on the planet who don't admit to the difficulties of juggling their home and work life. Even when they feel immense satisfaction at receiving their monthly salary cheque or engage in a mega-inspiring board meeting, I know for a fact that occasionally on a Sunday morning when they visit friends in the country or take a walk in the park with their children, they wonder what it would be like to give it all up.

I don't think Jennie, Lyn, Danni or I would claim to have all the answers. While Danni may occasionally long to be at home baking with her kids or watching her son in a football tournament, she knows deep down she'd be bored silly. While Jennie wishes occasionally for the buzz of raising £100,000 for charity, I know she wouldn't miss planting broad beans in the garden with Minnie for all the money in the world. The trick is to decide what works for you. As an avid consumer of feminist literature while a student, I had to swallow a lot of pride when I took the risk of leaving my safe day job to become an author. On the other hand, many career women who've been raised by the typical 1950s stay-at-home mum have to battle with massive guilt at leaving their teary toddler with a Romanian au pair. I think the trick is to make whatever path you take work for you and your family. For this reason I am going to dedicate the next three sections to embracing those different, but equally important work/life choices.

Mother knows best

'There was no way I'd have given up my job with my first child. In fact, I couldn't wait to get back. My son's colic and reflux had driven us all to despair and my confidence had suffered from lack of sleep and lack of contact with the outside world. Two years later, when I found out I was having twins, I had a huge shift in my priorities. After such a hard beginning with my first-born, we had really bonded over recent months and it suddenly felt hugely important to be around to help him adjust to the role of big brother, as well as to try to be an active mum to the twins. Combine this with the fact that my job as a teacher would never have covered a nanny's wage and left enough to call a salary. My mind was made up. I won't pretend it's not tough but I have no regrets, none at all.'

Full-time mum of three

The Career Mum

One thing's for sure, full-time career mums get an awful lot of stick. The media are only too quick to inform them that returning to work in haste 'damages' their child's well-being, while the government backs reports of the devastating effects long-term nursery and institutionalised care have on the under-fives, and this is all after a stone wall of silence from the mummy mafia at the school gates. It's not surprising that the boardroom must feel like some sort of refuge (and that's hoping that your boss hasn't slated you for taking an afternoon 'off' to attend the school nativity play).

The feminist wave of the 1960s opened doors for working women and raised the glass ceiling for ambitious, educated and determined females across the country. How many of us would have stated 'full-time housewife' as a career path? Unlikely, to say the least. Lawyer, doctor, journalist, actress, banker, chef, nanny, publisher, fashion designer, retailer or accountant would seem more apt. These choices all became well within reach; well, that's until motherhood became another string to our bow and maintaining these goals became harder and harder.

I am in no way advocating a full-time career and working life as the ideal scenario for mums, far from it. However, the choice to make this work should be well within a woman's rights. Who's to say that if you've spent twenty years getting to the top of your field, you should be required to give it all up to change nappies and impersonate the Tweenies? Who's to tell us that because we've given birth a few months earlier, taking on the new role of CEO is out of the question? And who's to say what requirements, working or otherwise, women need to make them feel complete?

My friend Sophie is the perfect example of late-feminist ideology. She regularly works a minimum fifty-five-hour week and is at the top of her profession. She busted a gut at her local grammar school, an inner-London university and then a leading specialist school to gain the perfect grades to graduate with her head held high. She then lived on four hours' sleep a night, as she wowed her first intern firm with her commitment and dedication. Boozy nights, dates and chats about recent episodes of *Friends* were about as far off her agenda as meeting for a sneaky weekday lunch. It was something of a surprise then, when at the age of thirty-three she entered a whirlwind romance which peaked with a beach wedding some eight months after their first date in Hyde Park, closely followed by a new baby.

Since then Sophie has maintained a career that stimulates her brain and ambition, while offering a six-figure salary year-on-year. She also has three kids, two dogs, a goldfish, a second home in Norfolk and a divorce. Today Sophie is the epitome of the 'multi-tasking mum'. Up at five-thirty every morning, she runs in her local park for forty minutes while her live-in au pair sleeps soundly in the room next door to her children. She then arrives home, showers, dresses in one of many grey pencil skirts, starched white shirts and kitten-heeled sling-backs, wakes the kids, checks her emails, feeds the dogs and shares breakfast with her brood. Most days this is followed by a manic bundling of all three kids into the car, a drop at two local schools and a just-about-legal dash into central London for a prompt eight-thirty start. I've been at Sophie's house on many an early evening occasion (I am an informal godmother to all her children) and I can vouch for the fact that although evenings are no less manic, they do almost always involve mum arriving home at around six-thirty, stripping out of her heels and pencil skirt and into a pair of old 501 Levis (paint and chocolate ice-cream stains obligatory) and morphing back into the most hands-on, engaged, interested and 'fun' mum I've ever seen. (She once came home from a hugely stressful court case, poured herself and me a large glass of plonk and proceeded to teach her youngest how to do cartwheels.) 'I don't know how she does it' is a phrase that often springs to mind.

For many women (me included), this amount of frazzled multi-tasking would be our idea of hell. Up at five-thirty? I'd much rather grab an extra hour in bed, thanks very much. Cooking beans on toast after negotiating deals all day? I'd much rather downscale and enjoy a little peace and a decent meal. Missing sports day, violin practice and your youngest's first steps all for a conference in Berlin? Forget it! However, for a large proportion of women, this is a reality they thrive on and for others it's a lifestyle that is totally necessary for survival. Sophie is a single mum and although her divorce settlement was sufficient to keep them all in their much-loved family home (where all the kids were born) she needs to bust her gut to make it work. Not only this, if she was to give it all up tomorrow, up sticks and move to rural Norfolk, sure she'd see her children more (and get rather fewer parking fines), but would growing her own vegetables and baking apple crumble for tea at six really fulfil her?

Sophie admits that without her 'life-saving uber-fabulous au pair' she'd be a dead woman. She also confesses to a necessary addiction to organic food delivery, black cabs and DIY on tap (care of Dan, her handyman who fixes everything from leaky taps to a broken BMX). For most full-time working mums this would read more like an issue of *Vogue* than their reality, which could well be more *Woman's Own*, but it illustrates how working women often need shortcuts and outside help (whether it be via their partner, mother, neighbour, carer or very own version of Dan) to make a viable full-time working life possible.

While Sophie confesses to a highly organised BlackBerry and a large stock of 'wind-down wine' to get her through the working week, many of you may also be wondering how to deal with the emotional strain and time restraints of juggling full-time motherhood with an expanding family life. The ideal person to ask about this is my old *Elle* pal, Paula. You may remember from my first handbook that Paula and I have shared many years of birthing stories, pregnancy cupcake fests and wild 'we're back' nights guzzling too much bubbly. (It has been our ritual that once we've finished breast-feeding our babies, are getting more than four hours' sleep per night and have the green card for a night 'off' from our husbands, we meet up for a 'we're back' evening of celebra-tions!) Although Paula and I have moved on from our days riffling through Manolos in the fashion cupboard at *Elle*, we have still remained great friends. Even though I work from my small study in North London, picking the kids up from school in faded jeans and Converse trainers while she smooches with the world's leading photographers and make-up artists from her trendy office in West London (no doubt wearing those Manolos), via our children, love of mother-hood and insatiable desire for gossip, we remain firm friends.

On top of being a great friend she's also a wonderful role model for working mums. Paula works full-time and has three children under the age of six (Toby is the eldest, followed closely by her twin girls, Phoebe and Daisy). Now the bril-liant thing about Paula is not only her collection of shoes or her talent for looking fab on very little sleep, it's the way she's managed her life choices and the amazing sense of confidence she has about them. Of course she'll occasion-ally fantasise about life in rural France, the kids happy at local French schools, her getting fat on sweet plum jam (picked and made that same morning from their very own orchard, *bien sur*) but by and large she exudes an air of absolute certainty that the work/life balance she has struck is right for her, her partner and their children. Guilt just isn't something that's allowed to creep into her daily consciousness. The bottom line is she loves her kids passionately, but also loves her job whole-heartedly. Of course a little give and take has to come into the equation, but making both her family life and working life a success go hand in hand.

It's damaging to imply that we can 'have it all' because women all over the country are regularly over-stretched in their pursuit of this. (After a long day at the office who needs extra pressure to then 'sparkle' for the kids and produce a Michelin-starred meal for the spouse?) What I will say is that if you plan well, cut back where necessary and strive for as much balance as is viable, it should be possible to have at least most of what you wanted. So what are the key formulae to getting that balance right? As a mum who has forgotten what the inside of an office looks like and has a publisher who is generous with deadlines, I can only offer speculative advice on how to rid yourself of that working mum guilt. What I can do is pour over the advice of multi-tasking super-mums Paula and Sophie, add it to the mix of anecdotes from other full-time working mum friends (Ros, Anna, Tanya, Sara and Danni) and come up with a hit list of tips to make the demands of work and play fuse with ease.

Childcare you're confident with

Every mum I spoke to unanimously agreed that good, trustworthy childcare is the key to a successful working life. Researching all avenues (even as early as pregnancy), budgeting for the necessary costs and taking the time to explore all the options available to you are essential to making the right choice. Continuity of care, a loving base and a secure framework in which your child can learn, play and grow must be an absolute priority for all working parents.

Rules that you stick to

Paula is an advocate of strict ground rules for encouraging the harmony of her work/life balance. Obviously, occasional flexibility is useful, but making 'family rules' will help you, your partner and your children know exactly what to expect from week to week. For example, Paula's rules include making the bedtime story at eight o'clock her domain (the children accept that supper will be given by their carer and bath by their dad but nine out of ten the times Mummy will be back for stories and bedtime cuddles); and saving weekends for sacred family time (the kids come first, so park trips, museums and picnics in the woods come way before shopping for Mum's underwear or being dragged around a garden centre with Dad).

Organisation is crucial

Although both Paula and Sophie admit to the occasional banana-smeared work blouse or mislaid document in the pile of finger paintings, they both agree that being organised is pretty crucial for the working mum who is seeking success. Each of you will have your own unique ways of drawing up lists (Sophie on her BlackBerry, Paula in her Smythson notebook, Sara on slips of discarded newspaper); whichever way works for you, organising your thoughts and planning for the day (possibly even the night before) helps you stay ahead.

Make life easy

By using things like Internet shopping for food and clothes, your lunch break to collect dry-cleaning and five minutes before you start work to list your 'must-dos' for the week ahead, you'll save time. You may also find these little cheats help you to enjoy more relaxed 'down-time' in the evening or at weekends.

Prioritise

As a busy full-time working mum you can't be everything to everyone, so prioritising events and people is key. Taking your daughter to her first ballet class may not be as important as clinching a top deal, but seeing the end of term show might be. Taking time off work for half-term might not be viable, but taking the day off because your youngest has whooping cough could be a necessity. You need to be clear about your choices and stand firm about them as much as is possible.

Separate your lives

I know when I went back to work, having the odd photo of my children on my desk felt comforting and helped with the transition from home life to work life. Having said that, keeping those lives distinct is essential to maintaining that work/life balance. Paula stresses this in her working ethos. She doesn't allow herself calls to home during the day (if there is an emergency, they will call her) and has just one family photo on her desk. Likewise, her work colleagues are under strict instructions not to call her at the weekend unless it is absolutely unavoidable and she rarely takes work home in the evening (unless it is life-or-death essential).

Support the school

Even though you may not be there for daily pick-up or at the mums' gathering at the local Starbucks, that doesn't mean you can't be actively involved in school life. Helping at summer fêtes, attending evening PTA meetings or offering your support for the annual quiz night will all help you feel part of your child's school world.

Guilt is counter-productive

A happy mum generally means a happy family. You may beat yourself up for missing the school bring-and-buy sale or seeing little Arthur score his first goal, but you're bound to make up for it one hundred times over in the time you do spend and value with your family. If you enjoy your job and all the benefits it gives you (in terms of confidence, self-esteem, sociability, career advancement, financial stability and lifestyle), then be proud of this choice. Love your children (and try not to compensate for lost time by spoiling them) and make sure you give them all the time that you can in order to show them that it's possible to be a busy working mum as well as a mum who adores and cherishes her kids to bits.

Nothing is set is stone

However hard you work and however much you value your job, nothing is ever set in stone. You may feel as your children grow, approach school age or enter their final year of GCSEs that you want to downscale your job or change tack altogether. Surely part of making choices is being able to change them when and if you need to?

I'm the last person to argue for a blanket workforce dominated by mothers (although a few more of them in top jobs would surely help society as a whole), but I am certainly a believer in backing mothers in all the diverse work/family choices they make. Full-time working mums shouldn't be beaten over the head for pursuing their own ambitions, just as full-time mums shouldn't be looked down upon for opting for childcare over their careers. As fabulous mums we should unite in recognising that each and every choice is valuable and viable in today's world. Less guilt and more celebration of the freedom to choose: what do you say?

Mother knows best

'My mother was a full-time mum and a regular face at the school gates. She ran the PTA, she cooked every meal from scratch and always looked like the picture-perfect housewife. It wasn't until my brother and I left home that we started to see cracks appear. Mum had lived her life through us and the family and as we grew up and forged our own lives, she was left feeling empty and alone. Although I want to be the best mum I can be, I also want a job that satisfies me and offers longevity in terms of the future. My children know I love them dearly and the weekends are full of fun and laughter, but they also know it won't be me serving homemade chicken casserole every night of the week after school. I know I'm biased, but I have very well-rounded, happy children and working at a job I adore hasn't harmed them in any way. If anything, it's made us value each other more.'

Full-time working mum of two

Finding a Balance that Works for You

I've talked about the fabulous mums I know who have made working nine to five part of their intrinsic mothering make-up. At times I look at them in their power suits and envy their charisma; often I hear of their working achievements and trips to New York on business and feel a swell of pride. I'm certain that for some women this is the best and only way to lead their lives. Having said that, it would take an awful lot of persuasion (and even more dosh) for me to ever consider going back to full-time work. Although some weeks I work far more than nine to five, many others I work a couple of days flat-out and enjoy the role of full-time mum for the remaining time. This flexibility for me, as a mum of two schoolchildren and with a newborn on the way, is what liberation is all about.

As I mentioned in the first section of this chapter, for many women a growing family means readdressing conventional hours and the idea of full-time work. For these same women, suddenly the idea of leaving the house when it's still dark, only to skid back in for a quick bedtime story five days a week is their idea of hell. Not only do they feel that the balance has gone totally askew in favour of work, but this sort of work ethic can lead to exhaustion and despondency with both your job and family life. In short, the conflict and demands of working full-time while caring for a family can make many women very unhappy.

So what other options do mums have when they reach a point of change in their working and home lives? For many mums this may be while they're at home on maternity leave with their second child, or even when they're considering their third or fourth pregnancies. As I've said before, for me the tide of change came after having my second child. I overwhelmingly felt that a better work/life balance was called for to give us all room to breathe and grow. I'd had enough of being worn down by work deadlines and felt an immeasurable longing for more time with the children. To be honest, I also think having my children made me more aware of a whole new variety of challenges waiting for me to explore with and without the children, something that was impossible to do or really imagine while chained to a desk.

It may be as a mum you just want more flexible hours and a more empathetic working regime, or it may mean you want a total change of career. I know that when my friend Rosie had her first child, it was certainly more flexibility and freedom to alter her working hours which made her feel better about returning to work. Alternatively, my switch was within the same realm of writing, but offered a totally different working life. As opposed to a desk-based office role, I created a home-based career structure for myself, one which was dominated more by writing books and less by writing articles or news snippets. You could even consider the other extreme and one taken by a good friend of Jennie's. She took the brave decision to retrain and switch careers altogether (she went from working for a legal firm to becoming a self-employed nutritionist). Again, it's all about making *your* choices work for you and your loved ones.

If you're feeling uninspired by your working life or feel slightly trapped by your straightforward office regime, here are some ideas you could consider to help you strike a more healthy balance:

Cut and paste your hours

It's more and more common for working mums to request flexible working hours. Just remember that, legally, requesting a 'family-friendly' working day is well within your rights. If this sort of arrangement wouldn't work for you or your company, then how about starting slightly earlier and therefore finishing earlier, or sacrificing that hour-long lunch break for an earlier finish time?

Shorten your week

When I returned to work, I reduced my working week by a day per child. (By this I mean I went down to a four-day week after my first child and then a three-day week after having my second.) For me, cutting down my working hours made total sense in trying to achieve a good work/life balance. In practice it may not help you climb the career ladder with the same speed and you may well have to put up with the odd snide remark or begrudging look from your childless colleagues, but I truly feel fighting for the right to a shorter working week helps you achieve a better balance.

Work from home

Although this isn't viable for many mums, if working from home is in any way possible, go for it! Presenting an attractive, detailed proposal to your boss (raising points such as where you'll be working, who'll be looking after the kids during those hours, how you can be contacted, etc.) will help you both figure out how to make it a success. By working one or two days from home, cutting out commuting and office chit-chat you'll be amazed at how much you get done, as well as how much more family time you're able to squeeze in.

Share it out

Sharing your job with another willing party can also offer a way out from the full-time work trap. If you can find a good job-share party who also understands your family commitments (a fellow mum is perfect) this can be a good solution for downscaling working hours.

Freelance freedom

Leaving your current employment to seek freelance work or adding to a part-time job with a few freelance contracts can suit some working mums. Many of my working mum pals have found that pursuing freelance work gives them the freedom they desperately seek. My stylist friend Gayle, for example, swears that working on a freelance basis allows her huge chunks of time with her twins, as well as the choice to decide what jobs she takes and when. She's adamant she'll never return to a conventional working life.

Re-evaluate and retrain

For many mums feeling stuck in a working rut doesn't seem to shift however many hours they negotiate 'off' or office days they lose here and there. Jennie's friend is a case in point. The demands of her legal job just seemed to sap more and more of her, leaving her energy at an all-time low. Retraining as a nutritionist on her Fridays off and two evenings a week, although draining at first, shed light on a future with far more flexibility and family time. Two years on and she's now fully trained, working from a practice at her home two days a week and, despite earning less, is happier than she's ever been.

There are many options to explore and it's worth taking the time to work out a solution that suits you. My neighbour Clare retrained as a teacher after falling out of step with the world of advertising and although my role as author isn't that far from journalist, it was about going for my goal and risking a change in my working dynamic. Clare, Gayle and all the mums I've mentioned were in dire need of change and more quality time with their children and they are proof of the possibilities that are there if you just take that leap.

Mother knows best

'I never seemed to get home for the kids' bedtime and I was sick of feeling tired and run-down. After a year of it I decided to cut back on household costs and go for a freelance life. I was petrified at first and things at home were incredibly tight; we even lived off soup and toast for the first month! Having said that, being my own boss spurred me on to make work come my way and I sold my soul to pick up on all and any relevant contacts. Graphic design will never grant us the life of the Beckhams but I certainly have far more time with my family and a hundred per cent more energy and job satisfaction.'

Full-time working mum of two

Self-worth as a Full-time Mum

Many of you will have read about Sophie and her five-thirty morning starts, indispensable au pair and city bound pencil skirts feeling she is a million miles away from your own mothering reality. You may skim over Paula's working mum rules and my suggestions for flexi-time with about as much interest as you have in *The Antiques Roadshow*. Some of you may have entered the world of mothering with a scattering of odd jobs on your CV, but above all a more prominent urge to be a mother. I should think more of you, however, will have come to this point, knee-deep in muddy rugby kits and maths homework, with a sparkling career or job aspirations somewhere in your past. Almost all the mums I meet at the school gates were once a nurse, lawyer, artist, surgeon, flight attendant, book editor or shop owner. However, they now state 'mother' as their main role. In all honesty, for a large proportion of mums, 2.4 kids and all the work that this entails means that caring for your brood is a full-time career (with no over-time, flexi-time, job share or New York business trips in sight!).

Just as I have an overwhelming belief that career mums should be admired and rewarded, I also feel that full-time mums deserve a medal for the work that they put into their role. Society tends to brush them under the carpet. How many full-time mums get thanks at the end of each day? How many get rewarded with a Christmas bonus or a pat on the back and a pay rise? Many mums I know would feel blessed to get a nod of recognition for doing the washing-up! It's hard for most men to imagine but for many of these women the school run, the sing songs at the weekly play-group, the endless rounds of fish fingers or pureed pear, the scrubbing out of grass stains on white summer frocks have replaced high-flying careers, jobs that fulfilled their creative flair or just the everyday social network of office banter. Don't get me wrong, you rarely hear them complain (we all know how that first after-school hug, that toothless high-chair grin or that 'I love you' last thing at night makes all the hard work worth it), but anyone can see the adjustment to full-time mum is staggering.

Since leaving my steady long-term job at *Elle* I've had periods between writing books or undertaking journalism projects where I've embraced full-time motherhood. After finishing my first handbook I immediately stepped onto a fast-moving PR machine. Most weeks included photoshoots or interviews at my home, radio and TV appearances and a vast number of written articles for women's magazines. To properly take in the success of the Fab Mum project and give myself time to reflect and move forward, I decided to take a chunk of time 'off' to be with my family and throw myself into full-time motherhood. My part-time carer at the time had left to have her own baby, so it seemed the perfect opportunity to step back and enjoy some quality family time. For five months (bar the odd article written in the evening or on a Sunday afternoon while my husband took the children to the park) I immersed myself in PTA involvement, afternoons picnicking at Highgate woods, muffin-baking and messy-play.

I confess, most of the time I was in heaven. Even though I normally only work part-time, having every second consumed by family life felt very different indeed. Having said that, there were times in every day when I craved the sound of my keyboard tapping out a chapter of my next book, or the sight of an email in my inbox confirming the next link up with crockery designer Emma Bridgewater or showing the page proof of my latest spread in *Grazia*. I missed the meetings with my agent or publisher (and the excuse they gave me to switch from my ballet pumps into a heel) and I longed for the buzz of being told by anyone over the age of five that 'you've done a good job'. On top of all that, as my husband came home from work in the evening and I stood knee-deep in wooden train track and Biff, Chip and Kipper reading books, I missed having an abundance of 'news' to share with him. It was on week seven, when all I was managing to discuss over supper was my daughter's eczema and the date of my son's sports day, that I realised I was rapidly in danger of becoming a mummy bore!

Not only was quality of conversation an issue (something I realised yet again when I had supper with my family and while my siblings discussed the latest Martin Amis novel, I was left wondering when anyone would raise the issue of my son's party entertainer?), but also the quantity of my self-confidence. However great I felt about being the one to meet my child's every need, with it came a feeling that my children were *my* every need. At times I forgot how much I love to sit around talking over a bottle of wine with a group of old girlfriends (I was much too knackered to stay up later than nine anyway) and how important it was for me to have a morsel of time alone each day (forget swimming; walking to and from school would have to fill the exercise quota). When there is no way to gauge your worth in the job you're doing, it's easy to see how many full-time mums begin to feel invisible to the outside world. In short, their confidence as a mum grows, but often at the expense of their confidence as individual, partner, friend, daughter, colleague and neighbour.

The answer to this is not, however, to dash out for the *Guardian* jobs section. Far from it. For so many women having a second or third child makes this an impossibility and something they feel just doesn't gel with the needs of their growing family. However, what it does mean is that as full-time mums you need to work on developing parts of your life that you may have neglected for some time. We can't change society overnight (and expect the government to miraculously announce the minimum wage for full-time mothers!) but what we can try to do is to work together to increase the self-worth of stay-at-home mums.

From my experience of full-time mothering, and that of my close pals (such as Jennie, Amy, Anita and Danni, to name a few), I think there are two crucial points to remember when trying to make it a successful role and one that evokes a feeling of self-worth. First, work on enjoying the time you have with your children and second, maintain small projects of your own within your day-to-day life. Now when I suggest 'enjoying' the time you have with your offspring I don't mean bounding out of bed to face-paint and sing nursery rhymes at full throttle before you've even put the kettle on. What I mean here is trying to work out a day-to-day family life that suits your needs as well as the kids'. As I've mentioned before, I see so many mums frazzled and resentful because they spend the week playing taxi to their children; this is totally unnecessary for the well-being of you both.

No child has ever come to any harm by missing their window for t'ai chi or Kumon maths and, more to the point, you're all likely to be far happier in the long run if these activities are replaced by a play in the park or a laze on the sofa with a handful of stories. I know my two would far rather scooter the two miles home from school, via the swings (stopping for ice cream en route), than sit in a hot car waiting to get to a course in French mime and drama! Similarly, no one will berate you for ditching their swimming class once in a while so that they can go home to play in the garden with a friend, while you have a good chat and a digestive with a fellow mum (or dare I say it, read the latest edition of *Red*).

I don't mean to start a backlash here, but you don't have to be the domestic ideal of supermum to have a happy family.

Admitting that *you* have needs within the family structure is the first step to finding an equilibrium that will make you happier and therefore have a positive knock-on effect for all the family. To tackle my second point, 'maintaining small projects of your own', you need to look outside the basis of the day-to-day routine and formulate creative projects beyond it. For Jennie this came in the form of doing the PR for her husband's art gallery opening (which she amazingly managed in the few hours in which her daughter went to pre-school), for Anita it means being active on the school PTA, for Danni it's training for a sponsored cycle ride, and for Amy it means undertaking a weekly dressmaking course at The London College of Fashion. These are all small projects which don't eat into family life too much, but have offered these full-time mums a purpose beyond childcare and a mission that enhances their creativity, their energy and their 'grown-up selves'.

For you it may be enrolling in an art class in the evening, possibly even taking on some freelance proofreading for extra cash, or even going for a jog once your partner comes in from work. After my full-time mum conversation evaporation at seven weeks, I realised I needed to take a leaf out of this book and rekindle some of my own pursuits. I put aside half an hour each day to research new topics, try out recipes or Google useful addresses for this book. I also scheduled a few mums' nights out and I became involved in organising a quiz night for my daughter's school and a bead stall for the summer fair at my son's school. Just by getting my teeth stuck into something other than playing My Little Ponies or defrosting bolognese sauce, I felt a boost in my self-esteem and certainly felt I could add a little to my conversation repertoire (even if it did involve trial Trivial Pursuit questions for the quiz night or the inner workings of a chicken soup recipe).

It goes without saying that being active with your kids and making time to meet and socialise with other mums is also crucial to a full-time mum's confidence and boredom levels. It's when you find yourself staying at home all day, alone with three under-fives, that you feel your anxiety about the outside world rising. Innately we are pretty sociable creatures and this doesn't change just because your life is a cycle of nappies and breast pumps! Admittedly, when your kids start school, the window for sociability increases dramatically (small-talk with twenty fellow mums is an obligatory part of every day), but that doesn't mean it's not worth seeking activities outside the home with your pre-schoolers. A weekly playgroup, coffee morning or music class are all great reasons for getting you and your teething toddler out and about. Failing this, why not knock on your neighbour's door and invite her and her twins around for a pot of Earl Grey and a custard cream?

The crucial thing in all of this is to remember your identity within this crazy world of mothering. When you have an office job to get up for every day (where people refer to you by your name and not just as Mummy) it's far easier to be reminded of who you were and who you still are. But we all deserve to forge our own lives, even if they are intertwined with those of our children. You're unlikely to get thanks anytime soon from the world at large so to value your own role and make it one you're happy and fulfilled with, you need to be pro-active. Why not start today?

Mother knows best

'After I gave birth to my second son we just couldn't afford for me to work and pay extortionate childcare fees. I spent the first year of full-time motherhood in a haze of snotty faces and tantrums and my self-confidence was at rock bottom. I felt incredibly depressed. After my doctor prescribed Prozac I was adamant I had to turn things around. I decided to do everything I could to build up my old passions and interests again and to try to rebuild my own identity. Slowly but surely I gained the momentum to start a weekly book club at my home, to join a local gym (which I attend two nights a week for spinning classes) and to organise a few girlie nights out with the local mums. These all helped immeasurably and I certainly feel I've turned a corner without dependency on prescription drugs.'

Full-time mum of two

Re-entering the Workplace after a Break

Whether your youngest child is five or twenty-five, many women who've taken time out to raise a family reach a point at which they start to consider going back to work. In my experience this is rarely while you're in the throes of full-scale toddlerdom (although at the third supermarket checkout screaming fit, you'd be forgiven for wishing you were back in the sanctuary of an office!). The vast majority of mums find this baby/toddler stage a time for downscaling, not upping, the work quota. However, for many women, as their youngest child waves goodbye at the primary school gates or catches the bus to their new secondary school, the feeling that work might once again be on the agenda becomes a prominent force in their minds. Sure, there are plenty of mums who carry on enjoying not working well beyond their kids leaving school – a life of lunches and yoga classes is a nice way to spend a Monday – but for others the child-free hours of nine until three pose a perfect opportunity for rejoining the workforce in some capacity.

The problem many of you will face when this time comes is what the hell to go back to? My neighbour, Amy, is still breastfeeding around the clock, but she's the first to confess that when her third and youngest child, Isis, goes to school she'll still be only a year shy of her thirty-fifth birthday and happy to embrace a new and exciting challenge. Her career pre-kids was one of a high-flying city banker and one that would be ridiculously demanding and incompatible now that she has three children. So her problem won't be a lack of drive and ambition, rather it will be the question of what type of work to do. Likewise, my friend Lissa, who earned a great salary and a wardrobe of designer frocks as a fashion PR, feels that her seven years as full-time mum have left her far too 'out of the loop' to even consider returning to the same career.

Not only can returning to an identical career seem impractical (who wants to be brokering deals at midnight with three kids tucked up in bed and a four-year-old who gets up at five-thirty every morning?) it can actually be tricky in terms of skills. For many women taking a five or ten-year break from the workforce means a return to a totally changed market. The skills they require for the job have shifted, the vocabulary is more diverse and the whole social climate almost unrecognisable from the one they left in the late 1990s. I know one mum whose old job as secretary would now be impossible without up-to-date computer skills. She hasn't touched a computer for eight years and is about as familiar with email as she is with outer space. This total distance from working life and the hours, the skills and the public persona it requires, inevitably leads to a lack in working confidence for mums. When you've been immersed in baby-talk, toddler-chat and school politics for the past few years, donning a power suit and applying for an office job is bound to feel about as alien to you as strutting down a catwalk in the latest Agent Provocateur underwear!

It's a catch-22 for thousands of mums all over the country: your kids are growing up, you want to re-enter some sort of workforce (even if it's just for a few hours a week), but you feel way too out of touch to even consider how to go about it. Even if you have begun to play around with possible open-ings or have attempted a flick through your dusty old contacts book, the idea of working long hours or requesting a working day that allows you to be home for school pick-up seems a long shot. Why on earth would a potential employer choose you, a thirty-something mum who hasn't worked for years and needs to leave the office at three, over an enthusiastic twenty-something recent graduate or trainee who positively beams at the thought of over-time. You see my point?

The issue here is that because there seem to be so many deterrents or reasons not to return to work, mums tend to be put off. The problems with this are obvious, but the main one that springs to mind is the simple fact that when your children start school, if you're not utterly content with a pile of washing-up, maybe a little charity work and the odd game of tennis with a girlfriend, you're going to be bored stupid. There's surely only a certain amount of ironing, chit-chatting and working-out one mum can do without feeling slightly limited? I know mums who'd argue with this, and I'm not going to disagree with them, but I know a vast number who would stand by my point that the school hours of their children pose a wonderful opportunity to do some sort of paid work, and stretch their minds a little. For these same women a life of household activities has often led to a life of small-talk and (I hate to say it) an unhealthy obsession with the lives of their children (we've all met the mother of three teenagers who spends most of her life in the gym and the rest of it telling you of her geniuses' achievements at school), so the window for change may well feel like a refreshing one.

The following advice is not aimed particularly at women with young children or those with school kids, but possibly more at women whose children are growing up and moving away, whose kids no longer need ferrying around between school, friends and extra-curricular activities. These same women may well begin to feel it's time to redirect their attention to some sort of work outside of the homestead. The tips I offer below are just devised to give these women confidence in their ability to step outside their role as mother and wife and into a different pair of shoes (even if just for a small part of every week). They are also written with a whole host of my mummy friends in mind, because the older my children grow, the more I hear a multitude of mums' voices asking, 'How do I begin to re-enter the working world again? Please heeeeeelp!'

Define your skills and interests

You may not want to return to the world of law or media, but then again using your extensive knowledge of quick, easy kids' meals may not drive you in the direction of becoming a dinner lady, either. It's important to define what your interests are and what skills, old and new, you possess in order to work out how you can utilise these skills and interests to create a working life you'll thrive in. Maybe you've got a flair for languages and, with a little extra training, translating could be your thing. Possibly you've gained an increasing knowledge and thirst for nutrition or homeopathy and with some real commitment you could make this into a career. Could you tap into some old skills like teaching, typing or creative writing and make these the basis for something new? Or maybe you could even consider utilising your years in law by undertaking a refresher course and going on to do some freelance consulting or part-time work for a small, family-friendly firm.

Consider retraining

One of the main ways to switch careers is to retrain. My mother, for instance, took several years out to raise us. When the time came to think about re-entering the workforce her career in the arts world just didn't seem to fit family life. She'd worked immensely hard as a mother to understand and combat both of my brothers' dyslexia and felt that retraining as a special needs teacher would offer her not only job opportunities she felt passionate about but also skills she could adapt to family life. The end result was a job in education that also came with the added bonus of fitting perfectly around the hours of her four kids.

Work out how much you can commit

There's little point applying for night work if you're a single mum with no overnight care for your children. Similarly, you can probably forget heading for the role of CEO at a new company in the city if viably you can only offer two days per week. Think clearly about the hours you can offer (and the childcare costs you can afford for any hours beyond this). It makes much more sense to aim for work that goes hand-in-hand with the needs of your family.

Talk with fellow mums and do some research

By discussing your ambitions or ideas with fellow mums and looking up 'working mums' on the Internet, you'll be surprised at how much advice and support you'll get. You may well find a neighbour who knows a great college where you could retrain as a teacher or you might meet a friend who could advise you on how to seek freelance work or another that offers you some contacts in a relevant field. Likewise, on the Internet you'll find tons of agencies and support groups for working mums all looking for work which can be done in family-friendly hours and in a family-friendly environment. (I've listed some of these in my 'Useful Addresses' section.)

It may not even be purely work advice you need, but support to venture out in the first place. Just chatting with a pal may prompt an offer of collecting the kids from school to free you up to go and see an editor about writing up an article or a headmistress about some part-time nursery assistant work. Just don't be too proud to lean on those around you.

Go at it as a team

You may find that working with a friend or acquaintance is a great way to share the workload. I seem to read a lot about famous female duos who've made it in the business world by leaning on each other (Sadie Frost and Gemima French, Sara and Aimee Berman, Lucie McCullin and Emma Milne-Watson to name a few), but even for mums like you or me, dividing the risk and possible success can make it all seem more 'doable'. If your dream is to set up a small boutique, then it's much more achievable if you share the workload, the cash flow and the brainstorming of ideas with one or more friends. Even something less ambitious, such as starting up a weekly yoga group, can be so much less daunting if there are two of you to share the research and commitment involved in starting something new. Not only does working as a team promote motivation, it comes with the added bonus of having someone to fall back on when one of your kids is ill or you're off on a week's camping holiday!

Re-define a working image and prepare your thoughts

If it's the conventional workforce you're returning to, or even a new field altogether, you'll need to give a little time and effort to thinking about your appearance and interview technique. You'll definitely get brownie points from a potential employer, investor or bank manager if you turn up with some ready-made questions, a business plan and an unstained blouse! Writing your ideas and queries down beforehand and slipping out of your ripped jeans and into a sassy knee-length skirt will also make you feel tons more equipped for a new challenge.

Don't expect too much too soon

Be careful not to expect too much of yourself. If you've set your sights on getting the lead in a West End musical (on the basis of an amateur dramatics certificate from your primary school drama teacher) you may be left feeling rather disappointed when the role goes to Martine McCutcheon! Take small steps towards your end goal, attempting to gain more and more confidence along the way. Remember also to congratulate yourself on every interview gained, business proposition accepted or grade achieved in your retraining – even if it's not the big 'wow' job offer you'd dreamed of you'll be making important steps towards regaining your status in the working world.

Follow your dreams

You may be lucky enough to make this your golden opportunity to try something you've always dreamed of doing. Writing a novel, importing French antique furniture, setting up a mail-order kids' clothing company or just offering a cake-decorating service to friends. If you have the time, motivation and financial security, then grab the opportunity with both hands and don't waste any more time dreaming about it!

Mother knows best

'All in all it's been ten years since I've worked in any capacity at all. Having four children has kept me so busy the years have flown by. Now my youngest is six I really feel it's time to reinvest in myself and a career of sorts. Prior to having my children I'd always worked in education, so teaching seemed a natural starting point. Although I didn't want to work full-time within a school, I decided that by retraining as a support teacher, I'd be able to work from home with hours that would suit family life. It took several years to get the up-to-date qualifications I needed, but I've finally found my feet. I now have around ten students aged from eleven to eighteen, who come to the sanctuary of my conservatory once a week. I give them extra help with maths and English and I gain an enormous amount of pride from my work. It also helps to finally be earning some money doing what I love.'

Part-time working mum of four

Lean on Me

When you have a busy family life, balancing a career as well takes a hell of a lot of effort. Not only do you need organisational skills by the bucket-load and excess energy in vast supplies, you also need a valuable support structure to back you up. Ask any successful working mum who her key supporters are and she's likely to list anyone from child-minder or mother, to neighbour or partner. You'd certainly be very unlikely to find any working mum who goes it alone. Sure, there are single mums (like Sophie) who manage to juggle a multitude of roles at any given time, without a partner or possibly even extended family member to lean on. However, you'll often find that they have a secret weapon in the form of a fabulous mummy network, whizzkid au pair or ever-obliging neighbour to turn to for help and advice.

In my experience, the trick to striking the (nigh on) perfect balance between work and family life is to have key friends, family and carers to lean on. When I worked four ultra-hectic, full-on, mind-frazzling days a week at *Elle* with a one-year-old and an eight-month-baby-bump in tow, my support structure consisted of my wonderful in-house childminder, Helen, my attentive and ever-obliging husband Michael, my on-call weekend children's entertainer and chef (aka my sister Fleur) and my large and superb network of fabulous mums. For my friend, Jennie, a thriving career was largely possible thanks to her mother-in-law and local mums, and for my boutique-owning neighbour Rainbow it's a fusion of sister, nursery teachers and best friend Amy.

There are no universal rules to building a support struc-ture around yourself and your working day; the only hard and fast rule is you need one! It doesn't take a genius to work out that to leave three kids even for just a few hours a week you need a dependable backdrop of helpers. These need to be people you like and trust and who understand your work and family ethos. Even if you're a full-time mum, you may find you need a little extra help to make the demands of running a family less of a burden and more of a pleasure, or just so you can have a few hours a week to yourself (to work out, buy some cotton undies unassisted by a two-year-old, or to start a retraining course to pave your way for the future). I've listed some of the support options below, so pick and mix from the list to suit your working hours, lifestyle and budget:

Mary Poppins

For many working families a full-time nanny is something far more likely to appear on an American sitcom than in their neighbourhood. Having said that, if you're returning to work, whether it be full- or part-time, most women need to rely on some sort of paid childcare. Whether this be a sole-charge nanny, a nanny-share, a live-in carer, a registered childminder, a nursery or a school, you really need to find the perfect solution for you and your child to instil maximum confidence in you both. My advice has always been research, research, research – everything from Ofsted reports and references, to local hearsay and location. You can never be *too* informed when it comes to deciding on care for your kids.

Babysitters

Even if you've found the dream nursery and have an obliging mother-in-law who'll help with the kids every Sunday morning, evening childcare can be a problem. You may need to work late, attend a PTA meeting, or you may just want to catch a movie or go for a run before you hit the sack. Having the phone numbers of a few local babysitters who'll help you achieve this is essential. We're lucky in that we have the lovely Gillian, who at a few days' notice will come in the evenings and help out.

Domestic help

The term 'cleaner', or dare I say it 'housekeeper', might be largely the domain of the uber-rich but that doesn't mean working mums like you or me might not need some extra domestic help now and then. I confess to employing a cleaner once a week. Sasha comes for a few hours to iron shirts and de-crust my hob and to be honest, with two children, another on the way and a demanding freelance job, I feel it's a justified luxury and one that I happily spend my well-earned pennies on. (Sasha's also come in very handy when I've had long periods without childcare and she's happily danced and hoovered at the same time to entertain my two kids, while I wrote a double-page feature for a women's magazine.)

Other odd jobs

Even if you can't part with that extra thirty quid a week, but feel overwhelmed with the demands of work, kids and the household chores, you may want to look into outsourcing some of those niggling domestic jobs. Sick of the ironing? Find a local company that will collect, iron and deliver those shirts, so you can get on with tending to the newborn and working towards that promotion. No time to flex those green fingers? Then unearth a local gardening firm to work wonders on your forty-foot 'pride and joy'. Or, how about something as simple as ordering your groceries online and having them delivered when the kids are there to help unpack?

Family and friends

Take up those offers of help! Make the most of willing friends and family, and reciprocate whenever you can! My two sisters-in-law (who have six kids between them) help each other out on a daily basis by sharing school runs and childcare. Unfortunately for me, my own sister and mum live on the other side of London, but during the week I lean on a handful of my fellow school mums for morning playdates and occasional help with school pick-ups, and I return the favour whenever they need it. I have to say that I've found this process of building up a support framework of friends has boosted my morale and belief in solidarity immeasurably. At the end of the day we're all in this mothering lark together!

Neighbours

It's rather old-fashioned I know, but I really believe in reviving the idea of a close-knit neighbourhood. Even if you live in splendid isolation or in a road jam-packed with student flats, there's likely to be a few young families somewhere not too far from you. My advice would be to tap into this network. I feel immensely lucky to have found myself in a street with a whole heap of like-minded, energetic young mums. We're constantly at each other's houses for tea and biscuits or asking for impromptu childcare while we attend a parents' evening or a last-minute work meeting.

Especially if you're new to a neighbourhood, it's well worth attending some local playgroups. Brave the mummy mafia, break the ice first and you're likely discover a whole host of friendly faces ready to welcome you in. (If you're on the receiving end to a newcomer, do what I did and take over a bottle of wine or bunch of flowers to a new mummy neighbour and welcome them into your parenting community.)

As with everything, it's a case of sharing resources and helping each other where you can. If you're lucky enough to have a super efficient and energetic nanny, then how about asking her if once a week she'll have your son's best pal over for supper (thereby giving his mum three hours to attend her secretarial refresher course)? If you live close to your sisters, then how about rotating Saturday morning garden play, so each of you gets some time to yourselves? Even if it's as simple as watching your neighbour's twins while she attends a job interview or when she's running late from her part-time job, leaning on those around you and allowing them to do the same is the trick to juggling family life with more ease and less stress.

Mother knows best

'My husband and I relocated to the North after he received a once-in-a-lifetime job offer. It was very hard for me to start afresh in a neighbourhood where I knew no one. In Essex I'd had both my mother and best friend within walking distance and suddenly I was in a new area, the kids at new schools, with a totally empty address book! It wasn't long, however, before I plunged myself into making friends with the mums at the local school and joined a weekend family swimming club where plenty of families lived close by. I found the only way of building up support was to rise above my initial shyness and attempt to make new friends and neighbours as quickly as possible. By leaning on those mums I've managed to start up a small business from home selling personalised party cakes. I can honestly say that without my fellow mums (and their regular offers of playdates and sleepovers) this wouldn't have been possible.'

Part-time working mum of three

Top ten working life tips

1. Prepare for the balance between work and family to shift with each child you have. Emotional issues as well as childcare requirements change and evolve with your growing family.
2. Deciding whether to return to work (and in what capacity) is a tough one and involves a lot of thought and planning.
3. Working full-time with a young family is the ultimate in multi-tasking. Try and formulate some ground rules

at home and in the office that will help you get the best of both worlds (without turning your hair grey overnight).

4. It's worth considering your options – part-time, flexi-time, job share, freelancing – to enable you to spend more time with your family.

5. Ever considered retraining? A career path doesn't have to be a life sentence, you know.

6. Maintaining your own identity within your role as a full-time mum is vital for your confidence and sense of self-worth.

7. Don't feel it's impossible to re-enter the work place after taking a break. You may just need to put some energy and effort into redefining your skills and areas of expertise.

8. Whatever your working dynamic, surround yourself and your children with a good support structure – reliable, trustworthy childcare is the key to working with confidence.

9. Lean on like-minded women for advice and friendship (not to mention that last-minute offer of after-school help because your meeting has over-run by an hour).

10. Remember that guilt is counter-productive. Either be confident with your work/home choices or make it a priority to change them to suit your life and family's needs better.

Grace's Guru: Gillian Nissim

Gillian Nissim is the founder of www.workingmums.co.uk, a jobsite and community for professional women looking for family-friendly, flexible, part-time, office and home-based job opportunities. She started Working Mums as a result of her own experiences and to cater for the businesses who did appreciate the vast experience and high calibre of professionals who had become mums and wanted to find more flexible work opportunities.

Prior to starting up her own business, Gillian was a senior manager in internal communications for financial institutions and also worked within the Home Office. She has two boys – Joseph (six) and Max (four).

What are your main work tips for the following mums?

A mum who can't decide whether to return to work after having a baby Whether to go back to work or not is rarely an easy decision. And it's not at all unusual to find that, despite having everything planned out before the birth, what you'd planned on doing isn't necessarily what you want to do once your baby has arrived. Even if you've loved your career, you may just feel 'differently' once you've had your baby. Everyone's circumstances and situations are different. However, it's important to remember that any decision you make is not irrevocable and, whether you choose to stay at home or go back to work, you can change your mind if things aren't working out.

Your decision will be influenced by a number of factors, including whether or not it is financially viable for you to stay at home, what childcare is available to you if you decide to return to work, and how much that childcare will cost. You may also make your decision based on whether or not you can return to work on a flexible basis, so make sure you're aware of your rights as an employee regarding flexible working and research other flexible working opportunities that are available to you.

Quite apart from the practical considerations, the decision to go back to work can be very tough emotionally, and will inevitably be accompanied by huge amounts of guilt. In the weeks before I went back to work after having my first son I was regularly in tears at the thought of leaving him and the guilt was made worse by the fact that my son cried every time I left him for the first three weeks he was at nursery (but, as I discovered, would stop crying within minutes of me leaving – and would spend a day playing while I left for work wracked with guilt). Being confident in your childcare and having a good network of 'working mum' friends around you will really help. You'll feel more confident and less stressed knowing your child is being well looked after and it's reassuring to have the support of people around you who have gone through the same decisions and same tumult of emotions as you're experiencing. It's important to realise there will be a period of adjustment – probably several weeks – as you all get used to your new circumstances and routine. It's also important to focus on the upsides too: working can have a very positive effect on self-esteem, confidence and sense of self-worth, as well as helping to ease financial pressures, all of which can contribute to a healthy work/life balance and happy family life.

Ultimately there is no 'right' answer and everybody's situation and circumstances are different. It's important to take your time and talk to your partner and family. Writing a list of pros and cons to see how different options weigh up can help you to make that decision. Here are some points to consider:

- Look at your financial situation and write a budget plan. Can you cope financially if you don't go back to work?

- Talk to friends who've had the same decision to make. What do they say are the pros and cons of their decisions?

- Would you like to work, but work flexibly? If so, understand what your rights are as an employee and research alternative flexible working opportunities.

- Think about childcare – this is absolutely key if you're thinking of going back to work. You must feel confident and happy about your childcare arrangements and have back-up, for example, for if your childminder is sick. This will make your return much easier.

- Get informed – make sure you have all the facts about flexible working, childcare options, etc. at your fingertips.

- Don't forget: once you have decided, you can always change your mind if it isn't working out.

- If you're going back to work, discuss with your partner/family how things will work at home so that the load is shared.

A mum who's desperate for a good balance between her work and home life Whether you're working or not, once you're a mother, life becomes a juggling act, but there are things you can do to make it easier.

- **Get organised!** This sounds very regimental, but having plans, lists and timetables helps create balance. If you know exactly what you're going to do and when/who needs to be where and when and have it all written down, it really does help reduce stress – and don't forget to plan some 'free' time for relaxation too!

- **Discuss working flexibly with your employer.** In many cases if you've worked over a certain amount of time with the same employer, and have children up to six years old or a disabled child under the age of eighteen, you have a right to ask to work flexibly. This will be extended by April 2009 to all parents of children under sixteen. Many employers are becoming more willing to find ways to help employees work more flexibly – and that can include reducing hours, allowing more home-working or job sharing. First of all, ensure that you have researched your company's policies and are aware both of your rights as an employee and also those of your employer. When you approach your employer, go with a business-minded proposition that works and benefits both you and your employer – and show how you can be an even more valuable and productive employee if you are able to work flexibly.

- **Find a new job.** Some jobs (like some careers) can be more stressful than others and you may find you can reduce some of the stress by finding a less pressurised job. This may involve finding a new job with your current employer, or looking for a brand-new job. It may mean temping, or going freelance, or even (as I did!) starting your own business.

- **Be confident in your childcare choices.** If you're happy with your childcare and know that your children are happy it will reduce a lot of stress.

- **Share the load.** Don't be afraid to ask for help, and consider more help at home whether that's a cleaner/someone to help with ironing or an au pair to give you that little bit more quality time for your family and for yourself.

- **Learn to 'let go'.** Realise that everything doesn't have to be perfect.
- **Learn to say 'no'.** It's very easy to take on extra tasks and responsibilities and want to be involved in everything that's going on around you, but learning to focus in on what's important in your life and 'de-cluttering' will help you to simplify your life.

A mum who wants to return to work after a five-year break Think about what kind of jobs you want to apply for and the kind of employers you'd like to work for. Do you want to work full- or part-time? Do you want to be office- or home-based? Look in the job sections of papers and at online jobsites for the kind of jobs you're interested in. You may find that the first job you do when you initially go back is not the role you'll end up in, but it may well be a good stepping-stone.

It's also important to identify any skills gaps and look for training courses that will help to ensure your skills are up to date. Attending courses is a good reintroduction to networking too and will help to boost your confidence. And if you're thinking about working from home you will find that, for most home-based jobs, being competent with using a PC, emails and the Internet is vital. There is a huge range of computer courses available through local colleges and also privately.

Don't forget to brush up your CV too – and think about what you've done in the interim such as being involved with the PTA, playgroups or organising fêtes. Prepare a covering letter in which you talk about your determination to get back to work and write a short paragraph about any training you've undergone to brush up your skills.

In my experience, many women who've taken a break find that talking to friends who've also done the same offers a lifeline of advice and tips. Ask them what they've done to re-integrate into the workplace, what they found hard and what helped them. You could also ask them to help you practise your interview techniques. The more you practise, the more comfortable and confident you will get.

A mum looking for a job that is ideal to do part-time or as flexi-time As I've explained in the work/life balance tips above, you should explore options with your existing employer to work on a flexible basis. Remember, parents who have a child aged up to six years or a disabled child under eighteen have the right to apply to work flexibly. This will be extended to parents of children under sixteen from April 2009. Their employers have a duty to consider these requests seriously.

If your existing employer can't help, there are alternatives. More and more companies are embracing flexible working practices. The Internet is a good place to start – jobsites such as www.workingmums.co.uk are geared up specifically to link employers looking for part-time professionals with mums who want to work more flexibly, and cover a vast range of roles that vary from full-time home-based work to term-time-only five-hours-a-week roles.

You should also consider contacting companies you want to work for directly – particularly if you know of companies with good flexible working policies. Local papers can also be a surprisingly good source of quality part-time jobs. And talk to your friends and mums network. You might find, for instance, that someone you know is looking for a job-share partner.

Before you request or start looking for flexible work, make sure you've thought through how flexible you want the role to be, how many hours a week you want to work and whether it is important that you can work from home either some or all of the time. You should also know what your childcare arrangements (and contingencies) will be and how you will cover things like the school holidays.

A mum looking for work she can do in the evenings or while the kids are at school to earn some extra cash There are a number of work opportunities for mums who want to work in the evenings or term-time only. And opportunities are as varied as jewellery and make-up party organisers to sales reps for educational products and running your own music classes. You need to think about whether you want to be an employee or whether you would prefer being a franchisee or business owner.

Just remember, when you look into these opportunities make sure you research the companies well and be clear about what the requirements of the job are. Be wary of any opportunities that ask you to make a financial commitment upfront, unless they are a recognised franchise.

The Internet is a really good source of jobs – as well as Workingmums, which offers a variety of term-time-only jobs, there are a range of other sites which offer evening work with reputable companies. Alternatively, you may spot a gap in the market and decide to set up your own business . . .

A mum who feels she'd been wrongly treated by an employer because of her family life It is unlawful for an employer to treat you less favourably than other employees on account of your family life, and if you feel you have been discriminated against by your employers because of being a mum, you should address this with them. There is a formal procedure to follow and it's important to ensure you familiarise yourself with this.

Once of the first things you need to do is get all your facts together and keep note of incidents you feel are relevant. You should then request a meeting with your employers and speak to them directly, raising these issues, explaining what you see as discrimination and asking for an explanation. If necessary, put your complaint in writing. You may be able to get help from an employee representative (such as a trades union official), and if your employer has an equal opportunities policy, you should ask to see it. In an ideal world, the issue will be resolved immediately; however, all too often this is unfortunately not the case. If so, you may need to make a complaint using your employer's grievance procedure. If you're still unhappy the next step is to apply to an Employment Tribunal. In the case of unfair dismissal, claim forms have to be filed within three months of the discrimination taking place. In other cases such as sexual harassment, the general rule is that a letter of complaint must be sent within three months of the action that is complained about and the claim form should be received at the Employment Tribunal within six months of the action that is complained about. The employer then has twenty-eight days to respond. Once you have received the response you need to consider your options.

Organisations such as the Equal Opportunities Commission,

the Citizens Advice Bureau and The Advisory, Conciliation and Arbitration Service (ACAS) all offer free advice and I would strongly recommend speaking with them about your situation from the outset. They will also be able to help you if you are unsure about what type of discrimination you may be experiencing.

What are the key dos and don'ts for the mum seeking the perfect work/life balance?

Do

- Be organised and plan your time carefully. Planning in advance will ensure that you always know where you are and can fit everything in, including some time for fun and relaxation.
- Consider changing your work patterns/job to free up more of your time. Make sure you know your rights and those of your employer, and go to your employer with a well-thought-out business proposition for flexible working hours.
- Be confident in your childcare – if you know your children are happy, you'll find yourself much more relaxed, positive and focused at work.
- Ensure you get proper legal advice if you think you've been discriminated against (ACAS, Equal Opportunities Commission and Citizens Advice Bureau all offer free legal advice).
- Be positive about the decisions you make – many women choose to return to work because they enjoy it as much as for financial reasons, and where a balance can be found I'm a firm believer that what's good for the mother is good for the child.

Don't

- Don't think it's all or nothing. If your existing employer can't offer you the flexibility you're looking for, there are other alternatives. Many more employers are now actively embracing flexibility within the workplace, and a recent survey by the CBI shows that forty-six per cent of employers in the UK are now offering home working compared with eleven per cent in 2006.
- Don't think you're on your own – millions of women face the same 'to work or not to work' dilemmas and issues of achieving a good work/life balance. Talk to friends, go online . . . you will always find a kindred spirit, a shoulder to cry on or someone to rant to over a glass (or two) of wine.
- Don't try to be supermum – ask for help if you need it and if you're returning to work, agree with your partner how you're going to share the load.
- Don't accept unfavourable treatment from an employer either when pregnant, on maternity leave, or as a result of having children. Discrimination is against the law and you can do something about it.

> **Gillian's fabulous mum's work/life mantra:** 'Being a working mum can be challenging and requires compromise, but it also offers great rewards. Be confident and proud of the decisions you make because a good work/life balance benefits everyone, including your family.'

Last, but by No Means Least, Me!

Who Am I These Days?

Last week my husband was away for seven days and seven nights. It's his fortieth birthday this summer and as part of his present I helped him to organise a charity bicycle ride through the rim of the Grand Canyon. While I washed endless whites, organised cakes for a stall at the school picnic and tried to cram in three interviews for an article I was writing (during which the children began World War Three over who ate the last Mini Milk), he was camping out under the stars with his best mates, experiencing immense physical and emotional highs along the way. After five nights of cooking myself cheese on toast for supper and going to bed before it was even dark outside, I got a crackly mobile phone call from him as their jeep headed through the desert towards Las Vegas. Charged up and euphoric, beer bottles clinking in the background, he sounded so invigorated I swelled with pride. However, as I put down the phone, an empty wrapper of Green & Black's butterscotch chocolate and a firmly leafed copy of Yehudi Gordon's *Birth and Beyond* beside me, a little voice inside wanted to scream, 'But what about meeeeeeeeeeeeeeeeeee?'

I lay very still and tried not to feel jealous; after all, this was something we'd planned together and as an amazing husband, father and boss he, almost more than anyone I know, deserved some time way from it all, bonding with his mates, experiencing once-in-a-lifetime sights and raising thousands for charity while he was at it. So why did I feel so left out? As my mind pondered over the last five years, I thought about my own highs and lows: having both my children and experiencing the wonderment of carrying a third, seeing their first steps, hearing their first words, letting go of my daughter's hand on her first day at school, hearing my son read his first book, receiving love letters from them both on Mother's Day. Sure, in the mix were watching the sunset in my husband's arms on our mini-break in Morocco, drinking too much bubbly at my gorgeous friend Ros's wedding last year, and of course seeing the first ever edition of my original *The Fabulous Mum's Handbook*, but by and large the majority of my recent memories and achievements have been those created in relation to my role as 'mum'.

At that moment I wanted more than anything else to be lying on a beach somewhere hot, surrounded by my best girlfriends, hearing the clink of our wine glasses as we chatted and laughed and confided and shared. No baby wipes, maths homework deadlines, school fees, dirty football socks or bumper bottles of tomato ketchup in sight. I wanted just for a second to feel more than anything like 'Grace', not Grace the mum, Grace the wife, Grace the author, Grace the class rep, Grace the kids' chauffeur or Grace the 'more fish fingers pleeeeeeeeeeeeeeeease!' provider. At this moment I picked up the phone and called my mum. She listened as I irrationalised and cried and asked her over and over again, 'Who am I these days?' until in the end she sighed and said, 'But Grace, you are the same person you've always been, only now you have some added strings to your bow.' Despite looking rather snotty and feeling rather more ridiculous than I had an hour previously (that's pregnancy hormones for you!), I then made my second call to one of my oldest and best friends, Katie, who lives a couple of hours from London in a small village in Wiltshire. 'It's half-term, I'm coming to stay for a few days with the children. Be there tomorrow at midday, OK . . . ?'

In true, old-friend form, Katie was waiting, six-month-old baby Archie in her arms, chocolate-chip cookies in the oven and a bottle of fizz in the fridge (just for half a glass mind you, before you condemn me for binge drinking while pregnant!). While my children rambled in the garden (oh, the joys of having more green out back than the fifty-foot which constitutes 'acres' in London) Katie and I chatted for hours and ate our way through almost all the hot, gooey cookies. We reminded ourselves of fun times gone by: nights at university when we'd attempt an essay after an all-night rave; the 'surprise' visit I made to her when she was working in New York (when we got matching tattoos in our excitement at seeing each other after a three-month gap!); and my wedding day when, with flowers in her hair, she'd shone as maid of honour. We stuffed another batch of cookie mix in the oven, laughed some more and with every second I sat at that kitchen table, sugar and the odd cheap champagne bubble swimming in my veins, I remembered with more clarity who I was.

Don't tell me as a mum of one, two, three, four or even more children you haven't had similar moments? Moments

374

when you're knee-deep in PTA letters, soggy nappies, bolognese sauce and your eldest wailing after cutting his knee in the garden and you just want to scream, '*Let me out!*' It can come at the most unexpected time. You could be flicking through a magazine in the doctor's surgery and come across 'romantic dinner for two ideas' and before you know it you're remembering a time when cooking lovingly for your (then) new date occupied at least three days' thought. Or it could be when you bump into an old work colleague as you're trawling the high street for maternity jeans, your toddler and rusk-smeared buggy in tow. Minus a partner or anything remotely like children, your old work colleague is wearing three-inch Manolos and just about to 'meet a client for lunch, daaarling'. As she whizzes to hail a black cab you're left looking down at your grubby Converse-clad feet thinking, just for that split second, *I'd like a taste of my old life back.*

You should know by now that I have embraced my role as mum with open arms. I certainly haven't had many backward glances as my role of fashion journalist on a glitzy and glamorous title has evolved into that of freelance writer and author who works largely from home in battered Levis. However, as my week rolls from writing a chapter on fashion for mums and planning the school summer fête, to buying navy socks for a four-year-old and seeking the best local midwives to cater for a home birth, there are the odd occasions when I want to break out of the mould and do something totally unexpected (like cycle through the Grand Canyon with my girlfriends). This doesn't make me a bad mother, it doesn't make me love my role or my family any less; in my mind it just makes me utterly human.

So, while you're pureeing the next batch of broccoli and butternut squash for your baby, surfing online for the perfect summer break with three under-fives, interviewing for the ideal nanny share so you can return to work, or discussing with your girlfriends where the best local secondary school is, why not ask yourself too, what tiny things you can do for yourself? Even in the mayhem and chaos of motherhood it's so crucial to maintain an essence of your own identity, your own passions, interests and skills. Failing this, you'll turn around in ten years' time (if not before) and be totally lost at the question, 'Who am I these days?'

Mother knows best

'I gave up work completely when I had my daughter and after the twins my life became totally consumed by the children. I immersed myself in playgroups, nursery activities and knowledge of child development; in short I became the epitome of a 'full-time mum' (in every sense). Now the children are all at school I am left slightly bewildered as to what to do next. I hardly recognise the person I am today and wonder at times if it's too late to merge my pre-children life with the one I have now. I try not to regret anything but in many ways I wish I'd kept up with some of my old friends and colleagues and continued with just the smallest amount of my own pursuits.'

Full-time mum of three

Carving out Time for Yourself

Yesterday I was a 'knightess' in shining armour for two of my great girlfriends. Sometimes when our fellow mums are in need the only thing to do is to whizz round there, relieve them of their kids (taking as many of them as will legally squeeze into the back seat of the car to the park, with an offer of 99s and wet sandpit play) and let your pal have an hour to breathe. In my close-knit group this is known as '999 mums' network'.

The reason I was on call for not only one but two of my good friends yesterday is simple: they were both in dire need of some time to themselves. And we're not talking an 'important' date with the hair colourist or personal trainer here; it was a case of needing some essential 'time out'. The first 999 mum call was made by my good friend, Jennie, three days before her due date with her second child. Her husband had been working all weekend, it had rained from morning to night and in between Braxton Hicks her three-year-old, Minnie, had been driving her up the wall. To top things off she had a ten a.m. appointment with the midwife to see if the baby's head had engaged and her neighbour (who'd offered to help with childcare that morning) had ended up in casualty with her three-year-old after an incident with a trampoline and a garden spade (ouch!). To cut a long story short, my SOS emergency pitstop to collect Minnie meant her mum not only made that ten o'clock appointment at the hospital but also managed to wash her hair and buy some toilet paper/plain flour/ketchup/cornflakes in peace!

The second 999 mum call was from my friend Florence, who had been home alone with her daughter for a full six weeks as the latter recovered from a broken leg. (Yet another unfortunate accident with a trampoline – can anyone remind me why I've just bought one for the garden?) Now her daughter had recovered and was raring to go, Florence had a mound of paperwork to get through, a tax return due in that day and at least eighteen clients to call to reschedule their appointments (she's a self-employed homeopath). She was the first to confess that ideally she'd really rather do all this with a peaceful house, a cup of herbal tea and some classical music playing in the background and not to the sound of *The Little Mermaid* DVD played at full volume and a three-year-old bouncing on the sofa!

I was only too happy to take all three kids to the park (seeing as taking playmates for my son means I don't have to whizz down the slide like an overgrown toddler in order to ensure he has a good time!). Plus the fact that in the past six months Jennie has stepped in to help when I've had no child-care and a deadline for a magazine article or a parents' evening at school, and Florence has had the children on several occasions when morning sickness got the better of me!

While I watched the children play chase in the park I started thinking about how hard it is to carve out time for yourself as your family grows. We expect ourselves to be these superhuman, multi-tasking perfectionists (you know, just like the 'supermums' depicted in glossy magazines with four kids, a full-time job, a gorgeous house in the country, a to-die-for body and designer wardrobe to boot!) who just breeze through our diverse roles with maximum efficiency and minimum fuss, when really and truly it's exhausting us! Working so hard at all these roles means in the end we're left knackered, on our knees, making 999 mum calls to our best buddy just so we can keep work afloat and go into labour knowing the baby is the right way up!

For most mums I know, carving out time for themselves is far more complicated than it ever was with one child. It no longer means enlisting their mother-in-law to help for an afternoon so they can go for a swim and read the papers in peace (as it did when family life meant an attentive partner and a six-month-old). No, 'time for ourselves' now means putting on CBeebies while we rush around for an hour cleaning the bath, writing up some kids' party invites, enrolling the children in a swimming club and possibly, just possibly, going to the toilet! The thought that maybe one day you could actually do something for yourself in that hour (a yoga class, a freelance feature, a browse in the bookshop, a cuppa with a friend, or a peaceful chill with your eyes closed, thinking of nothing) seems about as viable as winning this week's National Lottery.

I'm sure if I'd told Jennie and Florence to take a stroll to the local patisserie, sit with a cappuccino and eat a large cake, or read *Eve* with their feet up while I cared for the kids they would have choked on their breakfast. For most of us busy mums (the fully staffed yummy mummies who hang out in Harvey Nics aside) creating time for ourselves just doesn't even make it to the bottom of the 'to-do list' (let alone coming in anywhere as high as 'wash gym kit', 'talk to boss about leaving early on Friday for Tom's nativity play' and 'book doctor's appointment for Ella's eczema').

Having thought about all this as the game of tag evolved into kiss chase (with my son as the prince and the girls as the princesses), I decided to try a little experiment. I picked up my mobile and called Jennie and Florence. Both of them were at the tail end of their tasks and were gearing up to receive their muddy and ice-cream-stained daughters back. Instead of asking if ten minutes would do, I suggested that they both take an hour longer to do something for themselves. Both responded with silence followed by a long jumbled excuse as to why it was impossible and how they really ought to take the girls swimming/to a playdate/to their grandma's for a visit/or enjoy some 'quality time' with them. It was as if they felt that by acknowledging their own need for an hour 'off' (when they weren't tied to the maternity unit of the local hospital or laptop) they were being selfish or neglectful. In short, the thought of putting their own needs first for a change left them speechless and slightly dumbfounded. In the end, after much persuading and bargaining, I managed to hold off returning from the park for an extra hour and both friends did (I hope) enjoy a peaceful moment to themselves (although knowing them both as I do, they will have snuck in the odd bit of housework in that time as well).

I know I'm guilty of this too. Unless I'm working I feel utterly selfish for using my time with childcare to relax or enjoy myself. Only last week, I'd finished a chapter by four o'clock on a Thursday afternoon and felt like nothing more than celebrating with a latte and a flick through the newspaper at my local French brasserie. I confess, I got as far as the tillpoint (pain au chocolat in my hand, the *Guardian* under my arm) and felt a sudden wave of guilt that I should in fact be attending my daughter's swimming lesson or at least cooking some lasagne for her return. Who the hell did I think I was indulging in a relaxing coffee while my carer struggled to get my daughter's swimming hat on before she missed the lesson? Never mind it had been, oh, at least six months since I'd last had a window of 'me' time in which to enjoy every drop of a latte and catch up on current affairs. So what did I do? I abandoned my ridiculously huge pain au chocolat, retreated into Sainsbury's to buy fresh pasta and called my carer to tell her piping hot lasagne would be awaiting the kids' return. Surely even I can see that I should give myself even the teeniest, tiniest break now and then?

It doesn't take a genius to work out that once we've divided ourselves up to meet everyone's needs and all our roles, we're left with only the smallest part of the pie for ourselves. In my mind, this leads us in one direction and it's one heading for trouble. Not only do we feel zapped of energy but, I don't know about you, I start to feel rather resentful. I know that after an intense eight-hour day spent writing, an hour cooking fresh lasagne, forty minutes raising my voice on the phone to my mobile phone company (how can my bills really be so much?) and a long evening of horse-play with my eager-to-see-mum children, I am totally and utterly spent. And you know what I went to bed wishing? I wished I'd spent twenty minutes savouring that quiet time in the coffee shop and heated up some macaroni cheese for the kids instead. It makes little difference to them (macaroni cheese is gobbled up just as fast as lasagne) but a huge difference to my sanity.

After my pain au chocolat versus lasagne afternoon and yesterday's 'persuading my pals to utilise some time for themselves' encounter, I vowed to change my approach to 'me' time. So I have decided, as far as possible, to follow these five commandments:

1. **Don't kick a gift horse in the mouth.** If you get a window for time out, take it and run! Offers of help don't happen every day (or even every week).
2. **Don't feel guilty for enjoying a little time off from your kids.** Investing small pockets of time for yourself isn't a sin, so don't beat yourself up about it. You'll feel tons better for a little change in the daily routine.
3. **Plan ahead.** Trying to carve out small quantities of time for yourself will ensure you don't reach meltdown at the end of each month!
4. **Benefits all round.** It's not only you who will notice the difference after the odd swim or glass of wine and a natter with a pal. If you feel refreshed and revitalised those around you will benefit too.
5. **Because you're worth it!** Just because our role as mums comes before anything else, that doesn't mean we don't need time without our under-fives dragging behind us. You're still deserving of the odd night out or mooch in Topshop for that summer dress, you know!

Mother knows best

'Around my daughter's second birthday I realised it had been over two years since I'd even looked at a gym, let alone read a novel or been out for a romantic meal with my partner. With three kids, all my own needs just seem to be dissolved in one big family pot. To be honest, I was feeling really frumpy, fat and fed up and knew I had to find a little time, even just once a week, to

So Where Is a Good Place to Start?

Exercise

Before I go on to pinpoint exercise as a good starting point for time out for yourself, let me make one thing crystal clear: I am not an advocate of the unrealistic vision of the mummy body beautiful. Under no circumstances do I support the celebrity-led trend for uber-slim, ultra-toned post-maternity mums. I confess I like to get back into my pre-pregnancy jeans at sometime in the year following birth, but I enjoy cupcakes far too much to worry whether this happens ten weeks or ten months after birth (and I certainly don't beat myself up about the extra 'love handles' that might spill over when I do finally squeeze into those jeans again!). Enjoying exercise as a busy mum myself is pure and simple: I do it moderately and periodically because it makes me feel good about myself, it gives me time to relax and unwind each week and if it helps me tone up even the tiniest amount then this is an added bonus but certainly not a must.

Now I've cleared that up for us all, I think I'm safe to talk about the plus-side for mums of incorporating a little exercise into their lives. Sure, if you're a gym bunny or fitness freak training for this year's London Marathon, you may want to make this a daily ritual but for the majority of us I should think aiming to exercise once or twice a week is a realistic start and one that will definitely make a huge difference to your feeling of well-being and vitality. For many busy mums the days whizz past with school runs, commutes to work and many hours rushing around the house after toddlers and hoovers. What often happens is that at the end of each day you feel exhausted, but often not from any real physical exertion. The days are taxing and physically demanding but not necessarily from breaking into a sweat from a jog or cycle up a hill (possibly more from screeching at your teenager or running up the stairs six times to find a spare nappy).

I know that I feel a real difference in my physicality when I've walked all the school runs or done fifty laps in the pool instead of sitting at my computer all day. For starters, I feel much more revived and energised in the day (and even into the evening) once I've exerted myself a little, plus the fact that I always sleep better after a little exercise. I also find that when I walk the kids to school (it's a good forty minutes each way) we really get to chat about things and enjoy some good conversations (it took until the walk to school earlier this week for my son to properly fill me in on the details of his school play and a day in the life of his imaginary friend, 'Zeb'). Likewise, when I'm swimming I'll start off thinking about what to include in the next chapter, move on to creating recipes for the evening meal and finally go on to think about nothing at all, letting my brain shut off for all of eight minutes! It's not every day that it's viable to spend over an hour walking the school drop-off (especially when it's minus two and sleeting outside) or when it's a half-term and getting to the pool is just impossible (a day trip to the zoo is far more likely), but that doesn't mean you shouldn't attempt it when you can.

If, like my friend Danni, you have two kids, all of school age, you may find that you have an opportunity after drop-off (just before you do the food shop, plan your charity bike ride, meet with your son's form teacher and write up the minutes of the PTA meeting!) to go for a run or do a tennis class. If your kids are younger or you work full-time you may need to devise even more complex structures to get out and about. My friend Amy, for example, goes boxing on a Sunday morning and Thursday night while her partner looks after their one-year-old, three-year-old and nine-year-old. Likewise, my working pals Sophie and Paula manage to squeeze in once-a-week yoga sessions (Sophie in her lunch break or before work and Paula on a Saturday morning, while her husband takes the kids swimming).

Even if getting to a gym seems ridiculously tricky and taking a set yoga class each week equally as far-fetched, how about incorporating exercise into your day-to-day life? It's amazing how many people drive their kids to school when going by foot would actually take half the time (and save a heap of dosh on petrol and the excess air pollution); or how many working mums plump for a hurried desk lunch when they could take a stroll through a nearby park, or come the end of the day, could walk two Tube stops further towards home before jumping on board.

I must confess, having enough time to swim at my leisure, I never really walked before I had kids but now I find walking a life-saver for a mum (and kids) in dire need of exercise, fresh air and an excuse to slow down a little. I know my friend Katie feels the same. Before she had Archie she'd drive to the shop to buy a pint of milk but now she has moved to the country, has a babe and a dog, she'll often be found walking for miles each day. She actually started to in the middle of the night (finding midnight walks the only sure way to pacify a colicky baby) and the habit has stuck. She no longer treks the fields at two o'clock in the morning, but not a day goes by without a long walk, wellies and all!

I can't emphasise enough how exercise is the first key to unlocking a pent-up, maxed-out mum's stress box. I've met and heard from so many mums who've told me that since reading my specific advice on exercise in *The Fabulous Mum's Handbook*, they have felt a real change in their lives. Some have found it a great way to lose a little long-established baby weight, some have found it a wonderful tonic to counterbalance the demands of work and family life, and others, such as myself, have learned how to use it as a time to think more clearly without the fuzz induced by the telephone ringing, kids squabbling, emails flashing up and broccoli boiling over on the stove. Whatever box it ticks, I've yet to meet anyone who's started to include fun, moderate exercise (alone, as a pair or in a group) into their busy schedules and hasn't felt the benefits somewhere along the line. Even if it's just to get you out of the house to meet some other mums or as an excuse to lie still humming 'Ommmmmmmmmmm' in peace after a few yoga stretches, it's worth it to have some time of your own again.

Mother knows best

'I used to love my daily run but after having two kids and taking on a new job, the most exercise I got was walking the stairs at the underground station each day! I really missed exercising but just couldn't work out how to fit it into my life. It wasn't until a friend at work bought a bike that I considered doing this too. I got a cheap one at first, in case it didn't work out, and began cycling to work twice a week. Six months on I've now upgraded my bike and got one with a child-seat on the back so I can even drop my daughter at nursery first. I'll then head to the office, where I'll shower and change and be ready for the day. I love it and relish the fact that I beat the rush-hour traffic and get home early too!'

Full-time working mum of two

Relaxation and Fun

With three kids, a part-time job, a busy household and weekly swimming/yoga/Pilates/aqua aerobics, you'd be forgiven for baulking at the idea of adding 'relaxation' and 'fun' to the mix as well. I must be joking, right? Far from adding to the errands to run, jobs to do and 'perfect high-achieving mum' stereotype we're all supposed to live up to these days, my hope is that the prospect of a little more chilling and some added good times might well ease all these pressures somewhat. The aim for me is always to lessen the load, not add to the stress (I hope!). You only have to use the following as an example:

Maxed-out mum profile

Name: Lyn

Marital status: Divorced

Mother of: Three boys under the age of six

Job: Teaching assistant and mum (and general household dogsbody)

Last time you went out for the evening: January 2007 (but it may as well have been January 1987)

Last time you chilled in the bath with a glass of wine and a good book: Too long ago to remember what a long bath, glass of wine or good book look like

Reason for insanity: All of the above.

'Lyn' represents perfectly a multitude of fellow mums I know. Even if her predicament doesn't mirror yours exactly at least some of her profile is bound to strike a chord. (I sure feel it's been at least ten years since I chilled in the bath with a glass of wine and a good book. In fact, the last time I attempted it both my children stripped off and dived in too, leaving me to get out and clear up the red wine that had now sloshed all over my fluffy bath mat!) The sad truth is that the larger our families grow and the more we mums strive to balance work with children, exercise and solid personal relationships, the less time we have for relaxing and fun.

I just have to look at my diary for the month of July to illustrate this. Taking one week as a rough guide to how my summer is shaping up, in total there were: 2 kids' swimming classes, 1 midwife appointment, 1 appointment for daughter with homeopath, 1 haircut for kids, 1 ballet class for daughter, 2 kids' parties, 1 article to write for *Junior Pregnancy and Baby*, 1 chapter to write on work/life balance, 1 meeting with my agent, 1 interview with fashion guru, 1 PTA meeting, 1 summer fête, 1 school picnic, 1 school open day, 4 playdates, and 2 visits to Great-Grandma in hospital. The list goes on but what is sadly missing are the things I need more than any of the above, i.e: 1 supper at the local Thai with girl-friends, 1 housewarming party, 1 haircut (and God knows I need it!), 1 massage from loved one followed by long bath and home-cooked (by him) meal, 1 yoga class, 1 visit to the Tate Modern, 1 nip to Space NK to buy stretch mark oil, and 1 trip to a movie.

I'm not honestly expecting to be massaged and pampered and cooked for every night of the week, but once every so often should surely be a viable aim, don't you think? We all know how much better we feel about everything when we've had a dinner out with friends full of laughter or an hour in the evening where we're not filing bills or hand-washing ballet kits, but actually taking time to relax. It's so important for us mums to maintain these social and personal 'hobbies', if you like, so we don't feel like we're drowning in family and work responsibilities. We're not *so* different from those twenty-something women we once were, whose diaries were jam-packed with social arrange-ments and girlie treats. Sure, we may look that little bit wiser (note I didn't say 'aged and ragged'!) and may have to get up at six on a Sunday to fill bowls with Cheerios and plonk a Roald Dahl CD on, but that doesn't mean

389

our need for a little bit of down-time was lost in the labour room.

When I called a handful of my girlfriends to find out how they managed to prioritise a little time for fun and relaxation within their hectic family lives, I can honestly say we all scored 'nil points'! My pregnant pal Ros was feeling seriously down in the dumps at the overwhelming lack of the above in her diary (suppers at her favourite Italian were rapidly being replaced by visits to view prospective nurseries and childminders and then bed by nine o'clock). My neighbour Amy confessed she'd only been out three times since the birth of her daughter, Isis, last year (and even then she had to race home in time to breastfeed Isis at ten-thirty). As for the mums from school, most had seen far more of their kids' algebra homework than their own living rooms in recent weeks. Surely this calls for some serious action?

The first thing on my 'hit list for mum fun' was to organise a school mums' night out. A group email to all the mums and a booking for a large table at the local gastro pub (on a week night, so hopefully most of the respective partners will look after the kids) and we're well on our way. Even if we kill two birds with one stone and spend the first half an hour chatting about the logistics of the summer teddy bears' picnic, we're sure to go beyond that and all have a few laughs over some chunky chips and rocket salad.

The next morning, kids at school, two thousand words written of Chapter Five and it's time for my second mission: my lovely fellow pregnant friend, Ros. First I get a tentative confirmation from my Mary Poppins weekend babysitter, Gillian, for the following Saturday night and I then email Ros at work to convince her and her other half to meet me and mine for a Saturday night supper at our favourite feel-good Greek restaurant. I also throw in the suggestion that we get cracking with organising a summer brunch in her garden to celebrate her birthday (with all of her good buddies bringing the food, wine, juice and celebratory mood!). This has got to cheer her up. Lastly (and before I continue with another few thousand words), I ask Amy to join me for a swim tomorrow night while the kids are in bed (I know her mum can help her on a Wednesday evening). I'm sure once we get to the pool she can squeeze in a relaxing steam (even if I do sit with my big bump huffing and puffing outside while she detoxes in the steam) and possibly even a quick meal back at mine.

Within a short space of time, not only my diary, but that of some of my close friends looks far less family/work/school/household dominated and far more balanced out with a few fun treats. If I can just sneak in a long bath reading a few chapters of my new novel then I'll certainly feel rather more revived and human again.

I'm not saying I want to go and paint the town red every night (or lock myself away reading and applying a face-pack at every opportunity). Come on, almost no mums I know have the energy for such constant 'fun' but the odd burst of girlie times, meals out with friends and time for yourself (whether that be at the local meditation class, art gallery or boxing club) is good for the soul. Of course we still want to take the kids out to eat at the weekend and class the family picnic as 'fun', but on top of this I feel it's incredibly good for mums to enjoy a life outside of their role within the family. You should try it. Pinot Noir has never tasted so good!

'I'm not a hugely social animal and parties and big groups have never been my thing. Having said that, I did really miss sporadic grown-up social engagements once I had kids. Once they were both sleeping through the night and were at nursery for a few hours each day, I felt ready to start building on my other interests once more. My way of channelling this energy was to join a book club and a local wine-tasting group. Both of these are things I love and get me out the house and into groups of like-minded adults again.'

Part-time working mum of two

Relationships

Last, but by no means least, in my action-packed guide to an easy family life, we get to 'relationships'. To be honest, I ummed and ahhed about whether to designate a whole chapter to the complex and convoluted topic of relationships, love, sex and intimacy with your partner. Opinion was torn: many of my friends and readers thought a whole chapter going into great details about how to rekindle your sex life or keep sane through a break-up was essential to the mechanisms of family life, while others felt I'd covered much of this topic in *The Fabulous Mum's Handbook* and that a small section would be enough. In the end I reckoned I could give the topic of intimate relationships a good going over within this chapter (and failing that, it may warrant a whole *Fabulous Mum's Guide to Relationships* of its own!).

Whichever way you look at it your relationship with your partner changes immensely once you start a family. I love my kids to pieces, but sometimes I wonder why as humans we decide to start a family in the first place. Picture it: you have a great relationship, wonderful sex, good laughs and plenty of romantic nights out. As a couple you reap the benefits of good jobs and an income that enables you to enjoy fine wine, a new sofa and a week in Italy over summer. You sleep in until midday at the weekend and chill out with the papers after your brunch of eggs on toast and smoky bacon. So why on earth would any sane person bring a screaming, non-sleeping, demanding 'bundle of joy' into the equation? Well, that's love for you.

As ex-Blur musician (and father of three boys) Alex James so eloquently put it in an interview in *Red* magazine, 'Falling in love is a kind of madness. I was talking to a brain specialist about kids and she said love is the brain's way of coping with the fact that children are a really bad idea. It doesn't make sense from a logical point of view; life's going to suddenly become more complicated. But you fall in love with somebody and just think, I want to have babies with her.'* I think there is certainly some truth in that.

So, if making babies generally comes from love (or at least intense passion or companionship) then why do they so often cause relationship problems in the long run? We've all heard the statistic that one in three marriages ends in divorce and

* *With thanks to* Red *for their permission to quote this extract from their August 2007 edition.*

I'm sure it's pretty safe to say that many of these failed marriages have run into problems when kids are added to the equation. It's not the children per se but the way we as parents change within and towards each other when we breed. Even for that rock-solid marriage, keeping the spark alive with children in tow takes a lot of thought and effort. I know there will be a whole host of you who'll understand how, after a long stint in the office (or running around after three kids all day), a manic bath, stories and bed routine and a sweep of the mayhem left behind, the last thing you can muster is a smiley, happy grown-up supper or, God forbid, a cuddle and a little intimacy!

I feel very fortunate that (touch wood) I'm well into my predominantly 'happy' seventh year of marriage. With two kids only eighteen months apart and a third on the way, we've both done our fair share of work in building a stable family life. I'm not saying it's been a breeze but we're still standing here, wedding rings firmly wedged on our left hands. Sure, we've had our moments. (In one huge heated row I ran out the door for 'good', until I realised that it was raining torrentially and I was barefoot. My dearest too, has certainly slammed some doors in his time, not to mention accusing me of being 'neurotic' and 'utterly bonkers'.) But by and large it's pretty smooth sailing *most* of the time.

I think we're lucky in that we certainly feel we've found 'the one' and come what may there's no doubt for either of us that this marriage and this family is it. That doesn't mean, however, that it doesn't take constant effort from both parties, the regular input of positive energy and the occasional sense of surprise. I think the rule of thumb for every partnership is never take your eye off the ball. The moment you take the relationship or your partner for granted, you're heading for trouble. So, what are some tricks of the successful relationship trade?

Time alone together

Any mum with one or more children to care for will have to work pretty hard to create time alone with her man. However, that doesn't mean we shouldn't try. The only sure-fire way of increasing the amount of attention and interest you give each other is to prioritise a little down-time together. Whether this is to cook each other a meal every other night, ask a neighbour to babysit while you catch a film or book the in-laws for an afternoon so you can take a walk in the woods followed by a pint at the local pub, just try to make it happen! Even if it's only once a fortnight, because in leaving this important down-time together out of your family life, you're sure to find a distance will appear between you that is hard to bridge.

Keep the romance alive

I'm not talking roses every night or cards left on the bedside each morning (although both of these would be lovely!) but showing each other that you care is key. By sending the odd cheeky text, buying flowers once every so often, cooking a romantic meal for one another, booking your favourite restaurant for a treat or just saying something loving and complimentary before you leave for work (along with 'Pass the brolly' and 'Will you be going to Sam's sports day?') you'll remind one another that you care and you're a couple beyond your role as 'mum' and 'dad'.

Intimacy

I don't need to go into graphic details here to explain the importance of a kiss and a cuddle and possibly even some s-e-x! Few busy parents have the time and energy for a rampant sex life, but intimacy is crucial for a healthy relationship and a strong bond between couples. I know a big hug or an intimate embrace with my man still makes me feel utterly loved and special. Even if it's just a cuddle on the sofa while we watch the news, it's worth it. The physical touch and appreciation of one another's bodies is something we often leave behind as the marriage trundles on, and really and truly we shouldn't.

Respect

Listening to one another and respecting each other's lives and views is also something couples in a working partnership should bear in mind. Only too often you see relationships where one partner has stopped listening or taking interest in the other and the respect is soon lost.

It's up to both parts of the pair to make an effort to stay interested and engaged in the relationship. Ask questions and be involved in the parts of your partner's life you may be absent from. You may share the kids, but don't make this the only topic of conversation or interest! Respect is a key word to remember: respect of each other's roles as parents, workers, housekeepers and individuals.

It's totally normal to fantasise about Jude Law or the 'other life' (you know, the one where you're jetting off to New York with your rich, gorgeous lover); however, try to remember that in reality what you have is pretty damn good! Following your fantasies or acting out a desire for infidelity can lead to a hell of a lot more trouble than its worth and it can only cause a whole heap of hurt and heartache for all involved. In my mind the Jude Law/Justin Timberlake fantasies are best kept locked away in the inner workings of your imagination! Just remind yourself how your relationship started and cling on to what you've got. Look for ways to improve and enjoy what you have, not excuses to escape it.

Work at it

Be prepared to put energy and effort into your relationship. When the going gets tough don't hold your hands up and surrender before you've given it a good go. Turning to a third party (a counsellor or support group) when times are hard isn't a sign of failure, in fact it's a very admirable way of sorting through any 'excess baggage' and issues you may have as a couple. It's got to be worth some serious hard work and soul-searching to make things right for each other *and* the children.

This is all fair and well, but for many couples the end of the road is in sight and no amount of candle-lit dinners or weekends in Shropshire are going to save their relationship. Take my pal, Sophie. After ten years of marriage and three kids, we all thought they were set for a pad in the South of France and a 'happily ever after'. Unbeknown to all her close buddies, their marriage had been failing for the worst part of a year. A girlie dinner and a bottle of plonk to cry it all out wasn't going to reverse the inevitable, and divorce was in actual fact the best thing for all in the end. Sophie is certainly a million times happier and the kids, although shaken and shell-shocked at first, are now delighted to have a house with a sunny, happy vibe at long last.

Having divorced parents myself, I know how hard it can be to go through a separation in the family. Each person's role changes as the dynamic shifts and the reality sinks in that the family as you know it will never be the same again. It's hard as a child to get your head around the fairy tale of 'happily ever after' coming to a crashing end and facing the realisation that you're going to have to be 'shared'. Adjusting to weekends with just one parent and the week with another is tough, not to mention getting your seven-year-old brain around step-parents and step-families. However, anyone who's come from a family with a failed marriage will know that to see your parents unhappy, abused or just plain taken for granted only causes hurt. Somewhere and at some time, when the family has moved on and taken a new form, you find yourself taking a sigh of relief that all this is over and the pain has stopped. I certainly look back and feel my parents' divorce was for the best in the long run, however hard it was at seven to accept Daddy and Mummy would no longer be a pair.

For any couples who have tried and failed to make things work, the main priority in the end must be the children.

However much dear Sophie despaired at the end of her marriage, she tried not to let her resentment of her ex affect her children's relationship with him. She confesses that this was the hardest task she's ever faced as a mother. However, by biting her tongue (bar the odd outpour of rage and good hard cry witnessed by all three kids at one time or another) she did everything she could to make the divorce a billion times easier for the kids and allowed them to forge a relationship with their dad that will serve Sophie well in the long run (after all, who wants kids who grow up resenting you because you slagged off their dad and refused him access?).

Sophie reckoned the most effective way to get back at her ex was not to turn the kids against him, but to get her own life back on track and show him what a fool he'd been. After six months of tears, the best decision she ever made was to head to the coast with some friends for a week (leaving the kids with her mum) and begin the process of turning her life around. I know it sounds like a cliché, but a further six months later, a good few sessions with a shrink, a course in martial arts, a new haircut, a bronze suntan, a pair of Jimmy Choos and a promotion at work in the bag and, boy oh boy, her ex-husband's girlfriend doesn't look half as hot as his ex-wife!

If you're lucky a blip in your relationship or rocky ride down that family road may not lead to a session with Relate, or worse still the divorce courts, but as we grow up from newlyweds to new parents to a fully fledged family, working at our relationships is obligatory to their success. The plus side is that by putting a little energy and enthusiasm back into our love lives, we may be surprised at what we might find. Just under all that busy parent persona you may well discover that university graduate/fellow party guest/ brother of a mate/work colleague/gorgeous guy down the road who you fell for all those years ago is still there and, hiding patiently somewhere within you, is that carefree, leggy girl who didn't scream at him for not taking his shoes off in the hall. Isn't it about time you found out where those people have gone?

Top ten tips for the neglected (but innately fabulous) mum!

1. It's totally normal for busy, multi-tasking mums to ask ourselves (while knee-deep in dirty socks and craft activities), 'Who the hell am I these days?' Missing your 'old life' for that split second doesn't make you a bad mother.
2. Carving out time for yourself is crucial to easing feelings of frustration and despondency within your role.
3. Lean on friends and fellow mums for support. Helping each other is what it's all about.
4. Don't feel guilty for prioritising a little 'me time' in your life.
5. Investing in a little time for exercise is a wonderful tonic to the stresses and strains of everyday life.
6. Don't ignore your needs for relaxation (go on, let your son's PE kit go un-ironed and run a hot bubble bath instead).
7. Mums need fun too! (Calling your best pal, organising a babysitter and booking your favourite gastro pub for supper on Saturday night is long overdue.)

8. Designate a little time for your friendships. If you have a dispersed family (or can't rely on them for help and advice) these relationships will be your lifeline.

9. Making time for your partnership is crucial if you want it to stand the test of family life. It's so easy to neglect your partner when you feel tired and over-worked but taking them for granted will only end in resentment and hostility.

10. Every so often remind yourself of who you are and what you're all about. You may find this essence gets lost from time to time.

A Positive Look Forward

Writing this book has taken me on the most wonderful journey. I've relived humorous and heart-warming moments involving my nearest and dearest, captured the chaos and passion involved in raising a busy and dynamic family, and shared some of my solutions to achieving a happy and 'fabulous' family life.

I would never profess to knowing all the answers to the problems posed by the intricate complexities of family life. The truth of the matter is we never really know whether we're doing a good job. We may look older and wiser and fit the image of a 'grown-up' but underneath the power suits, the estate car, the greying hair and the armfuls of offspring we're still the big kids we once were, wondering if what we're doing is 'right' and seeking approval at some point along the way.

We confer, read, explore and question whether our parenting choices are good, bad or just downright damaging. One moment it's OK to give your baby pureed food; the next we're told we'll be stunting their taste palate. On the one hand we feel we should help our children learn; on the other we're told being too pushy will make them anxious and 'burnt out' before they're even ten. It constantly feels like we just can't do enough right. I know when my daughter looks up at me (her eyes all hope, faith and innocence) and asks 'Why does my friend's daddy live in a different house?' I should have an answer. I feel, as my son runs to me, his knees cut and bleeding, that I should be the one to make it better; and I know as I sign my second book contract and nurture my third baby-bump that really and truly I should feel like a genuine, certified 'grown-up'. But in all honesty, I often don't. I give the complex divorce answer to my best ability, tend to the cut knees and help with the homework, every so often wondering when someone will tap me on the shoulder and tell me 'the game is up'. That really my cover is blown and the big kid who likes to swim naked, lick the bowl clean of cake mix and get giggly on white wine has been revealed and I can stop pretending to be a fraudulent 'Fabulous Mum'.

As I confessed this to my close girlfriends I was surprised at how many felt the same. Suddenly an outpouring of questions about choosing schools, eating organic food, dressing ethically, making relationships work and adjusting siblings to a newborn came tumbling out and we realised that between us no one had the 'perfect' solutions. I'm certainly not the oracle on all this and wouldn't suggest for a moment that I'm an expert on parenting. But I reckon as mums the last thing we need is another expert or book telling us precisely *how* to be perfect mothers. For this reason, *Family Life Made Easy* isn't a step-by-step manual to achieving the ideal, happy, supermum family ideal. No, above all, what I hope is that it proves to be a funny, anecdotal, uplifting journey through parenthood and your growing (often hectic!) family. The result of all my research, shared advice and frank experiences of fellow mums, is an honest account of how I, and the many fabulous mums I know, have navigated our way through the expanding family model, the minefield that is eating well, dressing with an air of style savvy, living a green and healthy life, keeping sane in the world of competitive parents, striking a happy work/life balance, travelling *en famille* and last, but by no means least, carving out time for ourselves and our loved ones.

We feel confused enough about the choices we make as parents, and the last thing this book sets out to do is set another unattainable role model for mums to meet. In actual fact, the brilliant thing about the tips and advice in this book is that they are all real and doable, they've been tried and tested, and are aimed specifically at mums like you and me. There are no set rules or voices here dictating the 'right way' to achieve an easy family life, just a collection of anecdotes and experiences which should help along the way. It's meant to make you feel proud about your choices and empowered by your role. I hope, more than anything, that it's done just that.

Take from this a feeling of camaraderie and support. A feeling that the family life we lead and the roles we adopt through it (as a mother, partner, colleague, friend, neighbour and daughter) is a journey that we share together. Just keep reminding yourself that *you're doing a great job*, and I hope together we can celebrate this!

Recipes

Family Favourites

As my kids have grown from breastfed babies to messy eating toddlers to schoolchildren (who are hungry enough to eat a horse when I pick them up at three-thirty), I've become a culinary master at cooking some essential family favourites. Admittedly there'll be days when I'll simply bung a handful of fish fingers in the oven (and others when we'll all sit down to a lunch of salmon, Moroccan couscous and tender-stem broccoli) but no multi-tasking mum would be complete without an array of easy, classic feel-good family meals up her sleeve. Ask either of my children (and their dad) what they'd like for supper and nine times out of ten they'd request one of the following:

Delicious roast chicken

If I turn up at my own mother's house and can't smell chicken roasting I feel slightly crestfallen, so it seems only fair that at least once a week (usually Friday nights) my children return home from school to the smell of a roast in the oven. I used to baulk at the words 'roast supper'. I always imagined it entailed hours slaving over a hot stove but in reality this meal requires minimal effort. It's utterly delicious, the smell fills you with a warm 'Friday feeling' and it comes with the added bonus of leftovers (ideal for chicken salad or sarnies the next day).

Ingredients
Serves 6.

1 large organic chicken
2 garlic cloves, peeled and finely chopped
a handful of fresh thyme, roughly chopped
a handful of fresh rosemary, roughly chopped
125 g soft butter
celery salt
freshly ground black pepper
a dash of soy sauce
1 kg potatoes, peeled and cut into chunks
500 g carrots, peeled and cut into chunky strips
1 large onion peeled and cut into half moons

Preheat the oven to 220 °C/425 °F/gas mark 7. (Please check the packaging on your chicken for cooking time guidelines.)

Place the chicken on a baking tray, checking any giblets are removed first. Use your hands to mix the garlic, thyme and rosemary into the butter (keep aside some sprigs of herbs for garnishing). Once it's all one big fragrant ball rub it evenly over the chicken, going in between the meat and skin where you can. Garnish the top of the bird with herbs you kept aside and season with the celery salt, pepper and soy sauce (the soy always makes it a lovely golden brown at the end).

While the chicken is roasting in the oven, boil the potatoes for around 15 minutes and the carrots in a separate pan for three minutes. Drain the potatoes and carrots. Remove the chicken and scatter the potatoes, carrots and onion moons around the nicely melted butter that surrounds the chicken. Spoon some of the melted butter and herbs onto the potatoes, carrots and onions before placing it all back into the oven for a further 45 minutes.

Serve piping hot with its own delicious juices and some green vegetables. Now that tastes like Friday night!

Saunders' spag bol

My daughter in particular would eat this every day, seven days a week, for the rest of her life given the chance. I try and make the bolognese as meaty and packed full of fresh, organic vegetables as possible and I always use wholemeal pasta to make it truly nutritious. The trick is not to skimp on the sauce; I often give my kids more sauce than pasta as the ingredients make for a perfect, balanced mid-week supper and fill them up after a long day at school. If we're eating as a family I tend to also serve a large green salad (or a heap of broccoli) and shavings of Parmesan cheese.

Ingredients
Serves 6.

1½ tbsp vegetable oil
1 large onion, peeled and chopped
1 garlic clove, crushed

3 large grated carrots
750 g organic minced beef
200 g mushrooms, sliced
8 tbsp tomato puree

2 tbsp mixed fresh or dried
   herbs
450 g (or 1 tin) chopped
   tomatoes

450 ml beef stock
salt and pepper to taste
wholemeal spaghetti (enough
   to suit your appetite)

Heat the oil in a frying pan at a medium heat. Add the onion and garlic and sauté until soft (around 4 minutes). Add the carrots and sauté for a further 3 minutes. Add the minced beef and cook until it browns all over. Then add the mushrooms, tomato puree and herbs for a final 3 minutes. Finish off by adding your chopped tomatoes, beef stock and salt and pepper, cover and cook for around 15 minutes. You can either serve immediately with pasta or refrigerate in a sealed container for up to 24 hours, ready to reheat whenever suits.

Mmmmm for macaroni cheese

I confess until my daughter was walking I relied on Sainsbury's kids' ready-meals to give my daughter her mac-cheese-fix. One Friday afternoon the unthinkable happened: they had sold out and panic set in. It was that fateful November day that I was forced to think up my own macaroni cheese recipe and I've never looked back as it's become an absolute winner for both my children. I have to say that there is nothing nicer on a cold winter evening than tucking into a bowl of extra-cheesy macaroni cheese with the kids. Low-calorie it may not be, but feel-good-factor it certainly has. Serve with petits pois or garden peas and light that open fire!

Ingredients

Serves 6.

75 g white or wholemeal
    bread
200 g mature cheddar, grated
75 g Gruyère, grated
50 g Parmesan, grated

75 g butter
350 g macaroni
850 ml full-fat milk
75 g plain flour

Preheat the oven to 190 °C/375 °F/gas mark 5.

Using a food processor if you have one, whizz the bread into chunky crumbs (otherwise just tear it up into chunks with your hands). Mix 50 g of the cheddar and half the Parmesan into the breadcrumbs. Next you need to make the sauce: cook your macaroni on a back heat while making this. Warm the milk then melt the butter in a large pan and stir in the flour. Cook for around a minute and then remove from the stove. Pour in ⅓ of the milk and stir well until smooth and thick. Add another ⅓ and stir until smooth again and then repeat with the last of the milk. By this time your macaroni should be cooked. Using some of the butter, grease a good-sized oven dish. Drain the pasta and pour into the oven dish.

Simmer your sauce for a further 4–5 minutes, stirring occasionally, before adding all your remaining cheese. Beat in around 7 tbsp of milk and season before adding to your macaroni. Scatter the breadcrumbs over the top and heat in the oven for 15 minutes then put under the grill for a further 5 minutes to brown the topping. Serve while hot and melting, yum!

Fisherman's pie

This is another firm favourite in our house and one that is so easy to make, keep and freeze. I always seem to serve with peas and broccoli, not least because the kids end up willingly stirring all of the ingredients together making it a fish dish also packed with vegetables: a nutritional bonus I'm sure you'll agree! I should add here that if you fancy substituting either the cod or salmon with another fish (hake, tuna or even prawns) feel free. The more the merrier is my motto!

Ingredients
Serves 6.

550 g potatoes, peeled and diced
85 g butter
6 tbsp full-fat milk or double cream
Salt and pepper
1 onion, peeled and chopped

200 g of cod fillets, diced
200 g of salmon fillets, diced
a generous handful of chopped parsley
1 tsp Dijon mustard
140 g cheddar cheese, grated

Preheat the oven to 180 °C/350 °F/gas mark 4.

Boil the potatoes for 20 minutes then mash together with half the milk or cream, most of the butter and a good pinch of salt and pepper.

Heat the remaining butter in a saucepan and sauté the onions until cooked. (My kids seem to like them almost burnt!) Add the fish, parsley, mustard and a little salt and pepper, cover with the remaining milk or cream and simmer until the fish is cooked through (usually 4 minutes) then stir in the grated cheese until it melts.

Pour into a pre-greased dish, top with your mash and place in the oven until the top browns and the sauce is bubbling up from underneath (usually half an hour). I should add that ketchup is compulsory with this dish!

Sue's special stir-fry

This dish is a simple yet scrumptious invention by my sister-in-law Sue. She regularly feeds her three children with all their cousins (which at full-house means eight kids at a sitting) so has become a dab-hand at designing meals that are easy to make in large quantities and get gobbled up by even the fussiest of children. (That will be my daughter, then.) I must confess I've eaten the remains of this off the kids' plates while they tuck into pudding and have taken to making it in my home, making sure there's enough left for my husband and me to eat for supper.

Ingredients
Serves 6.

1 tbsp olive oil
6 small turkey breasts, cut into strips
2 tbsp of soy sauce
2 tsp Chinese five spices
1 tsp garlic salt
pepper

2 cloves of garlic, peeled and crushed
half a red onion, peeled and chopped
a large selection of fresh and frozen vegetables (enough for six servings), ideally cut

into strips – this is the perfect recipe for using up any veg left in the fridge. In her version, Sue usually includes: shiitake mushrooms, asparagus tips, pak choi, sugar snap peas and carrot batons.

three quarters of a thumb's length of fresh ginger, peeled and crushed

two bags of ready-to-cook noodles

Heat the olive oil in a large wok. When hot, add the turkey, soy sauce, five spices, garlic salt and some pepper. Cook the turkey until it's pink right through (around 2½ minutes).

Remove the turkey and place to one side. Add a little more olive oil to coat the wok and begin to cook your onion and garlic with a touch more of the Chinese five spice. After a minute or so add any veg that requires a little more cooking, such as carrots and broccoli, add a splash of soy sauce and cook for a further 2 minutes, mixing every now and then and placing a lid on in between to help the ingredients steam. Then add the rest of the veg. Cook for a further minute, add the ginger, noodles and turkey and cook for a final 2 minutes.

Make sure the stir-fry is seasoned to taste and all the ingredients are coated in the delicious juices before serving with chopsticks!

Ladies' Lunches

I say 'ladies' lunches' rather tongue-in-cheek because these healthy(ish) recipes are just as ideal for a quick lunch at home as they are for a light nutritious supper with your partner or some friends. The reason I entitled them 'ladies' lunches' is really because whenever I serve them up for a Sunday brunch with pals or a mums-meet at mine they always get gobbled up in no time (by the mums in particular) and I regularly get asked by fellow mums for the recipes so they can whizz them up for themselves. This certainly doesn't mean that these recipes can't be used for family meals with the kids too (the stir-fried vegetables and butternut squash and goat's cheese salad in particular are hot on my children's wish list, although I leave out the sesame oil and seeds when cooking for Bella). Feel free to improvise, serve and enjoy at will!

Ginger chicken salad

This is my ultimate lunchtime favourite. The combination of chicken, mango, ginger and spinach leaves is just mouth-watering and looks so appetising served in a big colourful bowl with some couscous or crusty wholemeal bread. You'll probably find if you don't go too OTT with the ginger, kids will love this too. I always find it's eaten up in seconds by grown-ups and children alike when I serve it as a summer alternative to the Sunday roast.

Ingredients
Serves 6.

- 4 chicken breasts, cut into strips
- a large bag of fresh spinach
- 2 large mangoes, cut into slices or chunks
- 1tbsp olive oil
- a handful of coriander, chopped
- balsamic vinegar

Marinade

2 thumbs' lengths of ginger, grated

200 ml runny honey

6tbsp soy sauce

4tbsp sesame oil

Mix together the ingredients for the marinade. Roughly divide into two bowls. Put aside one bowl and use the other to marinade the chicken

Wash the spinach and place into a large salad bowl with the mango scattered on top.

Heat the olive oil in a frying pan. Discard the marinade the chicken has been in. Dry fry the chicken for 5–10 minutes, depending on the size of the pieces, so that it caramelises. Once the chicken is sticky and golden brown all over, add the second bowl of marinade that you put aside earlier and cook until bubbling. Allow to simmer for a good 2 minutes.

Add the chicken and juices to the salad. Sprinkle the coriander over the top and if you fancy add some balsamic vinegar to the spinach to taste.

A squash and cheese salad

This is another of my favourite light lunches or summer suppers (with a glass of vino and a melon medley to follow). It's so simple to prepare and can even be kept in the fridge overnight if you fancy. My kids love butternut squash so if I miss my window for a romantic supper with the husband it can equally work as a family meal (just as long as you limit the quantity of green watercress leaves, you should get away with it!)

Ingredients
Serves 6.

2 red peppers, deseeded and halved
olive oil
1 squash, peeled and chopped
a handful of fresh rosemary, chopped

300 g mixed green leaves (rocket/watercress/spinach or all of the above)
140 g feta cheese
1 garlic clove, peeled and crushed
salt and pepper

Preheat the oven to 200 °C/400 °F/gas mark 6.

Place the red peppers on a baking tray and drizzle with olive oil. Cook for 15 minutes. When they're soft, remove from the oven and peel away the skin and cut into strips. While the peppers are cooking, heat about a tablespoon of olive oil in a frying pan, add the butternut squash and rosemary, cover and cook for around 10 minutes.

Put the green leaves into a large salad bowl. Add the still-hot butternut squash, peppers and crumble in the feta cheese (you could even add some pecan nuts if you fancy). Mix together the garlic, a few tablespoons of olive oil, some salt and pepper (and lemon if you wish) and dress your salad. Toss and serve.

Salmon salsa delight

I do love a little salmon to get me through the day, especially if it's a busy one, and this dish has just the right balance of protein and fresh goodies to keep up my energy and spirits through the madness of a 'normal' afternoon in the Saunders household. With the addition of some sweet potato wedges or herby couscous, this meal also makes an ideal healthy supper.

Ingredients
Serves 6.

6 salmon fillets
a handful of fresh coriander, finely chopped
200 g cherry tomatoes (ideally ones that come on the vine)

5 sundried tomatoes
2 tbsp olive oil
2 tbsp black pitted olives
a good handful of fresh basil
2 garlic cloves, peeled
1 tbsp sundried tomato puree

To serve

fresh watercress
a handful of chopped walnuts

a wedge of Roquefort cheese, crumbled
2 pears, sliced

Preheat the oven to 180 °C/350 °F/gas mark 4.

Cook the salmon on a baking tray with a splash of olive oil and a sprinkle on fresh coriander for 20 minutes, or slightly less if you prefer your salmon pink in the middle. Whizz up the remaining ingredients in a food processor or hand-held blender. Blend until the ingredients combine to make a chunky salsa (or, if you prefer, blend for longer to make a tapenade).

Serve the cooked salmon with a heap of the salsa and some fresh watercress sprinkled with walnut pieces, Roquefort cheese and pear slices.

Goat's cheese and vegetable couscous

This dish is all about maximum ease, speed and taste (the fact it's healthy and nutritious too is an added bonus). I tend to make a good-sized batch so I can tuck into it while working from home alone or root it out for a last-minute lunch with some fellow mums or when I need to conjure up an easy supper for me and my fella (I usually serve with some chicken or salmon wrapped in Parma ham if it's for an evening meal). This dish is also a great way to use up any old vegetables lurking at the back of the fridge. I've given a guide of what you can use in the ingredients list but it's really up to you what you throw in.

Ingredients
Serves 6.

1 red and 1 yellow pepper, chopped into chunks

2 courgettes, sliced

1 aubergine, chopped into chunks

1 butternut squash, peeled and cut into chunks

salt and pepper

olive oil

2 garlic cloves, peeled and finely chopped

a sprinkle of cumin

1 punnet of cherry tomatoes

500 ml chicken stock (although vegetable stock or even just boiled water will do)

400 g dried couscous

a handful of fresh basil, chopped

a handful of fresh coriander, chopped

a handful of fresh parsley, chopped

200 g goat's cheese

a dash of balsamic vinegar

the juice of 1 to 2 lemons

Preheat the oven to 200 °C/400 °F/gas mark 6.

Evenly spread out all the vegetables, *except* the tomatoes, onto a baking tray (you may even need two trays to fit them all). Drizzle with olive oil, sprinkle over the chopped garlic and cumin and season with the salt and pepper. Bake the vegetables for about half an hour or until soft and golden then add the tomatoes for a further 5–10 mins.

Heat the stock until it's simmering. Turn off the heat and then add the couscous and a tablespoon of olive oil. Leave to soak for a few minutes then fluff with a fork. In a very large bowl mix the couscous, roasted vegetables, fresh herbs, crumbled goat's cheese, a few lugs of olive oil, a few splashes of balsamic vinegar and the lemon juice. As you stir the ingredients together taste regularly to check that you have your preferred seasoning/oil/vinegar/lemon juice combination. Serve in a nice colourful bowl and eat with hot crusty bread, yum!

Crispy crust lamb

This dish is truly scrumptious and pretty low in fat too. It makes a perfect weekend lunch or evening meal and is so simple you'll wonder why lamb has been off the menu for so long.

Ingredients
Serves 6.

3 garlic cloves, peeled and crushed

1 tbsp sesame oil

1½ tbsp lemon juice

1½ tbsp soy sauce

a handful of fresh parsley, finely chopped

2 heaped tsp English mustard

750 g lamb, boned eye of loin   2 tbsp black sesame seeds
2 tbsp white sesame seeds

Preheat the oven to 220 °C/425 °F/gas mark 7.

Stir the garlic, sesame oil, lemon juice, soy sauce, parsley and mustard together. Brush the mixture over your lamb and cover with the sesame seeds. Cook the lamb in a really hot oven for at least 15 minutes or until it's browned all over (remember you may need slightly longer if you're cooking for the kids and don't want the meat too pink). Slice and serve with mash and some tender-stem broccoli.

Teatime Treats

As you'll know by now I'm not a member of the sugar police. Sure, my kids don't start the day with Coco Pops or munch their way through endless sticks of rock after school, but I see nothing wrong with them enjoying a yummy home-made cookie or flapjack at teatime. I admit I'm partial to these treats too and rarely a week goes past without a couple of tea parties where I'll share a cup of Earl Grey and a slice of ginger cake with a neighbour or mum from school. As far as I'm concerned life really wouldn't be worth living without Katie's cookies so if you're a sugar-free fanatic or insist on grapes for every snack-attack then you may want to bypass this section (glimpsing at the fruit kebabs if you're feeling brave) and head for your nearest fruit and nut stall instead. Everyone else can enjoy the following recipes; just don't count the calories!

Katie's cookies

These cookies have some serious heritage in my life. One of my closest pals Katie devised the recipe many years ago and whips them up with her eyes closed in a matter of minutes. I once blindfolded her after three glasses of wine to see if she could still accomplish the task in under five minutes and she managed it without even dropping an egg! Katie's cookies have marked the celebration of almost all the important occasions in my life. She made them to celebrate getting firsts in our university finals, to feed all my girlfriends at my hen night and to greet me post-labour after having my first child, her goddaughter. It seemed only fair then that these cookies should figure in my kids' lives as well, and I think it's safe to say your kids will love them too!

Ingredients
Makes roughly 12 cookies.

85 g butter
85 g brown sugar
85 g caster sugar
1 tsp vanilla essence

1 egg, beaten
200 g plain chocolate chips
170 g self-raising flour

Pre-heat the oven to 180 °C/350 °F/gas mark 4.

Mix the butter, brown sugar, caster sugar and vanilla essence together in a mixing bowl. Add the egg and stir into a smooth paste. Add the chocolate chips and stir these in evenly. Add the flour and mix into a stiff paste.

Grease a couple of baking trays with a little butter. Separate the cookie dough into teaspoon-sized blobs on the tray (they will expand massively so space them out well). Cook for 9 minutes or until golden. After removing the tray from the oven, drop it flat down on a surface to dislodge the cookies and encourage them into a firm cookie shape. Then remove and leave to cool on a wire rack. I told you it was simple!

Fruity flapjacks

These are utterly delicious and because they're packed with porridge oats and dried fruits they're a nutritious alternative to Katie's cookies. If you can stop the kids eating the whole batch piping hot from the oven they'll last a good while as after-school snacks or mid-morning fillers.

Ingredients
Makes 15 pieces.

140 g butter	85 g dried apricots, chopped
115 g golden syrup	55 g dried figs, chopped
55 g demerara sugar	85 g raisins
225 g porridge oats	

Preheat the oven to 160 °C/325 °F/gas mark 3.

Put the butter, golden syrup and sugar into a saucepan and heat on a low flame until the butter has melted, stirring frequently.

Mix the oats, apricots, figs and raisins together in a mixing bowl then pour over the warm syrup mixture. Stir well until it's all mixed evenly together.

Grease a quarter-inch-deep baking tray. Pour the mixture into the tray and spread it evenly out, packing it firmly into the edges. Cook for around 25 minutes or until the top is lovely and golden.

For a real treat, serve with ice cream or plain yogurt and a dusting of cinnamon.

A fabulous mum's ginger cake

I grew up on my very own fabulous mum's ginger cake. She used to alternate it with a hot chocolate brownie to greet me home from school and not only was our semi-detached house in Oxford soon *the* destination for four o'clock tea, but I rapidly became the most popular child in the class. I'm not sure quite how she managed it (raising three kids as a single mum with a demanding career to boot) but somehow the smell of baking filled the air most afternoons and my pals and I would devour her ginger cake before hanging upside-down from the climbing frame for the rest of the afternoon. I can't claim to be even half as fabulous as my mother, but I do try and recreate the fabulous ginger cake for my children whenever I get a window of half an hour to bake it. Team with poached apricots and honey, mascarpone or vanilla ice cream and you'll make many a tea/brunch/supper guest happy too.

Ingredients
Serves 10.

225 g plain flour
3 tsp ground ginger
1 tsp mixed spice
55 g sultanas
40 g brown sugar

55 g butter
225 g golden syrup
140 ml full-fat milk
1 tsp bicarbonate of soda
1 egg

Mix the flour, ginger, spice, sultanas and brown sugar in a large mixing bowl. Slowly melt the butter and golden syrup in a saucepan, but don't allow to boil, and stir frequently. In a separate pan gently warm the milk and stir in the bicarbonate of soda. Turn off the heat. Add the warm syrup mixture to the milk and allow to cool. Then add the egg and stir until you have a smooth batter.

Pour the cake batter into a greased cake tin and bake for approximately 25 minutes. It should feel springy to the touch and be golden brown. Allow to cool on a wire rack. It's delicious still warm too, if those eager eaters can't wait.

Fruit kebabs

Here's something for those looking for an alternative to chocolate or even as an accompaniment to that slice of cake or third cookie. My kids love *anything* that comes on a stick so these get gobbled up in no time, and it makes a change from blending up the same fruit for a smoothie.

Ingredients
Serves 6.

6 skewers
1 large pineapple
1 large mango
3 medium bananas

2 large kiwis
juice of a lime
a sprinkling of fructose
a sprinkling of cinnamon

Preheat the grill on a medium heat.

Skin and chop all your fruit into cubes or very thick slices (you could even buy freshly prepared pineapple chunks if you're feeling really lazy!). Thread the fruit onto 6 skewers, alternating the fruit to keep it colourful. Lightly rub the fruit with the lime juice and sprinkle them evenly with a little fructose and cinnamon.

Place under the grill and turn regularly for about 7 minutes. Remove when they're starting to turn golden. Serve with yogurt, ice cream or crème fraiche for a yummy dessert/teatime fix or even with some muesli for a delicious, fortifying breakfast alternative.

Useful Addresses for Fabulous Mums

The Growing Family

First Response
www.firstresponsefertility.com
Offers a midwife-led email helpline with advice on conception, birth and beyond.

For Parents by Parents
www.forparentsbyparents.com
Help and advice about choosing the right time to try for another child.

Gurgle
www.gurgle.co.uk
Expert advice and articles on dealing with more than one baby.

Tiny Prints
www.tinyprints.com
Good ideas on preparing for number two and even some novel tips on helping with sibling jealousy and rivalry.

Zita West

Tel: 0870 166 8899 (sales)/020 7224 0017 (clinic)

www.zitawest.com

Zita offers brilliant advice and a range of supplements for couples embarking on fertility and pregnancy – I swear by her vitamins before, during and after pregnancy.

Competitive Parenting

Amazing Moms

www.amazingmoms.com

The name says it all! A website for amazing mums jam-packed with everything you need to know on throwing a kids' party.

Directgov

www.direct.gov.uk

A great website for all state school listings, Ofsted reports and what you should look for in these schools.

Children's Party Shows

Tel: 01344 638501

www.childrenspartyshows.co.uk

This is the site to visit if you're searching for a children's party entertainer.

Cookie Crumbles

Tel: 0845 601 4173

www.cookiecrumbles.net

If you can't face the church hall and Cosmo the clown for

your child's next party why not have a few friends round
for a cooking party instead?

The Cupcake Company

Tel: 07815 873968

www.thecupcakecompany.eu

Why not order some cute, custom-made cupcakes for this
year's birthday party? Save yourself hours spent knee-deep
in flour and frustration!

Flutterby Cards Limited

Tel: 020 7751 3172

www.flutterbycards.com

This is the place to go if you want really special party invites.

Hats and Bells

Tel: 07775 924144/07979 261584

www.hatsandbells.com

If you do have a fortune to spend on kids' party food then
this is one great place to spend it in style. Failing that,
log on for inspiring themes and ideas to try yourself at
home!

Letterbox

Tel: 0844 888 5000 (order line)/0844 888 6000 (customer
service)

www.letterbox.co.uk

Has some cute ideas for party invites and goody bags.

Mystical Fairies

Tel: 020 7431 1888

www.mysticalfairies.co.uk
Heaven for birthday girls!

Office of Standards of Education (Ofsted)
Tel: 0845 640 4045
www.ofsted.gov.uk
Always check out these reports before viewing or deciding on a nursery or school.

Qualifications and Curriculum Authority
Tel: 020 7509 5556
www.qca.org.uk
Features an 'exam doctor' offering valuable advice on exam stress.

Party Directory
Tel: 01252 851601
www.partydirectory4kids.co.uk
A huge choice of party goodies for all ages.

Schools Guide Book
Tel: 020 7267 7002
www.schoolsguidebook.co.uk
All the advice you need on league tables, entry requirements, fees and uniforms for the independent schools sector.

Waitrose
Tel: 0800 188 884
www.waitrose.com
Great for kids' birthday cakes at pretty reasonable prices. My son had a fabulous pirate ship last year that cost far less than

a custom-made one and saved me the hassle of getting elbow-deep in icing!

Natural Living

Bare Faced Cheek
www.bare-faced-cheek.co.uk
Check out this website for all your organic beauty needs.

The British Medical Acupuncture Society
Tel: 01606 786782/020 7713 9437
www.medical-acupuncture.co.uk
For information on acupuncture and registered practitioners.

British Osteopathic Association
Tel: 01582 488455
www.osteopathy.org
If you're considering osteopathy here's a good place to go for more details and practitioners.

Chemist Direct
Tel: 0845 259 0175
www.chemistdirect.co.uk
Online discounted chemist products, including Dr Greenfingers plasters and ointment.

The Cloth Resource
www.theclothresource.co.uk
A non-profit website covering all aspects of using cloth

nappies. It also includes a list of real nappy manufacturers and retailers.

earthBorn
Tel: 01928 734171
www.earthbornpaints.co.uk
earthBorn natural paints are toxin-free and the company will match any existing pantone shade.

Environment Agency
Tel: 08708 506506
www.environment-agency.gov.uk
Log on for some really useful water-saving ideas.

Greenknickers
www.greenknickers.org
The most delightful, ethical, ecological undies on the market.

Holz Toys
Tel: 0845 130 8697
www.holz-toys.co.uk
Sustainable and organic toys.

Little Green Earthlets
Tel: 0845 072 4462/01435 811555
www.earthlets.co.uk
For a full range of natural, organic and essential care for babies, for mums and your home, look no further.

Jane Harter
Tel: 020 8365 2564

I'd highly recommend this brilliant homeopath to treat everything from childhood eczema to stressed-out mum syndrome!

Lutz & Patmos
www.lutzandpatmos.com
The place to go for beautifully designed knitwear made from eco-friendly merino wool.

Micro-scooters Ltd
Tel: 0845 258 7532
www.micro-scooters.co.uk
It seems no childhood is complete these days without a micro-scooter and we've made great use of them in my house by using them for the school run – cheaper than the car or public transport and far more eco-friendly!

Nappy Valley
www.nappyvalley.co.uk
A brilliant website for buying and selling baby gear.

Organics for Kids
Tel: 01865 725730
www.organicsforkids.com
Great clothes for babies and children made from organic textiles.

People Tree
Tel: 0845 450 4595/020 7739 9659
www.peopletree.co.uk
This is *the* leading ethical fashion brand.

Recycle This

Tel: 08701 163163

www.recyclethis.co.uk

Brilliant suggestions on how and where to recycle waste.

Register of Chinese Herbal Medicine

Tel: 01603 623994

www.rchm.co.uk

A good place to source a reputable Chinese herbal doctor.

Sharkah Chakra

Tel: 01392 662992

www.sharkahchakra.com

Fairtrade, naturally dyed, organic denim with ethically mined gold rivets.

The Society of Homeopaths

Tel: 0845 450 6611

www.homeopathy-soh.org

Log on here to find your nearest registered homeopath.

Steven Kippax

Tel: 020 7439 7332

Kippax is your man if you want a western herbalist to cure your ailments. He is the President of the National Institute of Medical Herbalists.

The Wildlife Trusts

Tel: 01636 677711

www.wildlifetrusts.org

The best place to get tips on composting and local conservation projects.

Worn again

www.wornagain.co.uk

Company selling guilt-free ethical shoes. You can buy cool, Converse-style plimsolls that use recycled materials and ethically sourced rubber.

Travel and School Holidays

Alexandra Palace

Tel: 020 8365 4386

www.alexandrapalace.com/icerink.html

Ice-skating fun for all the family.

Bewilderwood

Tel: 01603 783900

www.bewilderwood.co.uk

A curious treehouse adventure forest in Norfolk. This fifty-acre treasure hunt should keep them busy . . . !

The Big Chill

Tel: 020 7685 0525

www.bigchill.net

Why not try a relaxed festival *en famille* this year?

British Swimming

www.britishswimming.org

The place to go for listings of swimming pools near you.

Bushbaby Travel

Tel: 01252 792984

www.bushbabytravel.com
Brilliant for organising more adventurous travel and holidays
for the family.

Chickenshed
Tel: 020 8351 6161
www.chickenshed.org.uk
A wonderful interactive dance, song and puppet theatre
company that all children will adore – mine have been going
since they were six months old and still love it!

City of London
Tel: 020 7606 3030
www.cityoflondon.gov.uk
Go to this website for more information on what's on in
London (also the place to check out your nearest Lido for
the summer months).

Coastline Villas
Tel: 0844 557 1020
www.coastline.co.uk
Hand-picked family villas in Ibiza, Majorca and Corsica.

Cornish Tipis
Tel: 01208 880781
www.cornishtipiholidays.co.uk
Why not try a canvas tipi this summer. The kids will love it!

Crazee Kids
Tel: 020 8444 5333/07958 501919
www.crazeekids.co.uk

Brilliant dance and drama workshops for kids aged three to ten. A firm favourite with the Saunders children!

Extreme Academy
Tel: 01637 860543
www.watergatebay.co.uk
Surfing, kitesurfing, waveskiing and land boarding for your little adventurer.

Family Ski Company
Tel: 01684 540333
www.familyski.co.uk
The ski company designed for families.

Feather Down Farms
Tel: 01420 80804
www.featherdownfarm.co.uk
Camping at its most glam – we call it 'glamping' in our house!

Forestry Commission
Tel: 0845 367 3787
www.forestry.gov.uk
Get out and about with their nationwide activities listings – everything from pond dipping and cycling to survival days and horse riding.

Giffords Circus
Tel: 01451 820378
www.giffordscircus.com
If you only do one family day out this summer, it should be Giffords Circus. Just magical.

Holiday Nanny
Tel: 01494 772400
www.holidaynanny.org
A good place to go if you want to hire a trained and qualified nanny for your holiday.

Identity and Passport Service
Tel: 0870 521 0410
www.ips.gov.uk
All your passport questions answered.

Kamper Hire
Tel: 0845 226 7869
www.kamperhire.co.uk
I love the idea of hiring a VW camper van and heading to the coast for the Easter break.

Kids in the Med
Tel: 0845 277 3300
www.kidsinthemed.com
Heaps of kiddie-friendly holidays with the added bonus of a 'send-ahead service' that delivers all your nappies/baby food/wipes direct to your holiday door.

Legoland
Tel: 0871 222 2001
www.legoland.co.uk
If you can face the summer onslaught this is a really fun-packed day out.

London Aquarium

Tel: 020 7967 8000

www.sealife.co.uk/london

There can't be many kids who wouldn't love a trip to the aquarium, especially when you can get within inches of a shark!

London Eye

Tel: 0870 990 8883

www.londoneye.com

A brilliant focal point of any day out, just get there early or pre-book!

Luxury Family Hotels

www.luxuryfamilyhotels.co.uk

The place to look if you want a kid-friendly break in the UK but don't want to compromise on style or luxury.

Monkey Music

Tel: 01582 766464

www.monkeymusic.co.uk

A great introduction to music for babies and toddlers – also a good way to meet fellow mums in your area.

Paspic

Tel: 01273 704499

www.paspic.com

Email a digital picture of your newborn to Paspic and they'll produce a set of four passport-suitable photos. The beauty of this is you don't have to leave home!

The Peacock Theatre

Tel: 0870 737 0337

www.peacock-theatre.com

If you go to one production this Christmas, see *The Snowman* at The Peacock Theatre. It is truly magical and perfect for all ages (my newborn slept through it at two weeks old and my six-year-old begs to go each and every year). It's well worth making the trip to London to see this.

Perform

Tel: 0845 400 4000

www.perform.org.uk

Let the drama queens and kings act up care of these fabulous drama workshops.

PGL

Tel: 08700 551551

www.pgl.co.uk

Residential activity holidays for kids aged seven to seventeen.

Science Museum

Tel: 0870 870 4868

www.sciencemuseum.org.uk

Learning made fun and it's free!

Sovereign Luxury Holidays

Tel: 0871 200 6677

www.sovereign.com

Sovereign's Tiny Tots service delivers kids' products to your holiday-home door.

Stagecoach Theatre Arts plc

Tel: 01932 254333

www.stagecoach.co.uk

With more than 600 dance and drama workshops around the country you should find a place for your little ones to tap, pirouette and jive their way through summer!

Warwick Castle

Tel: 0870 442 2000 (recorded information)

www.warwick-castle.co.uk

When I was a child, my elder brother insisted we go here every year for his birthday and now I return religiously with my own kids. They adore it!

Whipsnade Zoo

Tel: 01582 872171

www.zsl.org/zsl-whipsnade-zoo

The chimpsnasium here is fab.

Willows Farm Village

Tel: 0870 129 9718

www.willowsfarmvillage.com

A firm favourite with my kids, this working farm is just bulging with things to see and do.

Yellow Moon

www.yellowmoon.org.uk

Hundreds of wonderful products to keep your children entertained.

Fashion

American Apparel
Tel: 020 3206 2046
www.americanapparel.net
Brilliant for staple T-shirts and vests in almost every colour under the sun.

ASOS
www.asos.com
A truly genius online fashion and shopping website.

Blooming Marvellous
Tel: 0845 458 7405
www.bloomingmarvellous.co.uk
Ideal for 'blooming' mums.

Donna IDA
Tel: 020 7225 3816
www.donnaida.com
With over twenty international denim labels, they promise to find you the perfect pair of jeans.

eBay
www.ebay.co.uk
Here's one place to buy or sell any assortment of goodies.

Elias & Grace
Tel: 020 7449 0574
www.eliasandgrace.com

If you're going to blow the budget on maternity wear or kids' clothes this really is the place to do it!

Entirely Everything
www.entirelyeverything.co.uk
I love this website that searches 200 shops to find your perfect pair of shoes, saving you the hassle of trawling the high street.

Figleaves Maternity
Tel: 0844 7700 999
www.figleaves.com
Maternity and breastfeeding underwear in abundance.

I Love Jeans
Tel: 0800 0834 713/020 8446 4299
www.ilovejeans.com
Input your basic details – leg length, waist size and body shape – and they tell you which jeans will suit you best (ranging from supermarket to designer brands). Genius!

JoJo Maman Bébé
Tel: 0871 423 5656
www.jojomamanbebe.co.uk
A brilliant one-stop-shop for kids' clothes and parents to be.

Matches
Tel: 0870 067 8838
www.matchesfashion.com
A nice mix of high-end and emerging fashion labels.

Mini Boden

Tel: 0845 677 5000

www.boden.co.uk

Sorry to be a middle-class cliché but Mini Boden does have lovely, original kids' clothes!

Net-a-Porter

Tel: 0845 675 1321

www.net-a-porter.com

Brilliant designer trends delivered to your door.

Pretty Ballerinas

www.prettyballerinas.com

Gorgeous flat pumps to see you through any occasion.

Sand in my Toes

www.sandinmytoes.com

A small but friendly website which will help you find your perfect beachwear. Just think, you'll never have to do bikini changing-room hell again!

Shoe Runway

Tel: 0870 850 7939

www.shoe-runway.com

When you buy shoes here, they'll donate a pair of flip-flops to a Kenyan disease-prevention charity, so you'll be doing a good deed while fuelling your fetish.

Topshop

Tel: 0845 121 4519

www.topshop.com

Everyone loves a good Topshop bargain and their website has daily updates of all its stock.

Top Tips for Girls

www.toptipsforgirls.com

Fun and informative advice forum that is especially useful for fashion and style tips and tricks.

Nutrition

Abel & Cole

Tel: 0845 262 6262

www.abelandcole.co.uk

Organic food and drink delivered free to your door.

All 4 Kids

Tel: 01707 659383

www.all4kidsuk.com

Check out this website for inspiring and informative kids cookery courses near you.

A Lot of Organics

Tel: 0845 094 6498

www.alotoforganics.co.uk

UK organic search engine for organic, Fairtrade, vegan, ethical and eco-friendly products.

Carluccio's
www.carluccios.com
Really delicious authentic Italian food that will inspire all ages, with the added bonus of a great wine list for us parched Sunday lunch mums!

Giraffe
Tel: 020 8457 2776
www.giraffe.net
Great world food for all the family and with an emphasis on yummy, fresh, healthy eating, how can you resist?

National Association of Farmers' Markets
Tel: 0845 4588 420
www.farmersmarkets.net
Check this website out for all you need to know about farmers' markets.

Organix
Tel: 0800 393511
www.organix.com
Delicious pre-prepared organic food for babies, toddlers and children – perfect for busy mums.

Peter Rabbit Organics
Tel: 020 7590 4640
www.peterrabbitorganics.com
Yummy organic snacks and food for your baby and toddler – and great fruit bars for mums on the go!

Pizza Express

www.pizzaexpress.com

One of the few places that does a healthy and relatively cheap kids' menu. Kids' margaritas with side salads all round!

The Food Doctor

Tel: 020 7992 6700

www.thefooddoctor.com

This team of specialist nutritionists give advice on everything from general nutrition to nutrition for peak fertility and pregnancy health.

UK Organic Living Directory

www.organicliving.uk.net

Ideas for organic food, wine and lifestyle.

Victoria Health

www.victoriahealth.com

A brilliant place to get your healthy goodies and supplements online, especially if you live miles from a good health food store.

Wagamama

Tel: 020 7009 3600

www.wagamama.com

My children love this place and with colouring and kids' chopsticks to keep them entertained we're all happy.

Baby World

www.babyworld.co.uk

Has some great tips for mums returning to work after having a baby or taking a break to raise a family.

Career Encouragement

www.careerencouragement.typepad.com

A really encouraging blog for mums going back into the working environment.

Citizens Advice Bureau

www.adviceguide.org.uk

All the advice you'll need on work-related issues.

Jobs4Mothers.com

Tel: 020 8537 3319

www.jobs4mothers.com

Check out this website for a broad range of job opportunities for mums as well as experts who can help you with everything from updating your CV to refreshing your interview skills.

Full-time Mothers

www.timeforparenting.org

Log on if you're a full-time mum; it's stuffed full of good advice.

Mumsnet

www.mumsnet.com

A brilliant place for any mum to get support, advice and a good laugh while you're at it!

Netmums
www.netmums.com
Offers some sound advice on retraining to return to work.

The Open University
Tel: 0845 300 6090
www.open.ac.uk
The only university dedicated to distance learning. This is a good place to find a course or training which you can fit around a family and work.

Working Families
Tel: 020 7253 7243/0800 013 0313
www.workingfamilies.org.uk
This site has some useful information about working flexi-time.

Working Mums
Tel: 020 8432 6094
www.workingmums.co.uk
Gillian Nissim's brilliant database of jobs, employers and business opportunities to suit working mums.

You Time

The British Wheel of Yoga
Tel: 01529 306851
www.bwy.org.uk

Check this website out for a listing of yoga teachers and classes in your area.

Coco de Mer
Tel: 020 7836 8882
www.coco-de-mer.co.uk
Spice up your sex life with a few treats from here . . . !

Cupcake
Tel: 020 8875 1065
www.cupcakemum.com
Cupcake is the first ever mums-only spa. Based in Putney, London it boasts a fabulous crèche, baby massage class and concierge service.

Natural Mother
Tel: 0800 008 6844
www.naturalmother.co.uk
Treat yourself to reflexology, yoga, massage or acupuncture, all in the comfort of your own home.

Pilates Foundation
Tel: 020 7033 0078
www.pilatesfoundation.com
The site to visit if you're interested in finding out about Pilates classes in your area.

Relate
Tel: 0300 100 1234
www.relate.org.uk

A good place to turn if your relationship with your partner is under strain.

Seat Choice
Tel: 01934 626 344
www.seatchoice.com
A one-stop-shop for theatre tickets nationwide.

Sitters
Tel: 0800 3890038
www.sitters.co.uk
All you need to find that perfect evening babysitter. Freeeeeedom!

Super Pages
www.superpages.com
You'll find a complete list of health clubs and gyms across the UK here – now you have no excuse!

Ticketmaster
www.ticketmaster.co.uk
Go on, you know you want front row at the next Take That concert!

Thank You

There were so many thank yous in *The Fabulous Mum's Handbook* that I felt rather like an over-indulgent, weepy actress during her Oscar speech. For this reason, I will try and keep these thanks short and sweet.

A huge thank you to . . .

My (still) amazing husband, Michael. Could you be any more wonderful? I think not. You are utterly supportive and inspiring in every way and the fact that you agreed to a third child knowing full well I am beyond crabby on little sleep and will only blame you at three a.m. (when we're woken for the tenth time), proves you deserve a diamond-encrusted medal, at the very least.

My three (yey, yey, yey!) children, I love you so much my heart could burst.

My close family (Fleur and Mum, especially you) for never tiring of my incessant parenting talk and for loving my children (almost) as much as I do.

My growing mass of mummy friends, all of whom provide unconditional inspiration, fodder and humour for the book – you are my lifeline.

A mention to a few special girlfriends who have at last joined the mummy brigade, and make it all the more fun for me (yes, that's you, Ros, Katie and Lucie). When are we having our next girls' night out?

A huge thanks to my stellar line-up of gurus and fabulous celebrity mums who have offered their wisdom and support with such ease, grace and honesty.
How could I not say a huge thanks to my utterly focused agent, Lorella Belli, and my editor Emma Rose and her team at Random House? You have not only helped to make the 'Fabulous Mum' concept such a huge success but have ensured this whole process has been an incredible journey for everyone concerned (not least me). I feel blessed.

Lastly I'd like to thank all those fabulous mums, known and unknown by me, who support and relate to my work. Your role as multi-tasking supermums may seem to go unnoticed by many but I hope by sharing this ride you'll feel slightly more empowered and slightly less weary by the end of it. Take my last piece of advice: put the kids to bed, run yourself a hot bath, poor yourself a large glass of wine and leave that ironing and those work emails until later; if anyone deserves it, you do!

Index

455